G000015862

FROM SADAT TO SADDAM

FROM
SADAT
TO
SADDAM

The Decline of American Diplomacy
in the Middle East

DAVID J. DUNFORD

Potomac Books

AN IMPRINT OF THE UNIVERSITY OF NEBRASKA PRESS

© 2019 by David J. Dunford

All rights reserved. Potomac Books is an imprint of the University of Nebraska Press.
Manufactured in the United States of America.

All photos courtesy of the author.

Library of Congress Cataloging-in-Publication Data
Names: Dunford, David J., author.
Title: From Sadat to Saddam: the decline of American diplomacy in the Middle East / David J. Dunford.
Description: Lincoln, Nebraska: Potomac Books, An imprint of the University of Nebraska Press, 2019. | Includes bibliographical references and index.
Identifiers: LCCN 2019005301
ISBN 9781640121577 (cloth: alk. paper)
ISBN 9781640122475 (epub)
ISBN 9781640122482 (mobi)
ISBN 9781640122499 (pdf)
Subjects: LCSH: Dunford, David J. | Diplomats—United States—Biography. | Ambassadors—United States—Biography. | United States—Foreign relations—Middle East. | Middle East—Foreign relations—United States.
Classification: LCC E840.8.D865 A3 2019 | DDC 327.2092 [B]—dc23
LC record available at https://lccn.loc.gov/2019005301

Set in Minion Pro by Mikala R. Kolander.

For Sandy, who is a full partner in my life
and all my diplomatic adventures

Diplomacy is always going to consist to some extent of serving people who do not know that they are being served, who do not know that they need to be served, who misunderstand and occasionally abuse the very effort to serve them.

George Kennan

CONTENTS

ACKNOWLEDGMENTS

Dr. James A. "Andy" Sheppard, president of Thomas University in Thomasville, Georgia, is the godfather of this writing project. We have been friends and collaborators since the day in January 2011 that I showed up on his doorstep (he was then dean of academic affairs at Southwestern College in Winfield, Kansas) as a Woodrow Wilson Visiting Fellow. He was aware that I had an itch that I needed to scratch, and he put me in touch with people in the publishing industry who helped me shape the basic idea of the book. He then guided me in how to put together the book proposal that found its way to Potomac Books. He read the entire manuscript, provided valuable suggestions, and caught many mistakes and omissions. Most important, when my morale needed a boost, Andy was always ready with encouraging words.

Many thanks to Tom Swanson at Potomac Books, who was willing to read and champion a book proposal that came in over the transom. Abigail Stryker was invaluable in guiding me through the many steps required to get the manuscript in shape for the editors. I was blown away by how quickly and comprehensively Abby handled my questions and requests for assistance. I am grateful also to my skilled and patient project editor, Ann Baker, and to my thorough and professional copyeditor, Walt Evans. Thanks also to the rest of the superb Potomac team who helped me along the way, including Rosemary Sekora, Annie Shahan, and Tish Fobben.

When my memory sputtered, I reached out to several former colleagues to fill in the blanks. Henry Precht, my boss in Cairo and my main point of contact in Embassy Cairo when I was director of the Office of Egyptian Affairs, read and commented on the first two chapters. Chas Freeman, my boss for more than two years in Riyadh, read the chapters on Saudi Arabia and the account of my bruising confirmation as U.S. ambassador to Oman. Ken Stammerman, friend and close colleague during the challenges of Desert Shield and Desert Storm, provided a wide range of helpful comments.

Larry Butcher, my main contact in Washington when I was back in Cairo trying to turn the decision to create a multilateral development bank in Cairo into reality, was a major contributor to the MENABANK chapter. Wafik Grais, Lorenzo Savorelli, and Janet Sanderson also contributed important pieces in that story.

Tim Carney, Allen Kepchar, Zaid Noori, and Jacqueline Lawson-Smith all read the Iraq chapter and set me straight on several events. Finally, my fellow LDESP faculty members, Michael Fahy, Mark Sargent, and Dodge Billingsley, all rallied with extensive comments when I reached out to them for assistance. Bob Tomasovic (Colonel T) generously took the time to read the chapter and to assure me that I didn't get anything seriously wrong in my account of his program.

I leaned heavily on the Foreign Affairs Oral History Collection of the Association of Diplomatic Studies and Training (ADST). The collection is rich in detail and insight and invaluable to historians and to authors like me who need assistance in fleshing out the detail and significance of past events. ADST president Susan Johnson pointed me in the right direction in my quest to understand how and why the State Department senior seminar disappeared.

This book would likely never have been written had I not signed up in the summer of 1997 for a week-long course at Ghost Ranch in Abiquiu, New Mexico, called "Writing the Land," taught by Bob Gish. Bob inspired me to start writing and offered much-needed encouragement over the years.

The book also wouldn't exist if my wife, Sandy, hadn't talked me into taking the job in Cairo instead of the one in Brasilia and if she hadn't made it clear to me that I belonged in Iraq, after the coalition toppled Saddam Hussein, rather than continuing to wring my hands in Tucson about what an awful idea it was to invade Iraq.

INTRODUCTION

In December 2016 I came across a long *Wall Street Journal* article about a Foreign Service friend and colleague named Robin Raphel.[1] I had known Robin for more than forty years and worked with her closely in 2003 in Iraq. Robin's home was raided by the Federal Bureau of Investigation (FBI) in October 2014 based on intercepts of her communications with Pakistani officials, suggesting to the FBI that she was working on behalf of the Pakistanis. She spent more than two years in the center of a Kafkaesque nightmare even though she was only doing what professional diplomats are supposed to do. She had established relationships with a significant number of influential Pakistanis and used her network of contacts to do her job, which was to promote U.S. interests. The State Department as an institution did very little to protect her, although her many friends inside and out raised money to cover her legal fees. Because of the national trauma we experienced on September 11, 2001, a whole new generation of law enforcement and intelligence officials that neither understood nor respected how diplomats operate had risen to the top of their agencies. The FBI eventually declined to file charges but did not apologize for what it had done to her life and her career.

When I read the article through I realized that what happened to Robin could easily have happened to me. The level of my security clearance made me aware that reports of my conversations with foreigners were often intercepted by our intelligence agencies. It never occurred to me that these reports would put me at risk of being investigated. By 2014 our surveillance state was criminalizing ordinary diplomacy. How did we get to this point?

This book seeks to answer that question and others by reflecting on the thirty years I spent trying to improve the U.S. position in the Middle East and to make the region a better place. I focus on the Middle East because that is what I know, but my personal experiences are relevant to our diplomacy in the rest of the world. The overall results of our Middle East adventures are beyond discouraging. We became mired in two endless wars.[2] The wars cost the United States thousands of lives and trillions of dollars. The country that most benefited from the conflicts was Iran. The Middle East peace process, which had seemed so promising in the early 1990s, had collapsed into violence, bitterness, and recrimination. The misnamed Arab Spring had led not to democracy and economic prosperity but rather to civil wars in Syria, Libya, and Yemen and further crackdowns on civil liberties in Egypt and Bahrain. The close U.S. relationship with Oman has survived, but the health of Sultan Qaboos is worrisome and the transition to new leadership after his death is problematic.

I started writing this book in 2017, the first year of the Trump Administration, but the book is not about what the administration has done to the State Department and the Foreign Service.[3] Like the majority of my colleagues, I was appalled by the Trump White House's disdain for the State Department and the Foreign Service. I will argue, however, that most of the damage to our diplomatic capability had already been done by past administrations, both Republican and Democratic. Resetting our diplomacy to what it was on the day Donald Trump was inaugurated will not fix all that is wrong.

I understand that not everything that goes wrong in the Middle East can be blamed on the United States. Given our unrivaled power position in the world after the collapse of the Soviet Union in 1991, however, we could and should have done far better. This book uses my personal experiences to illuminate the reasons why we have not fared better. I have three goals in mind. I want to show the reader, as opposed to telling the reader, what a diplomat does and what is distinctive about diplomacy as a profession. Second, I want to give the reader a sense of what the decline of our diplomatic performance looked like to a practitioner, in hopes of stimulating public support for greater reliance on diplomacy. Third, I want to give students or young people contemplating or entering a career in foreign affairs a window into what diplomacy consists of and what a career in diplomacy might look like.

One thing I learned about Middle Easterners is that they are much more like Westerners than they are different. Like the average American, they want a meaningful job that provides the income needed to support the family in a comfortable lifestyle. The major difference is that Middle Easterners often live in failed states and war zones. Far too many of them wake up in the morning having to think seriously about how they and their families will survive until nightfall. They make decisions about who can better protect them from harm. Democracy and human rights are fine concepts, but their immediate need is security. Throughout the years of U.S. military presence in Iraq, Afghanistan, and elsewhere in the Middle East, our ability to protect the ordinary people who live there has been woefully inadequate.

The flow of the book is chronological, beginning with my assignment to Cairo in 1981 to run the embassy's economic section. That led to my reassignment three years later to Washington to run the Department of State's Office of Egyptian Affairs. Following several months as a member of the State Department's Senior Seminar, I was posted in 1988 to Riyadh, Saudi Arabia, as deputy chief of mission (DCM). Saddam Hussein's decision to invade Kuwait gave that job a higher profile than it might otherwise have had. In May 1992 President George H. W. Bush nominated me as U.S. ambassador to the Sultanate of Oman. I survived a bruising confirmation process and served in Oman until my retirement in 1995. Twice the Department of State called me out of retirement, once to run an international team charged with setting up a multilateral development bank in Cairo in 1987 and once to help rebuild Iraq's Ministry of Foreign Affairs (MFA) in 2003. The latter experience led to seven years (2004 to 2011) working as a contractor, paid from Department of Defense funds, helping U.S. military units prepare to deploy to Iraq and Afghanistan.

During the thirty years of this chronology, I witnessed a thinning of the ranks of professionals devoted to diplomacy, a reduction in professional training, a significant increase in the politicization of the Foreign Service and State Department, and the militarization of foreign policy. Our political leadership often turns to the military as the first option instead of the last and then wonders why there are not enough capable diplomats to clean up the mess. If we are to restore U.S. influence in the world, bring more peace and order to the international system, and work with the international community to tackle critical global problems like climate change, we must invest in the professionalization of U.S. diplomacy.[4]

ABBREVIATIONS

2nd ID	U.S. Army Second Infantry Division
3rd ID	U.S. Army Third Infantry Division
AAR	after-action review
ABGR	American Business Group in Riyadh
AFRTS	Armed Forces Radio and Television Service
AFSA	American Foreign Service Association
AIPAC	The American Israel Public Affairs Committee
BIT	bilateral investment treaty
BUB	battle update brief
CAC	Cairo American College
CENTCOM	U.S. Central Command
CFLCC	Coalition Forces Land Component Command
CLO	community liaison office(r)
CODEL	Congressional visit
COIN	counterinsurgency
CPA	Coalition Provisional Authority
CRC	Civilian Response Corps
CSF	Egyptian Government Central Security Forces
CSO	State Department Bureau of Conflict and Stabilization Operations
DCM	Deputy Chief of Mission
DFAC	dining facility
EB	State Department Bureau of Economic and Business Affairs

EBRD	European Bank for Reconstruction and Development
ESF	Economic Support Funds
EU	European Union
FMS	foreign military sales
FOB	forward operating base
FBO	State Department Office of Foreign Buildings
FSO	Foreign Service Officer
GATT	General Agreement on Tariffs and Trade
GCC	Gulf Cooperation Council
HFAC	House Foreign Affairs Committee
IMF	International Monetary Fund
IO	information operations
IRDC	Iraq Reconstruction and Development Council
JECOR	U.S.–Saudi Arabian Joint Commission for Economic Cooperation
KATUSA	Korean Augmentation to the U.S. Army
KBR	Kellogg Brown & Root
KTC	Korea Combat Training Center
LCAC	landing craft air cushion
LDESP	Leader Development and Education for Sustained Peace
MB	Muslim Brotherhood
MDB	multilateral development bank
MEDRC	Middle East Desalination Research Center in Muscat, Oman
MENABANK	Bank for Reconstruction and Development in the Middle East and North America
MEU	Marine Expeditionary Unit
MFA	Ministry of Foreign Affairs
MPS	military police
MRES	meals ready to eat
MRX	mission readiness exercise
NCO	noncommissioned officer

NEA	State Department Bureau of Near East and South Asian Affairs (later Bureau of Near East Affairs)
NEA/IAI	Office of Israeli and Arab-Israeli Affairs
ODF	State Department Office of Development Finance
OECD	Organization for Economic Cooperation and Development
OIG	State Department Office of the Inspector General
Op Center	State Department Operations Center
OPM/SANG	Office of the Project Manager/Saudi Arabian National Guard
ORHA	Office for Reconstruction and Humanitarian Assistance
PECDAR	Palestinian Economic Council for Development and Reconstruction
PIR	priority intelligence requirements
PL-480	Agricultural Trade Development and Assistance Act of 1954
PLF	Palestinian Liberation Front
PLO	Palestinian Liberation Organization
POMCUS	Prepositioned Overseas Materiel Configured in Unit Sets
PRT	Provincial Reconstruction Team
REDWG	Regional Economic Development Working Group
RPG	rocket-propelled grenade
S/CRS	State Department Office of the Coordinator for Reconstruction and Stabilization
S/CT	State Department Coordinator for Counterterrorism
SAIC	Science Applications International Corporation
SFRC	Senate Foreign Relations Committee
SME	subject matter expert
TCFR	Tucson Committee on Foreign Relations
TRADOC	U.S. Army Training and Doctrine Command
UCMJ	Uniform Code of Military Justice
UNDP	United Nations Development Program

USAID	U.S. Agency for International Development
USERA	U.S. Embassy Recreation Association
USMTM	U.S. Military Training Mission in Saudi Arabia
USTR	U.S. Trade Representative (also Office of the U.S. Trade Representative)
WUS	World University Service

FROM SADAT TO SADDAM

1

CAIRO

Drinking from the Nile

Once you drink from the Nile, you are destined to return.

—Egyptian proverb

I had been in Cairo six months when a confrontation on a Nile bridge sparked an epiphany about Egypt and the Middle East. It was late 1981 and I was returning home from a day spent with my family at the farm of a prosperous Egyptian businessman. I was driving our Volvo, my wife, Sandy, was in the passenger seat, and my son, Greg, and daughter, Tina, both six-graders, were in the backseat. As happens so often in Egypt, the hospitality of our hosts led to us staying longer than we had intended. The rural roads were teeming with people and animals, horses, camels, goats, and *gamousas* (water buffalos). I was tired and tense from driving defensively on poorly lit roads and my knuckles were white by the time I got back to the west side of the Nile.

Crossing the bridge in heavy traffic, I knew I had to get into the right lane to take the route south to Ma'adi, the suburb where we and many other members of the foreign community lived. Just as I spotted an opening, a young Egyptian in a pickup bounced over the sidewalk and cut me off. I let loose a stream of curses in English (my Arabic was too basic for the task). The driver looked at me wide-eyed for a second and then took off his baseball cap and tipped it at me while flashing a wide smile. My anger evaporated, and I started to laugh. From that day forward, I felt at home in Cairo.

Cairo was my first Middle East assignment even though I was already fifteen years into a Foreign Service career. My job was to run Embassy Cairo's economic section. I had just completed nine years in the United States, mainly in the Bureau of Economic and Business Affairs (EB) working on trade and finance issues. My last eighteen months in Washington I had been detailed to the Office of the U.S. Trade Representative (USTR), with the pretentious title of deputy assistant USTR. It was time to fish or cut bait. I either had to leave the Foreign Service or accept a foreign assignment. I had earlier served in Quito, Ecuador, and still had ties in the Latin American bureau. The job of economic counselor in Brasilia was mine for the taking.

When I relayed this great news to Sandy, her reaction surprised me. She didn't want to go to Brasilia—it would be boring. I had visited Brasilia some years earlier to explain an obscure part of the proposed legislation that became the Trade Act of 1974. I liked Brasilia's climate and concluded that while it wasn't Rio, with a million Brazilians living there it couldn't be all bad. Sandy urged me to go back to the State Department and see what else was available. I agreed to check and found that a similar job in Cairo was open. Cairo's reputation as a dirty, dusty, noisy, and crowded city was well known. Apparently no other qualified senior officers were interested. I dutifully reported the opening to Sandy, assured in my own mind that she wouldn't want any part of it. To my shock, she thought Cairo was a great idea. She had lived in Tehran as a high school student while her father worked for the international oil consortium and had retained some nostalgia for the Middle East.

The next day I sought out my friend Arnie Raphel, then working in the Bureau of Near East and South Asian Affairs (NEA), to tell him I just might be interested in the Cairo job.[1] Arnie and I had joined the Foreign Service at the same time in 1966 and we shared a carpool from our northern Virginia homes to Rosslyn, where we received our basic training. Arnie went on to be ambassador to Pakistan and tragically died in a plane crash there in August 1988. My word to Arnie led within hours to a meeting with then–Deputy Assistant Secretary Maury Draper. Draper had been actively involved in the Camp David negotiations between Israel and Egypt and was nearing the end of a distinguished career. I was a little intimidated by his reputation and clumsily shook his thumb instead of his whole hand while trying to make eye contact. Our meeting was brief, as Draper promptly concluded that I was the warm body he had been looking for to fill the vacancy in Cairo. I was signed up to go to Egypt before I fully realized what was happening.

With Cairo now in my future, I still had to go to work every day at USTR. It might have made sense to assign me to a few weeks of basic Arabic training and maybe a few days of area studies, but I remained at USTR until the Friday before our family of four boarded a plane bound for Cairo, with both a golden and a Labrador retriever in the cargo hold. When we disembarked at the Cairo airport, the waiting area teemed with people, who parted like the Red Sea when they saw us leading the large dogs toward them. Egyptians, like most Muslims, are taught that dogs are unclean.

My first week in Cairo set the tone for all those years to come, living and working in the Middle East. Israel, on Sunday, June 7, 1981, staged a secret attack on a nuclear power plant under construction near Baghdad. This was an embarrassment for Egypt, which had signed a peace treaty with Israel two years earlier and was working hard to restore relations with other Arab countries who objected. It was also my introduction to the Arab-Israeli conflict. Some years before, I had jokingly told one of my colleagues in the State Department, a rabid hockey fan, that there were three things I wanted nothing to do with: hockey, arms control and disarmament, and the Middle East peace process. Both arms control and Middle East peace process negotiations had seemed from afar to be insanely complicated and at times counterintuitive. Now I was in Cairo, feeling as if I had been dropped into the deep end of the Middle East peace process pool and told to swim.

The first few weeks did little to reassure me about Cairo. June was hot, and Cairo was indeed dirty, dusty, and noisy. Happily, on the job side I had two experienced Middle East hands to show me the ropes. Roy Atherton, the ambassador, had been assistant secretary for Near Eastern and South Asian affairs and actively involved in the Egyptian-Israeli negotiations that led to the 1979 peace agreement. His kindness, his energy, and his ability were legendary. I never forgot watching him work cocktail parties and other social events. He would manage to make everyone present think that he was interested in what they had to say and still be gone in twenty minutes, off to the next event. Attending three social events in an evening was not unusual for him. I was more than twenty years younger and felt wiped out by an evening like that.

The deputy chief of mission (DCM) was Henry Precht. Henry hailed from Savannah, Georgia, and he worked hard to retain his Savannah accent. The Iranian hostage crisis had ended less than two years earlier. Henry had served in Iran and, as director of Iranian affairs in Washington during the crisis, he had become a lightning rod for congressional discontent. He was nominated but never confirmed as ambassador to Mauritania and had to settle for the job as DCM in Cairo.

Henry, who would be a constant in my life for the next four years, undertook to educate me on the realities of what could and could not be accomplished both in Egypt and with respect to influencing policy in Washington affecting Egypt. He listened patiently to my frustration with the difficulty of getting things done in Egypt, and he kept me in check when my ambitions to push Egypt harder on economic reform clashed with our political and security interests. He correctly diagnosed my tendency to smolder over perceived slights and encouraged me to be a little more open and sympathetic to those with whom I disagreed. I listened carefully and took his guidance with me to subsequent assignments, along with what I learned from watching him dealing with the diverse power centers of the large country team in Egypt.

I had a third mentor, although I considered him a competitor at the time. Don Brown was the director of the U.S. Agency for International Development (USAID) mission. The largest U.S. aid mission anywhere in the world, Cairo employed more than one hundred Americans. Part of my job as chief of the economic section, as I understood it, was to be an independent advisor to the ambassador on our aid program. Don was in his sixth year in the job and near the end of a thirty-year career in USAID. I knew I would face a daunting challenge having to go toe-to-toe with one of USAID's most senior officials.

While still in Washington, encouraged by my colleagues at USTR, I successfully persuaded the Department of State to change the diplomatic title of the job from economic counselor to economic minister-counselor. Reflecting on this years later, the initiative seems both audacious and somewhat reckless. My future bosses in Embassy Cairo pushed back with serious reservations about the need for the change. Henry, who also held the diplomatic title minister-counselor, was no doubt skeptical, and I am confident that neither my predecessor in Embassy Cairo's economic section nor the head of the political section with whom I would have to work were thrilled. Had the personalities awaiting me in Cairo been pricklier, I could have faced a very rocky start to my tour. Bob Hormats had been my boss for two years at the Department of State and then, as deputy U.S. trade representative when I moved over to USTR, my boss for another year and a half. A few weeks before my departure to Cairo, Bob, in the process of returning to State as assistant secretary of economic and business affairs, wrote a friendly but persuasive letter to Roy Atherton, and the reclassification took place. This upgrade in diplomatic rank made it easier for me to coordinate the agricultural, commercial, and science officers, all of whom bore the title of counselor. I doubt that Don Brown paid much attention to the drama of my title reclassification. He was remarkably tolerant of this young amateur looking over his shoulder at the work USAID was doing.

I had obviously found myself on a championship team. Roughly a half dozen of the Foreign Service Officers I worked with in Cairo went on to become U.S. ambassadors. The USAID mission also boasted some real talent; several went on to be USAID mission directors. Frances Cook, our consul general in Alexandria, replaced me as U.S. ambassador in Muscat when I retired.

The USAID administrator at the time was Peter McPherson. Peter had been general counsel for the Reagan transition team and he ran USAID for the entire six years that I worked on Egypt. He was a hard charger and, since Egypt was his most important program, we saw a great deal of him. For reasons I never understood, McPherson seemed to schedule his visits during the Christmas holidays, which led to some grumbling from me and my USAID colleagues. His first visit during my tour, however, was in early September 1981. I was invited to accompany, as notetaker, Ambassador Atherton, McPherson, and Don Brown to a meeting with Egyptian President Anwar Sadat at his "palace" in Alexandria.

Sadat was enormously popular in the United States. He was masterful in interviews with the news anchors of the time, such as Walter Cronkite, Barbara Walters, and Peter Jennings. My first impression was Sadat's booming voice as he walked down the stairs in his residence. He greeted Ambassador Atherton as "Roy." I was also taken by his firm handshake and direct eye contact, conveying the sense that he was truly interested in meeting me. The meeting began with a brief discussion of the political situation in the Middle East. Israel had yet to formally withdraw from the eastern half of the Sinai Peninsula, and talks between Egypt and Israel about Palestinian autonomy were going nowhere. Sadat spoke with the passion of a Shakespearean actor as he outlined Egypt's concerns. When McPherson introduced his agenda of economic assistance issues, Sadat's eyes seemed to glaze over a little and his responses became far less theatrical.

Sadat was less popular in Egypt. Conventional wisdom is that he was not liked because he had betrayed other Arabs by signing a peace deal with Israel that got the Sinai back but did nothing for the Palestinians. My impression is that his lack of popularity had more to do with his lavish lifestyle and failure to improve the lives of average Egyptians. The Reagan administration was in its first year and hadn't demonstrated much interest in working with Egypt to build on the 1978 Camp David achievement. Sadat had little to show his people for the risks he took with Israel, and he began to turn up the pressure on his domestic opposition, particularly the Islamic opposition. The Muslim Brotherhood (MB), operating in Egypt ever since it was founded in 1928, was a relatively moderate force. Members were not allowed to run in Peoples' Assembly (parliamentary) elections as MB members, but several of their members were elected as independents. There was also a more radical Islamic opposition, which became the Egyptian Islamic Jihad.

Anwar Sadat was assassinated on October 6, 1981, during a military parade commemorating Egypt's initially successful attack on Israeli positions across the Suez Canal eight years earlier. Ambassador Atherton attended, as did our defense attaché and other military members of the embassy. The assassins, affiliated with the militant Islamic opposition and armed with grenades and AK-47s, sprayed bullets at the VIP grandstand, mortally wounding Sadat, lightly wounding Vice President Mubarak, and killing ten others, including an Omani general.

I was at my home in Ma'adi because the embassy and all government offices were closed for the Eid al-Adha (Feast of the Sacrifice) holidays. Henry Precht called me, along with several other embassy officers, and asked us to come to the embassy. Driving there, I had an eerie feeling because the usual cacophonous traffic was not present and there were few pedestrians. At the embassy, Ambassador Atherton arrived looking shaken but determined to take charge. He reported that he had talked with Defense Minister Abu Ghazala, who told him that Sadat would survive. It turned out that Abu Ghazala knew better and, after several hours, press reports confirmed Sadat's death. Henry asked that some of us at the embassy drive past key government buildings to see if there was any activity. Two of us drove north along the Nile past the Ministry of Information but saw nothing worth reporting.

By the time I returned to Ma'adi in the evening, several of our neighbors who worked at the embassy had gathered at our house. Defense attaché (Navy) captain David Sperling and his wife, Judy, our neighbors across the street, were there. They had attended the parade, and David still had spots of blood on his dress uniform. None of us knew what to expect. Was this part of a broader coup? In the days to follow, still part of the Muslim holiday, the streets of Cairo remained relatively empty and calm. Experienced Middle East hands recalled that the city streets had been full of mourners when Gamal Abdel Nasser had died eleven years earlier.

We had little time to reflect because the mother of all funeral parties was about to descend on us from Washington. The delegation included Secretary of State Alexander M. Haig Jr., Defense Secretary Caspar W. Weinberger, former presidents Jimmy Carter, Gerald Ford, and Richard Nixon, U.S. Ambassador to the UN Jeane J. Kirkpatrick, former Secretary of State Henry A. Kissinger, Senators Thurmond, Percy, and Pell, House Speaker Jim Wright, Stevie Wonder, and Walter Cronkite.

Ambassador Atherton appointed Henry as overall control officer, with me as his deputy. Each delegation member was assigned a member of the embassy or USAID staff as an individual control officer. On the night of the funeral, October 11, the embassy organized an informal dinner just for the delegation and the team of control officers. A seating chart had former Secretary of State Kissinger sitting next to Sam Brown, a teenager who Sadat had met by chance in the United States and invited to visit Egypt as his guest. It was a heartwarming story, but Kissinger was unimpressed, declaring that he hadn't traveled several thousand miles to sit next to a bleeping kid. Sam, dressed in a white t-shirt, was moved to another table, where he sat alongside friendlier embassy staff members and enjoyed a cheeseburger. Kissinger was happy and so was Sam.

Each of the former presidents gave a speech. As I remember it, Carter led off with a very moving tribute to Sadat and what he had done for Middle East peace. Ford followed with a speech that I thought appropriate but not otherwise memorable. Nixon concluded with what he meant to be a tribute to all the support he had received from embassy staffs over the years. It rang a little hollow to me given his emphasis on logistical support rather than policy support. I didn't think we needed to hear that Foreign Service Officers always made sure that his luggage got to his room in a timely manner.

After a few days, Vice President Hosni Mubarak assumed the presidency. He was a former air force pilot and a colorless figure as vice president. He went out of his way to demonstrate that he would not live ostentatiously, as Sadat had. He remained in the same residence he lived in as vice president, although alterations upgraded its security. Egyptians joked that Nasser had changed the course of Egyptian society, Sadat had changed the course of Egyptian foreign policy, and Mubarak had changed the course of the streetcar line that ran near his home. Most Egyptians were relieved that the country remained relatively stable. The new president placed Egypt under a "state of emergency" that was not lifted until more than thirty years later, after Mubarak had departed the scene.

I first met Mubarak later that October, probably in conjunction with another McPherson visit, and he sported a large bandage on his thumb where he had been wounded during the Sadat assassination. He said the right things about maintaining the peace with Israel, and he listened attentively to our concerns about the Egyptian economy. Mubarak hoped to avoid drama and to slowly rebuild Egypt's relations with the Arab world without losing U.S. support.

As Mubarak settled in, my job as head of the economic section became more routine. It was our job to report on what was going on in the Egyptian economy and to execute instructions from Washington that involved economic issues. There were separate commercial and agriculture sections led by members of the Foreign Commercial and Foreign Agricultural Services. We had a science counselor who reported separately to the ambassador and the DCM. Our superiors expected us to follow what our colleagues in USAID were doing.

I had a very good team. Shaun Donnelly had worked for me in the Economic Bureau in Washington and I had persuaded him to come to Egypt as my deputy. Mary Gin Kennedy, a bright and dynamic officer, was already there. Liz McKune also lent her skills to the section. Liz was later my deputy in Oman. Both Shaun and Liz went on to be U.S. ambassadors, and Mary Gin was equally deserving if not equally lucky.

An average workday might involve one or two meetings with ministers or other officials in various economic ministries or the Central Bank. Tea or Turkish coffee with sugar served at every meeting provided calories but, considering restrooms were scarce, also required advance logistical planning. These meetings usually took place between mid-morning and mid-afternoon, so I became accustomed to eating lunch at 2:00 p.m. or later. During the month of Ramadan, when most Egyptians fasted from dawn to dusk, meetings often took place in the evening after the Iftar (breaking the fast) meal. We all knew that the most dangerous time to be on the roads in Egypt was during the half hour before sunset during the month of Ramadan. After fasting all day, Egyptians were both cranky and eager to get home for the Iftar meal.

We received many official visitors. Now that Egypt and Israel were at peace, senior and not-so-senior administration officials often visited, as well as congressional delegations. Most visitors included both Egypt and Israel on their itineraries. Appointments in Israel were not possible during the Jewish Sabbath (from sunset Friday to sunset Saturday). Our weekend was theoretically Friday (the Muslim sabbath) and Saturday, but it was convenient for visitors to schedule appointments in Egypt on Saturday either before or after a visit to Israel. The political and economic sections usually had to provide control officers. A control officer was responsible for putting together the logistics and itinerary for a visit. Mary Gin proved a superb control officer, always on top of every detail.

Since my previous job had been in the office of the U.S. trade representative, I took an interest in trade and investment issues handled in Washington by the USTR. The Reagan administration launched a policy of negotiating bilateral investment treaties (BITs) with developing countries. The argument was that getting these countries to provide basic guarantees of most-favored-nation treatment and protection against expropriation would stimulate more U.S. private investment and take some of the pressure off official aid flows. USTR provided a model treaty that I provided to Wagih Shindi, Egypt's minister of international cooperation. Negotiations proceeded at what seemed to me a glacial pace. The BIT, signed by representatives of Egypt and the United States in September 1982, was the first one negotiated under the new policy. It received a few modifications before being submitted to the U.S. Senate in 1986.

Another issue I took an interest in was Egypt's textile exports to the United States. Textile trade in those days was subject to special trade rules under the General Agreement on Tariffs and Trade

(GATT). USTR had on staff a textile negotiator with ambassadorial rank. A U.S. government delegation led by USTR visited Egypt to look at the country's textile industry. The major textile producer was a state-owned company in Mahalla al-Kubra located in the Nile Delta a couple of hours' drive north of Cairo. I accompanied the delegation to visit the textile factory. We received a warm welcome by the company's management and were provided samples. My lasting memory of that day was a picture I took of three young girls working at a loom and flashing dazzling smiles. The problem with the photo was that it documented that the factory was employing child labor. I don't recall that anything ever came of the delegation's visit.

My USTR connection resulted in one awkward moment. I was at a dinner party attended by both Ambassador Atherton and DCM Precht when somebody came into the room and sang out in a loud voice, "Mr. Dunford, the White House is on the phone and wants to talk to you." All conversation stopped, and I could feel Atherton's and Precht's eyes on me as I walked into the other room to take the call. It was a midlevel USTR official calling about the latest twist in the BIT negotiations. USTR, located across the street from the Old Executive Office Building, used the White House switchboard for official overseas calls. The mystery explained, the buzz of ordinary conversation resumed.

In those days the embassy was housed in what had been a private villa. The ambassador and the DCM shared a suite at one end of the bottom floor, while the embassy conference room was at the other end. The political and economic sections were on the second floor. Each morning the ambassador or the DCM chaired a country team meeting. Representatives of each of the embassy sections (political, economic, consular, and administrative) attended, as well as representatives of each U.S. government agency present in Cairo. The U.S. Information Agency was a separate entity then. The conference room was also the venue for briefings of important visitors. By the end of my tour, I could give the economic briefing in my sleep. I would explain that the population of forty-one million (more than twice that by now) lived on 2 percent of the land along the Nile. Egypt depended on four major sources of revenue:

oil, Suez Canal tolls, remittances from Egyptians working abroad, and tourism. Egypt was struggling to reform the centrally planned economy instituted by Nasser and to reduce subsidies for bread, electricity, and a host of other goods and services.

Before coming to Cairo, I hadn't given much thought to exercise. I played quite a bit of pickup basketball with my neighbor at a nearby high school. Once settled in Egypt, I started to run regularly, starting out from my home on Road 19 in Ma'adi, running over to the American school (Cairo American College), around the school track for several laps, and then back home. My son started running with me and we would try to complete the three-mile run in twenty-four minutes or less. I also played quite a bit of tennis. The Embassy Recreation Association found enough money to construct a clay tennis court, and they did so in the backyard of our house because we had the biggest yard. After I left in 1984, the embassy turned the property into an American club and added a swimming pool.

Henry would occasionally recruit me to play tennis with official visitors who were looking for a game. I remember losing badly to Steve Solarz, a hard-charging congressman from Brooklyn and much-feared member of the House Foreign Affairs Committee (HFAC). Solarz was the congressman most responsible for the State Department splitting the Bureau of Near East and South Asian Affairs into two separate bureaus in 1992.

Even more memorable than the Solarz match was the time I was recruited, along with the CIA station chief, to play then–Secretary of State Al Haig and then–Assistant Secretary of State Nick Veliotes. Sam Lewis, our ambassador in Israel, had traveled to Cairo to meet with Haig and Veliotes, and he watched the match from the sidelines. The first two sets were competitive, but we punished Haig's weak backhand and won each by a score of six to four. Both men had a meeting scheduled with Egyptian foreign minister Kamal Hassan Ali, but they opted to send word that they would be late and play a third set. The result was the same.

Perhaps a year later, Nick Veliotes was named to replace Roy Atherton. He had sharper edges than Atherton, but he was also a true professional and he was happy to let those of us in the political and economic sections do our jobs. Shortly after he arrived he called me to arrange to play tennis with someone else on the court at my residence. I explained to him carefully that there was a sign-up sheet and I didn't exercise any control over it. I thought later that perhaps I should have been more helpful. Ambassador Veliotes had not forgotten our earlier match, and he wanted a rematch with the station chief and me. At the appointed time, he appeared with a partner who worked for USAID. His partner had both a backhand and a forehand and they beat us convincingly. Revenge accomplished, Ambassador Veliotes never asked us to play again.

President Mubarak would visit Washington about once a year, and I was asked on more than one occasion to fly back to Washington and help NEA prepare for the visit. By chance, I arrived just in time for the NFC Championship Game in January 1983 when the Washington Redskins of Joe Gibbs, Joe Theismann, and John Riggins beat the hated Dallas Cowboys. I was still there when the Redskins, featuring a 44-yard run by Riggins, won the Super Bowl over the Miami Dolphins. I flew back to Cairo with Betamax tapes of both games and was received as a hero. The administrative counselor scheduled a showing of both games in the embassy auditorium, and the place was packed with mostly Redskins fans. This was before the days when the embassy had access to the Armed Forces Radio and Television Service (AFRTS).

Cairo was my introduction to Middle East culture, and I learned lessons there that served me well throughout the rest of my career. Traffic was chaotic, and driving was an adventure. While I could use an embassy car and driver for official meetings, I had to do personal travel and errands in my Volvo. There were, strangely enough, traffic lights but they rarely worked and, when they did, they were ignored. Once a car nosed even slightly ahead, it could cut into your lane. You had to use the horn when you passed anyone. If for any reason your horn stopped working, the only safe thing to do was pull over and wait for help. Though some cars had rear-view mirrors, they were not necessary and even distracting. The good thing about traffic is that it moved slowly, and an accident rarely resulted in death or serious injury. This was not true on the Desert Road from Cairo to Alexandria, where cars traveled at high speed and had to pass badly overloaded buses and pickup trucks. Periodic dust storms (known as *hamseens*) could also make the Desert Road a death trap.

Learning to drive in Egypt was one thing but learning where to park was a separate skill. Sandy needed to complete two years of accounting practice to become a certified public accountant. She found a job with a Cairo branch of a major U.S. accounting firm. On her first day of work she found herself in front of the office in downtown Cairo with no place to park. She was late, so she double-parked and locked the door, hoping the car's diplomatic plates would protect her. When she returned to the car at the end of the day, she found it covered with stickers. An Egyptian emerged from the shadows and pleaded with her never to do it again. He would always see to it that she found a parking space. His living was finding people parking spaces for a small fee, universally known in Egypt as *baksheesh*. We quickly learned that this method also worked at other crowded places, like the popular downtown market district called the Khan al-Khalili.

Navigating Cairo traffic as a pedestrian was also challenging. There were no signs counting down from thirty while pedestrians walked safely across. It was necessary to make eye contact with an oncoming driver, cup the palm upward and move it slightly up and down. Every Egyptian is familiar with this gesture, which means, basically, "cut me a little slack." After crossing four lanes of traffic in this manner, it was normal for your heart rate to be accelerated. When traffic was completely stalled, a not unusual occurrence, it was best not to get overconfident. I once exited the embassy and, seeing gridlock in front of me, confidently crossed between two stationary cars and was knocked down by a motorcycle weaving through the space between lanes. Concerned Egyptians immediately surrounded me and helped me up, brushed the dust off my clothes, retrieved my glasses, and made sure I wasn't hurt too badly. I limped back into the embassy and went to the Health Unit, where they monitored my heart rate until it returned to normal.

As the head of an embassy section, part of my duty was to entertain. We received a staff for that purpose. Sandy went through a couple of cooks before finding one that was reliable. Although we sent out invitations for most of the dinners we hosted, some people responded and some didn't. Some of those who said they were coming didn't and some of those who didn't respond came anyway. We quickly learned to be flexible. I remember one ambitious dinner where we had invited forty or more people. We pulled out the stops and assembled thirty-two place settings. To my horror, thirty-one people had arrived when it was about time to serve dinner. I knew that a minister and his wife would still be coming. As we were about to panic, the minister appeared at the door and apologized that his wife was not able to join him. We told him how sorry we were, and the dinner went swimmingly.

Meetings with government officials in Egypt also required some cultural adjustment. One of my earliest meetings was with an undersecretary in the Ministry of International Cooperation. He was talkative and friendly, and I may have appeared to him a little stiff. We were sitting close together and he put his hand on my thigh to make a point. All I could think of over the next several minutes was that hand on my thigh, wondering where it might go next, and I pretty much lost the thread of whatever points he was trying to make. Americans unconsciously leave a bubble of space around them in such situations and the undersecretary had invaded mine. After I settled in, I grew to be comfortable with Egyptians who moved to within inches of my face to make a point. It was fun to watch newly arrived Americans in conversations with Egyptians, inadvertently moving backward until they had backed into a wall.

Meetings with ministers could be somewhat chaotic. These were the days before mobile phones, and ministers would usually have several phones in their offices. Some of them were not monitored by secretaries and the official would answer the phone directly. Secretaries would often bring papers in during the meeting for the official's signature. Some officials would have several meetings going on in their offices simultaneously. Both Minister of Electricity Maher Abaza and Chairman of the Central Bank Aly Negm would often greet me at the door, sit me down in a corner of the office, see that I got some coffee or tea, and then rejoin another meeting already under way. I came to assume that the meeting would last at least an hour, but I learned that I would only get about ten minutes of that hour to accomplish what I came to do.

Expatriates would often complain about what they called the "IBM" mentality. IBM stood for *insha'allah* (God willing), *bukra* (tomorrow), and *ma'alesh* (loosely translated as "never mind"). After a little time in Egypt I came to understand that insha'allah was simple recognition that despite one's best efforts, things can go wrong. We have a similar phrase—"God willing and the creeks don't rise." To this day, whenever I promise anything in any cultural situation, I add a version of insha'allah. Bukra was described to me as the same as the Spanish *mañana* but without the sense of urgency. Arabs, including Egyptians, don't like to say "no" to anyone. Bukra is an acceptable substitute and it at least allows you to put off saying "no" until another day. Ma'alesh is more a philosophy than a word. It means roughly that what just happened or whatever inconvenience you have just suffered is no big deal in the greater scheme of things. It is a philosophy that has allowed Egyptians over the years to be resilient in the face of a formidable array of obstacles to survival.

Following the Sadat assassination, my time in Egypt was not marked by any grave crises. Our colleagues in Beirut, Lebanon, were not so lucky. On April 18, 1983, a suicide truck bomb exploded outside the American Embassy in Beirut, killing seventeen Americans and many others. That led to the Inman Report, which funneled considerable amounts of money into hardening American embassies all over the world against attack. The American embassies in Egypt, Jordan, Saudi Arabia, and even Oman are now fortresses. An even worse attack took place in Beirut in October of that year, killing 241 Marines. The Lebanese Shi'a group responsible later became known as Hezbollah. These events were triggered by the Israeli decision to invade Lebanon in June 1982. There was speculation that Secretary of State Al Haig had given the Israelis the "green light." The Egyptians certainly believed that. Later, in

June 1982, President Reagan announced that George Shultz would replace Haig as secretary of state. Shultz came to Cairo following the embassy bombing to attend a memorial ceremony for the victims. I remember reaching out to local clergy—Christian, Muslim, and perhaps Jewish—to offer prayers at the event.

On January 18, 1984, Malcolm Kerr, president of the American University in Beirut, was killed outside his office. His wife, Ann, subsequently came to live in Egypt. Their son Steve, then a freshman at the University of Arizona, chose to suit up for the Wildcats basketball team two days later and became one of the best and most popular Arizona players and went on to have a highly successful career as an NBA player and coach. We followed these events closely, because many of the Middle East hands in the embassy were close with some of the victims.

Having secured the title of minister-counselor, I was the third-ranked American in the embassy, and a day arrived (it was two days) when both Ambassador Atherton and Henry Precht were out of the country. An embassy telegram announced that I had assumed charge (technically, I was the chargé d'affaires ad interim), with my name at the bottom. This is heady stuff for a relatively young Foreign Service Officer. Fuad Mohieddin, the Egyptian prime minister, had just died, and it fell to me to represent the United States in the funeral parade. Mubarak never appointed a vice president, so the prime minister was arguably the next most important Egyptian official. Practically, however, prime ministers in Egypt come and go and don't make a big impact. It was June and Ramadan, and Egyptian funeral parades are somewhat disorganized, as those who marched in Sadat's funeral parade can attest.

My two days were also memorable because of how I traveled to work on my first full day as chargé. I usually traveled to work in van C, an embassy van that picked up embassy employees who lived in my neighborhood in Ma'adi and drove us to work. A USAID officer who was a fellow rider, along with a friend of his in the embassy security section, managed to borrow the ambassador's vehicle, a big black Cadillac, and driver. I was out front of my house waiting for van C when the ambassador's Cadillac pulled up, followed by van C. My friends leaped out of the Cadillac and muscled me into the backseat. The Cadillac set off for the embassy with van C trailing behind as the follow car. When we arrived at the embassy the gates opened magically as they would for the ambassador. I was pleased that my friends were confident enough to arrange this joke and I took it as a message to not take myself too seriously.

As chargé I chaired the daily country team meeting. Our science counselor, Dr. Tom Vrebalovich, was always an active participant. Dr. Tom had genuine technical credentials, having graduated from Cal Tech with a PhD. Scientific cooperation between Egypt and Israel was a lively subject in the early years after the peace treaty was signed, and it seemed less vulnerable than other areas of cooperation to the chill in Egyptian-Israeli relations after Israel invaded Lebanon in 1982. One subject I remember Tom explaining was the problem of bilharzia (schistosomiasis) in the Nile River. Tom was very enthusiastic about the subjects he was following, and he was eager to share this enthusiasm to the point where the eyes of other country team members would begin to glaze over. If Roy Atherton became impatient, he never showed it. I took advantage of my temporary elevation to the chair to ask Tom to wrap up his presentation after he had gone on for five minutes. Several other members of the country team quietly commended my initiative after the meeting.

We did what we could to get to know the city and the country. Egypt is justifiably famous for pharaonic monuments such as the pyramids at Giza, the Sphinx, the monuments in Luxor, and sites all along the Nile in Upper Egypt. The Islamic monuments in Cairo were also impressive and more accessible. The Mosque of ibn Tulun, the al-Hakim Mosque, and the mausoleums in the City of the Dead are impressive examples. Far from being dead, the City of the Dead was home to many poorer Egyptians.

We made it a point to travel outside Cairo when we could. One of our early trips as a family was to Hurghada on the west coast of the Red Sea. We spent a few days there at the Club Med. It was our first flight on Egyptair. I remember trying to get on the plane with a huge crowd. There were no assigned seats, and as it turned out there were more passengers than seats. Our son and daughter, then eleven and ten years old, burrowed through the crowd and got on the plane early enough to claim seats for all four of us. As I recall, there were a few passengers who stood during the flight, as if passengers on a bus. At the Club Med some women were topless, and my son was wide-eyed.

Egypt was a very secular society in those days, more conservative than the United States and Europe but nowhere near as conservative as the Gulf countries or as conservative as Egypt would become. The *hijab* (pronounced hee-gab in Egypt), or headscarf, was rarely seen on Cairo streets.

We made at least two trips to Upper Egypt, taking the train on one. The most common brand of beer in Cairo was Stella, so I was surprised to order a beer on the train and find it was brewed in Israel. Our last year in Cairo, we booked a cruise from Luxor to Aswan. From Aswan, we flew to Abu Simbel to see the twin temples, which are well over three thousand years old. The temples were relocated in the 1960s to the west bank of Lake Nasser, the huge reservoir created by the building of the Aswan Dam.

On another occasion, we drove to Mersa Matrouh, a sleepy beach resort with a dramatic coastline on the Mediterranean close to the Libyan border. We also made two trips into the Sinai. The first was a visit to St. Catherine's Monastery at the foot of Mt. Sinai. It featured a remarkably well-preserved "burning bush." After a short sleep in monastic cells, we took a guided hike of three to four hours up Mt. Sinai, arriving at the top in the chill of dawn in time to view the sunrise. The route back down included hundreds of steps that were just a little bit too far apart. My calves were sore for days afterward. On the second visit, we traveled to the beach resort of Sharm al-Sheikh in the southern part of Sinai looking across the Strait of Tiran toward Saudi Arabia. During the time of Israeli control, some effort was made to develop it as a tourist destination because of its sheltered beaches and wonderful corals. It was still relatively undeveloped when we visited, and we elected to camp on the beach. It later became a major tourist resort and the site of several international conferences. Tourism there has suffered in recent years owing to terrorist attacks.

We also took advantage of our time in Cairo to visit nearby countries. Our family visited Cyprus, Turkey, and Israel. This was my first of three trips to Israel. We traveled by bus with a church group. The bus took us across the Suez Canal on a ferry, and we continued through the northern part of Sinai to Gaza. We were met at the Israeli border by an Israeli guide. The itinerary might be described as following in the footsteps of Jesus, but our Israeli guide made sure that we understood well the Israeli side of the Arab-Israeli conflict. We visited Tel Aviv and several places along the Israeli coast, continuing to the Sea of Galilee. Our journey continued up to the Golan Heights, driving up to the ceasefire line with Syria. We then turned south to Jerusalem, visiting the Old City, the Dome of the Rock, the Western Wall, and the Church of the Holy Sepulcher. Finally, we went to the Dead Sea and to Masada.

I traveled without the family to Sudan, then a unified country. Our Defense Attaché Office had its own plane, and the staff's responsibilities included Sudan. The office kindly invited Mark Hambley from the political section and me to go along. U.S. Ambassador to Sudan Bill Kontos was our host. We spent some time in Khartoum and visited the Kenana sugar plant farther south. I was amazed to see the Nile River choked with water hyacinths. We then flew to Malakal and on to the location of a massive French digger. The Jonglei Canal was a project to carve a canal through the huge marsh in the south known as the Sudd. The project was designed to increase the flow of Nile River water downstream and improve transportation between north and south. Political instability and violence in 1983 led to a suspension in construction, the year after I visited, and it has never resumed. The digger is reportedly still there.

My friendship with Capt. David Sperling paid off in other ways as well. He invited Sandy and me to visit one of our aircraft carriers, the uss *John F. Kennedy*, as it was passing through the Suez Canal. After Israel invaded Lebanon, the carrier had been ordered to the waters off the coast of Lebanon, ostensibly to support the possible evacuation of Americans from Beirut. We boarded near Ismail-iya, climbing up ladders and stairs. Standing on the flight deck as we passed through the canal, it appeared as though we were sailing through the desert. The water of the canal itself was not visible. We met several of the pilots of the VA-75 attack squadron. At Suez we disembarked and looked back to see the crew lined up along the edge of the flight deck, looking down at us.

Looking back on our time in Egypt, we were there at an opportune moment. Following Sadat's assassination, Egypt was calm. There were tensions with Israel, Libya, and Sudan but no crisis erupted. We lived in a pleasant suburb, about a mile from the Cairo American College (CAC), which turned out to be an excellent school. The campus provided the venue for youth and adult sports. An American friend and I put together a youth soccer team, made up of boys and girls in the middle-school grades. We didn't have an extensive schedule, but we competed against other teams in the Cairo area made up of expatriates' children. The school had a swim team, and I can remember my daughter traveled with it to a meet in Israel. I was part of an adult slow-pitch softball team that played every week. I still hear the cries of "Stella" whenever any player popped up. In theory, anyone who popped out had to buy a Stella beer for everybody else on the team.

The American Embassy had an annual softball game against the Japanese Embassy at CAC. Yukio Okamoto, a charismatic diplomat who went on to be a very influential adviser to at least two Japanese prime ministers, was the driving force in the Japanese Embassy. While our embassies would no doubt have kept in regular touch at any rate, the annual softball game created a closer bond that was a real asset for both embassies. My first year, we won handily. The second year, the Japanese Embassy brought along a ringer who hit a home run every time he came to the plate. The third and final year I was there, every member of the Japanese Embassy came to the game wearing bright yellow t-shirts lettered with "We beat the American Embassy, ha, ha!" Thus provoked, we put together a convincing victory.

One of the interesting aspects of the Egyptian economy in those days was the existence of multiple exchange rates. There was an official exchange rate and an actual exchange rate, the latter of which we called the "gray" market rate. We didn't use the term "black" because it was not illegal. At the official rate, a U.S. dollar was worth about seventy piasters, or 0.7 Egyptian pounds. In the popular market (*souk*), a U.S. dollar was worth well more than one Egyptian pound. In addition to the distortions an economist can describe, this caused at least two problems for us. First, almost every official American imported a car into Egypt when he or she arrived. Upon departure the employee would typically sell the car for more than they paid for it because auto imports into Egypt were heavily taxed. Then the American could take the Egyptian pounds received from the buyer to the embassy cashier and convert them to dollars at the official exchange rate. Once word got out, arriving Americans were bringing the most expensive cars they could afford (Mercedes were popular), driving them for two to four years and selling them for well more than they paid for them. This practice eventually attracted the attention of the American press, and the embassy drew up regulations to prevent it.

A Department of State employee whose job it was to oversee budget and fiscal operations at U.S. embassies surveyed the exchange rate situation and devised what he thought was a foolproof embezzlement scheme. It involved using a personal banking account to buy Egyptian pounds with dollars at the gray market rate and selling them back to the U.S. government at the official rate. It turned out not to be foolproof, and this individual was prosecuted.

My assignment in Egypt was for three years, and I hoped to return to the United States for the four years that my children would need to graduate from high school. With support from Ambassador Veliotes and Henry Precht, I was offered the job of Director of the Office of Egyptian Affairs in the State Department. My superiors encouraged me during my last months in Cairo to expand my understanding of what we were doing in Egypt beyond the economy and the USAID program. I was not ignorant of political and political-military issues, having sat through numerous country team meetings where these issues were discussed. I did go with Edmund Hull, then the Embassy Cairo political-military officer, to an Egyptian air base where the U.S. military had a presence.

The State Department also funded an orientation trip for me to

Jordan, the West Bank, and Israel. I can remember meeting a junior officer assigned to our embassy in Amman named Bill Burns, who rose up the ranks to be the deputy secretary of state. The embassy in Amman transported me down to the Allenby Bridge over the Jordan River. A guard directed me to walk across the bridge with my luggage. An unsmiling female Israeli immigration official awaited me on the far side. She was all business. I was carrying a separate diplomatic passport to be used for travel to Israel. Doug Keene, who had been Embassy Cairo's political-military officer and was now the deputy principal officer of our consulate-general in Jerusalem, met me at the border. He took me to several West Bank cities where I met with Palestinian officials. It was my second trip to Israel but my first real exposure to the Palestinian side of the conflict. I learned of attacks by a Jewish terrorist group on the Palestinian mayors of Nablus and Ramallah that maimed them for life. The same group was apparently contemplating blowing up the Dome of the Rock, a Muslim shrine erected in the seventh century on the Temple Mount (Haram ash-Sharif to Muslims). Such an act would clear the way to build a third temple on the Temple Mount.

Back in Cairo, it was time for Sandy and me to summon our stamina for the farewell parties and pack up and head back to Washington. Egypt had been rocked by Sadat's assassination four months into my tour, but the country had remained calm over the balance of it. One bad sign was an attack in the early summer of 1984 on an Israeli diplomat near the home of the Israeli ambassador in Ma'adi only a few blocks from my home. As I left, thoughts of what might have been, had I gone to Brasilia, were long gone. I had learned to comfortably navigate the culture in one of the most important Middle Eastern countries and I had worked for three years with some of the finest professionals in the career Foreign Service. I had also drunk from the Nile, at least metaphorically, and there was little doubt that I would return to the Middle East.

2

WASHINGTON

Egypt and Crisis Management

On my first day back to work in DC as director of Egyptian affairs in early August 1984, the U.S. government was grappling with reports that ships exiting the Suez Canal into the Red Sea were running into mines. My new office was at the center of the crisis. The U.S. response was to put together a naval task force in cooperation with several European countries to clear the mines and protect shipping. Libya, then ruled by Muammar Qaddafi, was the suspected culprit, but it took about a year to confirm the suspicion completely.

I would be disingenuous if I claimed to have done much that day other than to watch in amazement as the capable team that I was inheriting dealt with what needed to be done. At that point, I had neither the contacts nor the background to be of much help other than to proofread memos. I was now director, however, so leaving while the rest of the staff was still working would have been bad form. I stayed until the work was done at about 9:00 p.m. that evening. When I was on the phone to Sandy, explaining the latest delay, Arnie Raphel came in to discuss a memo prepared by our office. Arnie was now the principal deputy assistant secretary (#2 in the Bureau of Near East and South Asian Affairs). Arnie and Sandy knew each other well from our early days in the Foreign Service, so I handed him the phone and gave him the job of explaining why I was still in the office.

When I started this new job, the Reagan administration's foreign policy machinery was running reasonably smoothly. George

Shultz had settled into his job as secretary of state. Dick Murphy, a highly respected career diplomat, was the NEA assistant secretary, with Arnie as his deputy. My immediate boss was Deputy Assistant Secretary Bob Pelletreau, another career diplomat who had earned the respect of his colleagues with service at several tough Middle East posts. My job, and that of the four Foreign Service Officers (FSOs) who worked for me, was to manage the relationship between the United States and Egypt. This involved daily contact with our embassy in Cairo and near daily contact with the Egyptian Embassy in Washington. Nick Veliotes and Henry Precht remained in Cairo during my first year in Washington, making my transition to the Office of Egyptian Affairs practically seamless.

The Egyptian ambassador in Washington, Ashraf Ghorbal, had held his position since U.S.-Egyptian relations were reestablished more than ten years earlier and was one of the best known and most respected foreign diplomats in Washington. It was now time for him to retire, and I received an invitation to one or more farewell events per day for several weeks. It was a real advantage, early in my tenure, to meet socially the people in the Washington area involved in U.S.-Egyptian relations and to bask in Ghorbal's reflected glory. Ghorbal finally departed in November and was replaced by Abdel Raouf el-Reedy. El-Reedy was smart, fluent in English, and a genuinely nice man. Now that the legendary Ghorbal was gone, el-Reedy and I were both finding our way in Washington and we did what we could to help each other. I made sure that he was kept in the loop on various elements of the relationship being dealt with by Washington agencies and Congress.

Every year, State and other agencies would put together a budget proposal for foreign assistance. Israel and Egypt got at least half. As noted in the previous chapter, Egypt received $2.115 billion plus perhaps $200 million in U.S. wheat under PL-480. Israel received $3 billion ($1.2 billion in economic assistance or ESF and $1.8 billion in military aid or FMS). These numbers had strong congressional support, so there was little need for an administration lobbying campaign. Other recipients of U.S. aid and their corresponding regional offices in the State Department were not so lucky. I would periodically get visits from my regional counterparts pleading for us to release a few million for what they considered an essential foreign policy initiative. Surely, we could spare such a small amount. I would listen sympathetically but would then have to explain the harsh political reality. Aid to Egypt and Israel was a "sacred cow." Occasionally, a powerful congressman like David Obey, chair of the House Foreign Operations Committee, or Tom Lantos, a Holocaust survivor and strong supporter of Israel who served on the House Foreign Affairs Committee, would suggest leveraging some of our assistance to encourage better behavior from Egypt. But the aid figures were far too political to be budged during those years.

While there were political limits on my freedom of action, I was never bored during the three years I spent in the Office of Egyptian Affairs. There were things I could control and initiatives I could take. The State Department was officially open from 8:15 a.m. until 5:00 p.m. I would usually drive in from my home in Fairfax, normally a commute of about an hour. My job came with a much-coveted parking pass for the State Department underground garage. I walked up the stairwell to the sixth floor for exercise and stopped at the NEA communications center to grab the sheaf of telegrams that had come in overnight. I tried to be in the office by 8:00 a.m. Ambassador el-Reedy soon learned my routine, and my first act of the day might be to take a phone call from him and talk through his latest crisis. While I read through the messages, the rest of the office would trickle in and we would agree on morning assignments. Media stories were a priority. A front-page story by the *New York Times* or the *Washington Post* involving Egypt could often trigger unhelpful congressional initiatives and had to be dealt with promptly. Draft press guidance was due in the NEA front office by 9:30 for approval and use by the State Department spokesperson in the noon briefing.

Henry Precht remained in Cairo, and I was now on the Washington end of his daily phone calls. Cairo was normally six hours ahead of Washington time, so our phone calls usually had to happen by late morning. We had by now been working together on

Egyptian issues for more than three years and we could often fin-ish each other's sentences as we discussed how to manage the daily challenges.

Most days, the hours between noon and 3:00 p.m. were rela-tively calm, allowing time for exercise and lunch at my desk. I tried running early in the morning but there wasn't enough time to run, spend time with my family, and get a decent night's sleep. I learned to play squash and paid for a membership at George Washington University's Smith Center, an easy walk from the back entrance of the State Department. I often played squash during the lunch hour with my USAID counterpart, Dick Brown, and the walk over and back to the Smith Center gave us a chance to talk through the differences between State and AID on Egypt economic issues.

By 3:00 p.m. the Washington bureaucracy was gearing up to send instructions to our embassy in Cairo on a variety of issues. Outgoing telegrams had to be written, cleared with other parts of State and other agencies, and, if important enough, approved by the NEA front office and perhaps even by the secretary of state. I learned quickly that the best way to control the substance of an instruction was for our office to volunteer to write the initial draft. The clearance process often required multiple telephone calls, vis-its to other offices in the building, and multiple rewrites. My last act each day was to sign off on the official-informal telegram (o-i) to our Cairo Embassy. Usually, everybody in the office had one or more items to contribute to the o-i. Sandy had issued strict instructions that, absent a major crisis, I would be home for the family dinner with my kids, now high school students, no later than 7:40 p.m. at home in Fairfax. I made it a practice to depart the office by 7:00 p.m., even though many of my fellow office directors hung around well beyond that time. Because rush hour was over by then, I could make it home in thirty-five minutes.

Word processing was still in its infancy in the State Department in 1984. Department offices all used Wang computers, which were state-of-the-art in the early 1980s. In Cairo I wrote messages on a legal pad and office secretaries would type them on telegram forms. Now, I found myself typing messages on a computer monitor with two fingers. Periodically, the system would crash, or I would hit the wrong key and the text would disappear into the ether forever. Eleven years later when I retired in 1995, the State Department was still using WANG computers, while the rest of the world had upgraded to the now more familiar brands of Dell, Apple, and Microsoft.

During the summer and fall of 1985, NEA was in almost permanent crisis mode. On June 14, TWA flight 847 departed Cairo destined for San Diego, with several stops along the way. After a stop in Athens, it was flying to Rome when it was hijacked by Lebanese Shi'a terrorists from the organization that came to be known as Hezbollah. The plane was diverted to Beirut International Airport and, over the course of the seventeen-day crisis, made two round trips to Algiers and back. After the plane initially landed in Algiers, the Algerian government managed to negotiate the release of the women and children onboard. The hijackers ordered the pilot to fly back to Beirut. Checking identification documents during the flight, they discovered a U.S. Navy Seal named Robert Stethem. The hijackers beat him badly and, after the flight landed, they shot and killed him and dumped his body on the tarmac, presumably as a signal of their seriousness.

Joined by some of their compatriots in Lebanon, the hijackers flew back to Algiers, where negotiations with the Algerian government resulted in the release of two-thirds of the remaining hostages. The plane flew back to Beirut and the remaining hostages were disbursed to locations throughout the city. Negotiations ensued, involving Lebanese Shi'a prisoners being held by the Israelis, and the hostages were eventually released. No one wanted to admit that these talks were negotiations because U.S. policy precluded negotiating with terrorists. The hijackers melted back into Beirut neighborhoods. The Americans were flown to Frankfort and on to Washington, where they were met by President Reagan. Of the 139 passengers and eight crew members, Stethem was the only one who died during the ordeal.

For those of us in NEA, the crisis consumed our lives for the next seventeen days. During such an event, a crisis center would be set up in the State Department in a conference room, equipped with phones for each seat at the table. The room was located on the seventh floor next to the Operations Center (Op Center), the nerve center for communications with all State Department posts around the world as well as with all other U.S. government agencies. The NEA bureau, the Bureau of Consular Affairs, and the Counterterrorism Office (S/CT), along with several other bureaus, would be represented. The center was staffed 24/7 and almost every NEA officer would do shifts on the task force in addition to their regular jobs. Information was hard to come by and the most reliable source was the television on the conference room wall broadcasting CNN. The news network was only a few years old then and it had no real competition. The major networks would interrupt their regular programming occasionally to report on dramatic events, but CNN was reporting all day and all night.

I remember talking by phone to embassy officers in Algiers and Beirut and getting snippets of information that we would plug into a periodic sitrep (situation report) prepared for senior State officials. While talking to an Embassy Beirut officer the day Stethem got killed, we heard the ominous information that the hijackers were checking passports for Jewish-sounding names. Consular Affairs handled phone calls from concerned relatives of the passengers but the rest of us helped as needed.

It is instructive to zoom out and consider the overall atmosphere in the summer of 1985. The Reagan administration was at the beginning of its second term. It saw Middle East issues primarily through the lens of the U.S.-Soviet rivalry. The Israeli invasion of Lebanon in 1982 led to our military involvement there. We had pulled out of Lebanon in early 1984 having lost multiple civilian and military lives without accomplishing anything positive. The Lebanese civil war was raging, and Hezbollah was holding seven Americans as hostages in unknown locations. The Reagan administration had announced in 1982 a Middle East peace plan (Reagan plan) that proposed Palestinian self-government in association with Jordan. We refused to talk with the Palestinian Liberation Organization (PLO) until it accepted UN resolutions supporting a "land-for-peace" solution and renounced terrorism. Reagan had responded in a press conference that he didn't think Israeli settlements in occupied territories were illegal, contradicting a long-standing U.S. policy. The PLO, Jordan, and Israel had little enthusiasm for the Reagan plan and Israel clearly had no intention of freezing settlement growth. Two years later in 1987, Palestinian frustration would boil over into the uprising dubbed the *Intifada* (or shaking off) in the West Bank and Gaza. Grievances abounded and none of the Arabs saw the Reagan plan as a serious way forward. The atmosphere was ripe for terrorist attacks. The hijacking of TWA 847 was far from the only terrorist incident that summer. There were bombs in airports in Frankfort and Tokyo and the destruction of an Air India flight killing more than three hundred.

The summer passed into fall. Henry Precht's tour in Cairo was coming to an end and he was replaced by Bill Clark, who had spent most of his career in East Asia. Bill was coming from Japan, where life for a senior diplomat was considerably more orderly than what Henry had experienced in Cairo. Bill held some unrealistic expectations about the housing and domestic staff that would await him in Cairo. Henry, well into his fourth year in Cairo, was inured to the chaos and disorder of life in Cairo. He shared with me the gist of his communications with Bill and his concerns that Bill would have a tough time adjusting. Bill stipulated that he would have to visit Cairo before agreeing to take the job. The State Department balked at funding the trip, but Nick Veliotes very much wanted Clark for his deputy and talked the department into making it happen. Bill made the trip and, to my mild surprise, agreed to take the job. His was a very different personality from Henry but he was smart, professional, and he made the adjustment to Cairo. The close relationship between Egyptian Affairs and Embassy Cairo continued.

On October 1, Israeli F-15s attacked and destroyed PLO headquarters in Tunis, killing at least forty-seven Palestinians and Tunisians and wounding even more. The Israelis were responding to a September 25 Palestinian attack off the coast of Cyprus that killed three Israeli tourists. President Reagan's initial statement about the October 1 attack called it a "legitimate response to terrorism." Arab governments in general and the Tunisian government were outraged. On October 5, the UN Security Council condemned the Israeli attack in a fourteen to zero vote, with the United States abstaining. That same day, an Egyptian soldier shot seven Israeli tourists including children at Ras Burqa, a Sinai beach resort. The hijacking of the *Achille Lauro*, an Italian cruise ship, was the next event in this ongoing cycle of violence.

On October 7, the *Achille Lauro* docked in Alexandria and the majority of passengers went off to Cairo to tour the Pyramids of Giza. After the buses departed, a crew member surprised four members of the Palestine Liberation Front (PLF), a faction of the PLO, cleaning their AK-47s in their cabin. The hijackers were not planning to act until the ship reached its next stop, the Israeli port of Ashdod. The hijackers, once discovered, forced the captain and the crew to depart Alexandria. They demanded the release of Palestinians held in Israeli prisons. The ship headed for Syria, but the Syrian authorities would not allow it to dock. The hijackers then shot Leon Klinghoffer, an elderly Jewish American confined to a wheelchair, and threw his body over the side. The hijackers tried to take the ship into port in Cyprus but were again rebuffed. They headed back to Port Said in Egypt, where they established radio contact with the Egyptian authorities, and a deal was cut. The Egyptians were not aware at this point that Klinghoffer had been murdered.

By now Abu Abbas (Mohammed Zaidan), head of the PLF faction, had arrived in Egypt along with a sidekick. The Egyptians agreed that if the hijackers released the hostages, they would be provided safe passage out of the country. With that understanding, the hijackers disembarked in Port Said and turned themselves into the Egyptians.

When initial word came of the hijacking, NEA reassembled the seventh-floor crisis task force, and our office and others in NEA went back to staffing it 24/7. There wasn't much to do at first except watch CNN and answer queries from worried friends and relatives of the passengers until the ship returned to Port Said. Ambassador Veliotes took a team from the embassy to Port Said, where they boarded the ship. Nick learned from the shaken captain and passengers what had happened to Klinghoffer. He called Bill Clark on an unsecure ship-to-shore telephone that, unbeknownst to him, was monitored by the press. Nick told Clark to contact Egyptian foreign minister Esmat Abdel Meguid and tell him to "prosecute the sons of bitches." "Sons of bitches" does not translate well into Arabic, and those few words unfortunately defined Nick Veliotes in the Arab world from that day forward. Nick frequently used salty language and, after spending a considerable amount of time with emotionally distraught passengers, including Marilyn Klinghoffer, he can hardly be blamed for using the term during what he thought was a private conversation.

The Egyptians clearly wanted no part of prosecuting the hijackers, who would be viewed by many Egyptians as heroes, and hit upon the idea of sending them to PLO headquarters in Tunis to be dealt with. When we asked about the hijackers, the Egyptians, who by then knew of Klinghoffer's murder, told us they had left the country. We knew from intelligence sources that this was not true. We also learned of Egyptian plans to fly the hijackers, along with Abu Abbas and his associate, on a chartered Egyptair 737 to Tunis to be turned over to Yasser Arafat and the PLO.

A young lieutenant colonel named Oliver North, who achieved quite a bit of notoriety the following year in the Iran-Contra scandal, suggested to his bosses in the National Security Council that, because we had enough information to identify the plane, why not intercept it and force it to land, where we could capture Klinghoffer's murderers. President Reagan reportedly quickly approved the operation. North's bosses, National Security Advisor Bud McFarlane and his deputy, Admiral John Poindexter, also played major roles in the Iran-Contra scandal.

While this was happening, I was not in the crisis room but back in my office on the floor below trying to do my day job. I received a call to go upstairs to see Mike Armacost, the undersecretary for political affairs. Armacost was the third-ranking official in the department and responsible for overseeing regional bureaus like NEA. When I arrived in his office, Armacost was animatedly talking to his aides. He waived me in and told me that U.S. Navy jets (F-14 Tomcats) were in the air over the Mediterranean flanking an Egyptair plane carrying the hijackers. How did I think the Egyptians would react if we intercepted the aircraft? It was a lot to take in, but I knew immediately that the Egyptians would react with a mixture of embarrassment and anger, and I told Armacost as much. Armacost wasn't about to try to stop the interception and I certainly didn't blame him. I was grateful that he had the wit to make sure that the Office of Egyptian Affairs was looped into the action.

Pilots ordered the Egyptair plane to fly to Sigonella Air Base in Sicily. After a long standoff with the Italian authorities, we allowed the Italians to take the four hijackers into custody, along with Abu Abbas and his deputy. Much to our consternation, the Italians allowed Abu Abbas and his companion to depart Italy. Abu Abbas found his way to Baghdad, where he was still living eighteen years later when U.S. forces invaded Iraq. He was captured during the first days of the invasion and died eleven months later in U.S. custody, reportedly of natural causes.

Although much of the drama was over on October 10, the crisis task force kept functioning for several more days. I remember four nights later I was taking a shift on the task force. I snuck over to the Op Center, where there was a small group watching the Dodgers and the Cardinals in Game 5 of the National League Championship series. I had been a rabid Cardinals fan since I was nine years old and was bummed that I had to work when I wanted to be home watching. Shortly after I arrived in front of the screen, Ozzie Smith, one of my sports heroes, hit an improbable home run to help the Cardinals win three to two. A mixture of cheers and groans rang through the center as people working the phones looked up in annoyance.

The real work was now back on the sixth floor in the Office of Egyptian Affairs. Our interception of the Egyptair flight and subsequent events strained relations not only with Egypt but also with Tunisia and Italy. The administration elected to send Deputy Secretary of State John Whitehead, who had only been in the job for two months, to the three capitals (Cairo, Tunis, and Rome) to soothe the anger. The press stories about Veliotes's characterization of the hijackers as "sons of bitches" allowed President Mubarak a way to deflect some, but not all, of the Egyptian criticism of the way the incident had been handled. There were demonstrations in Cairo provoking a massive military and police presence on the streets. Americans too were angry about the murder of Klinghoffer and at Mubarak because he had lied to us and had been caught in the lie.

For about ten days, Americans and Egyptians exchanged barbs. Mubarak claimed that Egypt had acted in good faith to protect the cruise ship passengers and that Americans stabbed him in the back, and Americans accused Egyptians of intending to let murderers go free. I watched Ambassador el-Reedy on television struggling with tough questions from Ted Koppel on *Nightline*. Whitehead arrived in Egypt on October 21, but Mubarak professed to be too busy to meet him until the third day of his visit. Cooler heads eventually prevailed, considering the relationship was too important to both countries to be allowed to fail. Following the visit, contacts between Americans and Egyptians gradually returned to normal, although the episode left scars.

The *Achille Lauro* affair overall was a major success for the Reagan administration. It was a case study in the capable gathering and effective use of intelligence in real time. The NSC made a bold decision to act and the U.S. Navy executed the plan flawlessly. Unfortunately, it may have given the NSC leadership too much confidence in Ollie North's judgment because the plan that led to the Iran-Contra scandal was not only highly flawed, but ultimately judged illegal.[1]

A month later I was back on the seventh floor working in a new crisis task force. On Saturday, November 23, three Palestinians associated with Abu Nidal hijacked Egyptair flight 648 after it left Athens bound for Cairo. When the hijackers tried to take control of the plane, an Egyptian air marshal on the flight opened fire and in the ensuing gunfire the air marshal, two crew members, and a hijacker were wounded. The hijackers had originally planned to take the plane to Libya, but Libyan government reluctance and low fuel forced the hijackers to divert to Malta. The Maltese government did what it could to prevent the plane from landing, but the pilot managed to land at Luqa Airport near the Maltese capital of Valletta anyway.

My colleague Phil Wilcox, who was director of the Office of Israel and Arab-Israeli Affairs (NEA/IAI), had been selected by the NEA front office to direct the *Achille Lauro* task force. I had grumbled a bit about this to Arnie Raphel because it appeared that most of the action would involve Egypt. That may have played into Arnie's decision to tap me for task force leadership on the Malta hijacking. The events of the next forty-eight hours reminded me to be careful what I wished for. I was co-leader of the task force with Ambassador Bob Oakley, who was at the time the State Department coordinator for counterterrorism.

The Maltese prime minister came to Luqa Airport to lead negotiations. The hijackers released some passengers initially. Without warning they brought a female Israeli passenger to the cabin door, shot her, and dumped her on the tarmac. She survived by pretending to be dead. The hijackers had collected passports and over the next day, four more passengers, another Israeli woman and three Americans (two women and a man), were shot and dumped on the tarmac. Two of the three Americans ended up surviving, although one of the American women sustained permanent injuries.

I remember learning of the shootings from telephone conversations with Embassy officers in Malta. Bob Oakley was busy coordinating military medical support and a U.S. offer to send a special-forces team to deploy to Malta. While this was going on, I answered the phone and Secretary Shultz was on the line asking for an update. I told him what I knew and, considering I wasn't totally up to speed on what Oakley was doing, I made sure that the secretary also talked to Oakley. While the Maltese were negotiating with the hijackers, other negotiations were going on between us, the Maltese, and the Egyptians. The Maltese, I was told, refused to allow the U.S. team to come but did agree to accept an Egyptian commando unit that had been trained by the U.S. military.

The Egyptian government asked us to provide an air escort to the plane carrying their commandos to Malta, ironic given that the previous month the U.S. Navy escorted an unwilling Egyptian plane to Sicily. The Egyptians also asked that we send along members of our military advisory group in Egypt.

The Egyptian commandos, on Monday, November 25, blew a hole in the luggage compartment and stormed the plane. The U.S. advisors were not involved in the Egyptian decision to act, nor were they included in the action. The hijackers fought back with grenades and soon the plane was engulfed in an explosion. Roughly fifty people were killed, including all but one of the hijackers but mostly passengers, including children. It was a tragic outcome. There was an embarrassing lack of soul-searching after the incident concluded, in my opinion. We could point to the lax security at the airport at Athens, to the stubborn refusal of the Maltese to accept our help, and to the ham-handed actions of the Egyptian commandos. While these issues were addressed in the aftermath, by the time we returned from the Thanksgiving weekend, most of our time and energy was taken up with new challenges.

All three of these hijacking events were examples of the use of terrorism as a tactic. All three groups of hijackers singled out American and Israeli passengers for retribution. Although Hezbollah (Party of God, in Arabic) is Islamic, none of the incidents featured the use of terror in the name of Islam that we have come to be familiar with after the September 11, 2001, attacks. Both Palestinian-inspired attacks were carrying out by secular Palestinian organizations.

Terror is an attractive tactic for groups that are weak militarily, and don't possess carrier battle groups and high-performance fighter jets. In the mid-80s, passenger airlines and cruise ships were vulnerable targets. It was also no accident that the two hijacked planes departed Athens, where airport security was then easily bypassed. We are fond of describing terrorist acts of violence as "senseless" and "evil," blinding us to the reality that terrorists have political agendas. All three of the hijackings in the summer and fall of 1985 were related to Israeli occupation. In the case of TWA 847, the hijackers were Lebanese Shi'a. Israel invaded Lebanon in 1982 and continued to occupy the southern part of Lebanon where Lebanese Shi'a make up the majority of the population. One consequence of the Israeli invasion was the massacre of hundreds of Palestinians in refugee camps near Beirut called Sabra and Shatila. While a Lebanese Christian militia was responsible for the slaughter, they entered through a perimeter set up by the Israeli Defense Forces to do so. The *Achille Lauro* and Egyptair 648 were both hijacked by splinter Palestinian groups, the PLF and Abu Nidal respectively.

Though the hijackers made demands for the release of passengers taken hostage, such as the release of prisoners in Israel jails, their main motive was to attract the attention of the world to their cause and to make that cause relevant. As Tom Friedman wrote in *From Beirut to Jerusalem*, Yasser Arafat's genius was to take the Palestinian movement "out of the deserts of obscurity into the land of prime time."[2] Arafat was head of Fatah and chairman of the Palestinian Liberation Organization, an umbrella group that included Fatah and the Palestinian Liberation Front (PLF), the group that hijacked the *Achille Lauro*, but not the Abu Nidal organization, which was responsible for the Egyptair hijacking. Abu Nidal was responsible for simultaneous attacks in the Rome and Vienna airports, roughly a month after the Malta incident, killing twenty people. Arafat claimed to be out of the terrorism business by 1985, and while I am confident he did not coordinate with Abu Nidal, I am less confident that he was not aware of the *Aquille Lauro* plot given the close relationship between the PLF and Fatah.

The emergence of CNN in the late 1970s was a huge boon for potential terrorists. A terrorist attack is indeed senseless if the world never finds out about it or ignores it. CNN's blanket coverage of terrorist events had the world sitting on the edge of the couch waiting to see what would happen. Journalists had long before understood that coverage of violence sells newspapers, but CNN took that truth to a new level. The news coverage of the hijackings rarely if ever included an analysis of the hijackings in the overall context of the Arab-Israeli struggle, including the extension of Israeli law to the occupied Golan Heights, the Israeli invasion of Lebanon, the Sabra-Shatila massacres, the Israeli attack on the PLO headquarters, and the expansion of Israeli settlements in the West Bank. Reagan administration officials were not about to provide this context. The pro-Israel lobby was at the height of its power and would sharply attack any statements that suggested moral equivalence between Arab terrorism and Israeli actions.

The winter holidays came and went, and the early months of 1986 produced new challenges for the Office of Egyptian Affairs. Oil prices, which had peaked during the time of the Iranian Revolution in 1979, dropped sharply in early 1986, impacting most of Egypt's sources of foreign exchange. On February 25, conscripts of Egypt's Central Security Forces (CSF) rioted and targeted tourist sites, including hotels and nightclubs. Most lived in camps on the outskirts of the city, explaining why the rioting started near the Giza pyramids. The rioting was set off by rumors that three-year compulsory service would be extended an extra year without any corresponding benefits. The CSF forces were conscripts, uneducated young men from rural Egypt. They were poorly paid, badly treated, and looked at with distain by urban Egyptians. While I was now far away in Washington, having served in Egypt, I was familiar with the situation of the police conscripts. I always had two or three shabbily dressed guards stationed across the street from our home in the Cairo suburb of Ma'adi. They had rifles, but we were never sure if they were loaded with ammunition. I worried some days that they were loaded and other days that they weren't. Our household staff would see to it that they got sugar for their tea and did what they could to maintain a positive relationship with them. One evening, while our family and household staff were away, our guards did a thorough job of harvesting the mangoes growing in our back yard.

The Egyptian government called out the regular military to suppress the riots, and it succeeded in doing so after three days. Remarkably, the rioting did not spread to opposition groups or other elements of Egyptian society. There wasn't much we could do from Washington except to stay in close communication with the embassy. The embassy's basic preoccupation was the protection of American citizens. The Bureau of Consular Affairs did set up a task force to respond to inquiries about American citizens in Egypt. Those Americans working in the embassy and the downtown area who had their families in Ma'adi, well south of Cairo, were particularly anxious. Bill Clark, in charge of the embassy during this incident, contacted Defense Minister Abu Ghazala, who arranged to escort a convoy of embassy vehicles taking embassy employees back to their families in Ma'adi.

My first reaction to the news of the police rioting was that the unsustainable problems of the Egyptian economy were now leading to political instability. While the military did a credible job of restoring order, much to the relief of most Egyptians, it did stimulate those of us concerned with Egypt to give more attention to how we could work with USAID, the IMF, and the World Bank to get Egypt more firmly on the path to economic reform. This issue dominated my third and last year in NEA, but in the weeks and months after the police riots, the Office of Egyptian Affairs was consumed by the issue of Taba.

Taba is about 250 acres of beach bordering the Red Sea near Eilat, Israel, and Aqaba, Jordan. Israel turned over the eastern half of the Sinai Peninsula, pursuant to the Egyptian-Israeli peace treaty, on April 25, 1982, but chose not to withdraw from Taba. Israel's position was that, back in the days of the Ottoman Empire, the boundary between Palestine and the Sinai had been incorrectly delineated. Israel had not raised this when it signed an armistice with Egypt in 1949, nor did it raise Taba when Israel withdrew from the Sinai after the Suez Crisis of 1956.

Israel's flimsy legal justification seems to have been constructed after Israel decided not to withdraw. There are various explanations for this Israeli decision. There was an obvious economic motive. Taba was a popular tourist destination for Israelis when Israelis occupied the Sinai. The Sonesta, a five-star hotel, was being constructed in Taba in 1982 to give tourists an alternative to a beach village, owned by a colorful Israeli with a glass eye and a cowboy hat named Rafi Nelson. There were political motives. Some argue that it gave Israel leverage to deal with Egypt after withdrawing from the Sinai, and that it blunted Egyptian attempts to link the Egyptian-Israeli relationship to Palestinian autonomy. Another theory was that Israel wanted to leave a thorn in Egypt's side, a warning that Israel could reconquer Sinai if Egypt didn't behave. Yet another theory is that it was to signal that Israel was under no obligation to withdraw from all occupied territory under the terms of UN Security Council Resolution 242 dated November 22, 1967. That resolution calls for "withdrawal of Israel armed forces from territories occupied during the recent conflict (1967 war)." Israel stressed that it doesn't say "all the territories."

Disputes between Egypt and Israel were subject to resolution in accordance with the terms of the 1979 Egyptian-Israeli peace treaty, which provides for negotiation followed by conciliation or arbitration. Not surprisingly, the Israelis preferred conciliation because the U.S. government would be the conciliator and the Israelis believed that the United States would not press for a solution unsatisfactory to the Israelis. The Egyptians preferred arbitration because, once the arbitrators were chosen, the Israelis could no longer control the outcome. It didn't take long before Taba became a huge political issue within both Egypt and Israel and served as the linchpin of the overall relationship. Talks between Israelis and Egyptians over Taba inched along in a desultory fashion for a couple of years, hostage to the overall coolness in the relationship. Egypt had withdrawn its ambassador from Israel owing to the Israeli invasion of Lebanon in 1982. While the talks languished, Israeli border and regular police controlled Taba, and the Sonesta Hotel was completed.

When I came to the Office of Egyptian Affairs in the summer of 1984, Israel had just formed a National Unity government. Labor Party leader Shimon Peres became prime minister, but the agreement stipulated that, after two years, Likud Party leader Yitzhak Shamir would replace Peres for an additional two years. Peres wanted very much to hold a summit meeting with Mubarak and end the freeze in relations with Egypt. Mubarak refused to hold such a summit and to return the Egyptian ambassador to Tel Aviv until Israeli forces withdrew from Lebanon and Taba was returned to Egyptian control. These political developments injected new life into the Taba negotiations.

Peres knew that the legal claim was baseless, but he had to deal with Israel's hardliners. He restarted the talks with Egypt. Mubarak backed off his maximal demands and told the Israelis that they only had to accept a timetable for arbitration. Shamir had little interest in Peres getting credit for restoring relations with Egypt, and he fought Peres every step of the way. The talks limped along, interrupted periodically by events such as the various terrorist attacks and Israel's attack on the PLO headquarters in Tunis. The Egyptian negotiators reacted to criticism that they had been rolled by Menachem Begin and Israeli negotiators at the 1978 Camp David summit. Sadat acted as though it were beneath him to haggle over each word of the agreement, while Begin had no such reservations. The result, according to critics, was that Begin was able to water down language designed to benefit the Palestinians to the point where it became meaningless. Now, in 1984, Egyptian negotiators were determined to be as tough and uncompromising as the Israelis, and they largely succeeded. They had one major point of leverage. Peres wanted to do a deal and he had a deadline. He would have to turn over leadership to Shamir in October 1986.

The Egyptian-Israeli peace treaty provided that the United States could act as an intermediary in dispute settlement talks if both sides agreed. Both sides did. I was spared much of the mind-numbing detail of the Taba dispute because David Greenlee, my deputy director, handled our office's participation in the issue. The chief U.S. negotiator, during the final year of the negotiations, was Abe Sofaer, the Department of State legal advisor. Greenlee had served in Tel Aviv and had been in NEA/IAI (the Israel desk). I understood that David, given his background, would also work with others in NEA on peace process issues. David kept me posted on these extracurricular activities, and we worked well together.

A break came in the Taba talks in early 1986, when Peres kept the Israeli cabinet in session all night until Likud accepted subjecting the dispute to arbitration. Likud exacted a price, however, requiring that Egypt comply with thirteen different demands involving normalization of relations. For example, Egypt would have to end hostile press treatment of Israel. Egypt predictably refused to link normalization of relations with Israel to Taba. U.S. negotiators eventually persuaded Egypt to agree to a separate committee to look at normalization issues, maintaining the fiction that the issues were not linked.

Then the negotiations turned to the question to be arbitrated. Would the arbitrators be asked to determine the "correct" location or the "exact" location of the boundary pillars? The compromise was to not have any adjective at all. Arbitrators would be instructed to determine the location of the boundary pillars. Next came the problem of selecting three international arbitrators. Lists of candidates were solicited repeatedly from the Egyptian and Israeli governments until two candidates appeared on both an Egyptian list and an Israeli list. The two arbitrators then selected the third. The technical mapping of the location of each party's claimed boundary pillar set off another round of talks. The Egyptian position was simple—the existing boundary pillar was the correct location. The Israelis had no exact position in mind, so they proposed that their position be described as a fixed area (which was referred to as a polygon). Egypt refused to agree to the polygon but did agree to give the Israelis two locations.

As the negotiations came down to the wire, our office had to provide daily briefing papers and press guidance. I recall at some point during the summer of 1986, I was in the State Department every day for nineteen straight days to deal with a Taba-related issue. Once the arbitration agreement was sealed, it was clear to us that Egypt would get Taba back. The arbitration panel ruled in Egypt's favor sometime in 1988, long after I left the Egypt desk, and Israel turned the territory over to Egypt.

Mubarak, after initially demanding major modifications of Israel's positions on negotiations with the Palestinians, agreed to a summit with Peres without further conditions. He, no doubt, was worried about the U.S. Congress and U.S. assistance. Congress had long demanded the summit and the return of the Egyptian ambassador, who was withdrawn after Israel's 1982 invasion of Lebanon, to Israel. Mubarak finally met Peres in Alexandria in September and the Egyptian Ambassador returned to Tel Aviv. Mubarak, like Sadat before him, was criticized at home for again selling out the Palestinians for 250 acres of sand that few Egyptians could afford to visit. The Egyptian-Israeli peace had survived a major test, but clearly the "cold peace" would continue with Shamir returning as Israeli prime minister.

During my time in the Office of Egyptian Affairs, there were several changes in the leadership of NEA and in the embassy in Cairo. Roscoe (Rocky) Suddarth, coming off an assignment as DCM in Saudi Arabia, replaced Bob Pelletreau as the deputy assistant secretary to whom I reported in the summer of 1985. Rocky was tall and lanky, and I would joke to my close friends that he reminded me more of Bullwinkle than Rocky. He was a hands-on boss, and I had to spend much more time explaining what we were doing in Egyptian Affairs than I was accustomed to doing with Bob Pelletreau. Once I had adjusted to Rocky, I came to respect his judgment. He always listened carefully to my arguments, and he was very supportive when it came time to look for an ongoing assignment.

I was pulled out of Egyptian Affairs that summer for a few weeks to chair a promotion panel. It was an important part of my growth as a Foreign Service professional, although I recall being bleary-eyed from reading evaluations all day. I had to learn to read between the lines of each Officer Evaluation Report (OER) and learn to distinguish between various gradations of both faint and gushing praise. It is never easy to identify with confidence genuine admiration for an officer's abilities. Reading large numbers of these OERs and making sure that the right officers got promoted was challenging but, by the end of the process, I had learned the art of writing evaluations from reading evaluations prepared by Foreign Service Officers stationed all over the world. An evaluation of a talented subordinate must be glowing but believable. It should have a positive impact on both the employee's morale and future career track. At the same time, an evaluation of a less talented employee cannot be so blunt as to damage his or her morale but candid enough to guide the promotion panel to the right decision. During my subsequent assignment in Riyadh, I had to write ten such evaluations every year, including on all the embassy section chiefs as well as the consuls-general in Jeddah and Dhahran. One of the charges of a promotion panel is to publish commendations of rating officers who did a notably good job in writing an evaluation. One year while in Riyadh, I led the entire Foreign Service in such commendations, with seven.

David Greenlee's tour was up in the summer of 1986. He succeeded in getting an assignment to the National War College. Later in his career he served as U.S. ambassador to Bolivia and to Paraguay. Dan Kurtzer replaced David Greenlee. Dan had been a political officer in Cairo when I arrived in 1981. Dan and his wife Sheila were assigned as our sponsors, and they did an admirable job of seeing to it that we broke the code on how to take advantage of embassy services and learned the basics of surviving in Cairo. Dan, like David before him, was also expected to assist the NEA office charged with following what little activity there was in the Middle East peace process. It was clear that Dan was an officer going places, and he went on to be U.S. ambassador in Cairo and Tel Aviv before retiring. Dan is an Orthodox Jew, which complicated my life somewhat. He strictly observed the Sabbath, which meant I had to cover Friday nights and Saturday mornings, times when NEA was invariably humming with activity. To balance the scales, I left Dan in charge on many weekday evenings so I could attend my kids' sporting events.

Nick Veliotes elected to depart Egypt and retire from the Foreign Service in April 1986. Frank Wisner was promptly nominated to replace Nick. Frank had been ambassador to Zimbabwe and principal deputy assistant secretary in the Bureau of African Affairs at a time of intense diplomacy in southern Africa. Frank's confirmation was held up as part of Senator Jesse Helms's running battle with the State Department. Helms was the chairman of the Senate Foreign Relations Committee. Frank didn't get confirmed until August, so between April and August, he was a near daily visitor to our office. I took a deep breath when I saw Frank come in the door because I knew that he was bringing us several new ideas for what we should do with Egypt. I joked to my friends that he came in with one hundred new ideas every day, and every day at least one of them had to be taken seriously. Some of his ideas could be easily dismissed but the others had to be staffed out, keeping all five of us in the office hopping. Frank was smart, genial, and unbelievably energetic.

Jock Covey, who had served a couple of tours in NEA and was working at the NSC, was chosen to be Frank's deputy (DCM). Jock came by our office for briefings, and we quickly established a close working relationship. He went out to Cairo in June and, following the tradition Henry Precht had encouraged, we were in more-or-less daily contact by telephone and o-i telegrams in the months to come. Jock took the initiative to invite me to return to Cairo for a brief trip. I went to meetings with former contacts and Jock hosted a dinner for me, which benefited the embassy by putting new life into relationships I had cultivated but had languished. I stayed at Jock's house on the island of Zamalek. I found myself one morning having breakfast alone with his two young boys, perhaps six and nine years old. I poured myself a bowl of cereal and asked for the sugar. One of the boys stared at me wide-eyed in amazement and exclaimed, "You put sugar on your cereal?" I knew immediately I had set a horrible example for the Covey children.

Both Frank and Jock took very seriously my admonitions that Egypt faced an economic crisis, and they worked very hard to persuade Mubarak to come to agreement with the IMF on economic reforms Egypt would implement in return for balance of payments support. As noted earlier, three of Egypt's main sources of revenue had fallen sharply—oil, remittances, and tourism. Egypt was falling into arrears on its foreign debt of nearly $40 billion. It was billions of dollars behind on servicing its military debt to the United States. When the debt was incurred, interest rates were in the double digits and annual interest owed alone was now about $500 million. Debt forgiveness or renegotiation was out of the question except in the context of what is known as the Paris Club, an informal group of creditor countries that meet to resolve the debt problems of borrowing countries in difficulty. Generally, an IMF agreement is a prerequisite for Paris Club action.

Egypt began discussions with the IMF about a possible agreement in the fall of 1986. An agreement with the IMF ten years before had led to riots and was quickly scrapped by the Egyptian government. Mubarak had witnessed this as vice president and remained very cautious about economic reform. His approach was "reform by stealth." The IMF wanted the Egyptian government to allow the pound to float (ending multiple exchange rates), to cut the budget deficit to below 10 percent of the GNP, to increase taxes, to cut the public-sector payroll and to reduce government subsidies. Mubarak kept looking for an escape route, but we were not able to give him one. He persuaded the Soviets to offer debt relief, but we were unmoved. He postponed an expected U.S. visit. Mubarak had visited at least annually for several years. He had already postponed a 1986 visit likely because the *Achille Lauro* incident was still fresh in the minds of both Egyptians and Americans. He signaled that a 1987 visit was off because we wouldn't budge on military debt relief. There were many internal discussions within the U.S. government about how hard to push. Treasury, USAID, and State were the principal players.

During my tour as Egypt director, we put together a strategy that included a one-time supplemental appropriation of $500 million (roughly the size of the annual interest payments on the military debt), and we agreed to provide a proportion of Egypt's annual assistance ($200 million) as a cash transfer. The Egyptian government had long complained that our project aid was slow-disbursing and subject to multiple restrictions while Egypt had to service its debt from its limited cash reserves. In return, we expected Egypt to commit to serious negotiations with the IMF.

Egypt and the IMF reached preliminary agreement in February 1987, but the final details were not ironed out until May. Clearly our political interest in maintaining the Egypt-Israel peace and the large economic assistance program allowed Egypt to postpone economic reform for several additional years. The requirements of the 1987 IMF agreement were also considerably less strict than the IMF and U.S. economic agencies like Treasury and AID would have wished. Despite AID administrator Peter McPherson's best efforts, the leverage that our assistance program provided on Egyptian economic policy was nowhere near commensurate with the size of the program. The agreement with the IMF did spell the end of multiple exchange rates, and the modest reforms prepared Egypt to take advantage of favorable economic and political developments that were on the horizon.

The IMF agreement came during my sixth year of chipping away at this issue, and I celebrated it as a nice way to wrap up three years as director of Egyptian affairs. I had spent most of the Reagan administration focused on Egypt. The United States had helped stabilize Egypt, and the peace treaty with Israel held. There wasn't much else the Reagan administration could brag about. The administration was more focused on the Soviet bloc and Central America. The Lebanese Civil War raged on and Israeli and Syrian troops remained in Lebanon. Iran and Iraq were in the seventh year of their bloody war. The Saudis were unnerved by our botched attempt to negotiate with Iran, although they continued to cooperate with our effort to help Afghan mujahideen drive the Soviets out of Afghanistan. The Palestinians had gotten the world's attention, but they were nowhere close to having a state of their own. The Israelis continue to consolidate their position in the West Bank and the Golan Heights. The Middle East was dry tinder waiting for someone to light a match.

At some point in the fall of 1986, Arnie Raphel asked me if I would be interested in going to Kuwait as ambassador. I said it was not possible because both my son and daughter would be seniors in high school the following year. Had I said yes and made it through the nomination and confirmation process, I might have been in Kuwait on August 2, 1990, when Saddam Hussein took over Kuwait and kept U.S. employees effectively imprisoned within the embassy compound. I instead lobbied successfully for a year in the State Department senior seminar.

As I departed the Office of Egyptian Affairs, I felt good about how I had left the U.S.-Egyptian relationship. The strains of the relationship from the *Achille Lauro* hijacking and our inability to forgive Egypt's military debt had been managed. The IMF agreement and the subsequent rescheduling of debt in the Paris Club gave Egypt breathing space to manage its enormous economic problems. Our security cooperation with Egypt had never been better. Looking back at those three years, I believe that it was a golden age of professionalism in the State Department in general and the NEA bureau. Subsequent years would witness a steady decline in both professionalism and effectiveness.

The now defunct senior seminar was the State Department counterpart to the military war colleges. About two-thirds of seminar members were senior officers of the Foreign Service, while the other one-third were members of the CIA, the FBI, the military services, and other Washington agencies. The program was a mix of lectures punctuated by a trip every month or so, mostly within the United States. One of the purposes was to reacquaint officers with their own country before sending them off to represent the United States in leadership positions abroad. The trips provided many vivid and lasting memories. I spent twenty-four hours on a family-run dairy farm in Winona, Minnesota, rode around with the night shift in a police patrol car in Detroit (participating in a brief high-speed chase), and I spent another evening in a Border Patrol vehicle near El Paso (getting the opportunity to question a detained border crosser before he was sent back to Mexico). We were all given the month of February 1988 to research and write a paper on a topic we chose. I chose to write on geographic illiteracy in the United States. As a student in the senior seminar, I got to spend most evenings and weekends with my family and attend high school soccer and basketball games to watch my kids play.

This idyllic interlude ended abruptly in April 1988. I had been selected to go to Riyadh as DCM, working for Hume Horan, who had arrived there as U.S. ambassador the previous fall. I had planned to complete the senior seminar in June and then proceed to Saudi Arabia. Because of the Chinese missile crisis (more in the next chapter), Hume Horan was forced to depart immediately from Saudi Arabia. Ed Djerejian, who had replaced Arnie as the senior deputy in NEA, called me and told me to pack my bags and get on a plane to Riyadh.

3

RIYADH

Chinese Missiles

arrived in Riyadh in the middle of April and walked out of the airport into the rain. Riyadh is built around an oasis in the middle of the Nejd, a desert region that gets roughly four inches of rain per year. The rain can come as a sudden and surprising downpour, but I wouldn't see much rain during the rest of my tour. King Khalid International Airport was a modern architectural marvel. The unimpressive sedan assigned to the deputy chief of mission (DCM), which would be mine for four years, was festooned with dents from a hailstorm a few days earlier. Riyadh had a very modern look, what I imagined a twenty-first century city on the moon might look like. My predecessor, Edward "Ned" Walker, had left the post the month before for his new assignment as a deputy assistant secretary in NEA. As I arrived, Ambassador Hume Horan was preparing to depart, so Ned had been sent back to Riyadh to help with the transition and to introduce me to key contacts.

I dropped my luggage at the DCM's residence near the Riyadh Air Base and went directly to the embassy. When I returned to the residence that evening, every piece of clothing in my suitcases had been washed, ironed, and hung up or put away by Selas, the Eritrean housekeeper. Sandy remained in Virginia because both my son and daughter were finishing their senior year at Fairfax High School. Selas and the three other members of the household staff took excellent care of me. In the second half of May, the month of Ramadan came to an end and the Saudi Arabian government closed for about a week. This is a time when Saudi families celebrate an end to a month of fasting from dawn to dusk. Selas no doubt felt sorry for me because my family remained in Virginia. She invited me to join her family one evening for an Eritrean meal, and I gratefully accepted.

Horan was the Arabist's Arabist. He spoke and read Arabic fluently. He had been DCM in Saudi Arabia for five years when the American Embassy was still in Jeddah. Horan's birth father was an Iranian diplomat. His parents were divorced, and his American mother remarried. Horan was raised in the United States.

In March the United States discovered that the Saudis had purchased CSS-2 intermediate-range ballistic missiles from the Chinese and were installing them in the desert south of Riyadh. I learned that enterprising members of our Defense Attaché Office had found their way to the location and photographed the missiles. The Chinese had configured this class of missiles to deliver nuclear weapons. This discovery caused a great deal of consternation in Washington and in Israel because Israel was within the range of the missiles. Not much thought was given to the fact that Tehran was also within range. Saudi Ambassador to the United States Prince Bandar bin Sultan had negotiated the deal with the Chinese. The context was Saudi unhappiness with Israeli-inspired limitations on the types of weapons the United States was willing to provide and Saudi concern about the threat from Iran. Iranians had disrupted the *hajj* (annual Muslim pilgrimage) in Mecca the year before, and Saudi-Iranian relations were particularly tense. The deal was worth hundreds of millions of dollars at minimum, and there was widespread speculation that Bandar had personally pocketed a lucrative commission.

On March 12, Horan received instructions to tell King Fahd that we wanted the Saudis to freeze all construction and training related to the missiles. This was a difficult request, and Horan checked with NEA to be sure it reflected our policy before conveying this message to the king's office on March 15. Two days later, Horan received word that the message conveyed in Washington to Bandar was entirely different in tone and substance and that, as a result, King Fahd was displeased with Horan. The charming and free-wheeling Bandar had no doubt met with the NSC and perhaps with President Reagan himself and presented the best possible case for the Saudi decision to purchase Chinese missiles. The way in which the White House responded opened a huge disconnect with the State Department. Horan was instructed to take no further action until an envoy from Washington arrived. Washington leadership selected Phil Habib as the envoy. Habib was an experienced career diplomat who had come out of retirement on several occasions during the Reagan administration, most notably to handle the delicate negotiations between the Israelis and Arabs in Lebanon in 1982 and 1983.

Habib arrived in Saudi Arabia with Bob Oakley, still running the terrorism office, and a representative from NEA, Bill Kirby. Horan accompanied Habib to a meeting with King Fahd. The meeting was going well until Habib divulged that the United States wished to look at the missiles. The king responded that there was no need to inspect them because they were non-nuclear. Habib pressed, saying that we needed for our own reasons to confirm they were non-nuclear and that construction had stopped. The king then launched into a tirade about how Horan must be continuing to meddle in the issue even though the king had been assured otherwise. He went on to attribute the meddling to Horan's "Iranian blood." According to Horan's account, Habib did little to defend the ambassador.[1]

Horan returned to the embassy and sent a recommendation that he be replaced because no ambassador can be on the king's "shit" list and still be effective. In addition to Horan's ancestry, his Arabic skills contributed to the king's animosity. His knowledge of Arabic and the Qur'an was good enough for him to go toe-to-toe with the Kingdom's religious conservatives, something that unnerved King Fahd and other members of the royal family. Horan recommended that, to signal our displeasure, there be a large enough gap before the nomination of a new ambassador. Washington ignored that recommendation and, before Horan left his post on April 22, he received instructions to request agrément (approval by the accrediting state) for the return of his predecessor, Walt Cutler. One more humiliation! Horan, the department's leading Arabist, found himself in limbo with virtually no prospect of ever returning as a diplomat to the Arab world. The Saudis must have concluded from the incident that they had little to fear from future U.S. ambassadors.

Cutler's confirmation took longer than expected, and he did not arrive until August 1. I found myself in charge of one of our largest embassies, if not the largest, counting all the military components, for more than three months. Horan had been very popular among the embassy staff, and a number directed considerable anger at both the Saudis and Washington at the way he had been treated. Four members of the embassy leadership team were of great help in getting me functioning. Allen Keiswetter was the political counselor, Anne Patterson, who had worked for me years earlier in the Economic Bureau, was the economic counselor, Mike McLaughlin the administrative counselor, and Stephanie Smith the counselor for consular affairs.

I had to get up to speed quickly on our substantial U.S. military training missions, as well as a Treasury-run assistance program. The U.S. Military Training Mission (USMTM), headed by a two-star general, worked with the Ministry of Defense and Civil Aviation while the Office of the Program Manager/Saudi Arabia National Guard (OPM/SANG), headed by a one-star general, worked with the Saudi National Guard. We also had a large Army Corps of Engineers presence in Saudi Arabia to construct, among other things, a large Saudi military base. The Joint Economic Commission Riyadh (JECOR) was a large technical assistance program headed by Charles Schotta of the Treasury Department. It resembled a USAID program but was paid for by the Saudi government rather than the U.S. government. Schotta lived in the DC area but visited Riyadh periodically.

The embassy complex was a new construction, very modern and spacious, and contained a large swimming pool and tennis courts. One of my early priorities was to make appearances in all parts of the compound, to be a visible leader to the embassy staff. I also needed to at times leave the embassy to meet with staff of the two consulates general in Jeddah and Dhahran, and with all U.S. government agencies having offices outside the embassy compound, as well as with the many Americans and their families who worked in the oil, military, health, and education sectors. I am very much an introvert, so this was a challenge, but made easier considering that the American community, official and non-official, was eager to get to know me and were seeking leadership. I scheduled a meeting with the secretaries who worked in the embassy and arranged to meet regularly with administrative counselor Mike McLaughlin, regional medical officer Tom Wiegert, and with the community liaison officer (CLO). I wanted to ensure that I had a good sense of the post's overall morale.

I learned as DCM and later as ambassador that one of the most important people in your professional life is your secretary. Foreign Service secretaries became known as office management specialists after I retired. My secretary during my first three years in Riyadh was Debbie Paolini-Huff. Her unprepossessing manner concealed an iron will to manage access to me and to organize my time in a way that maximized my effectiveness. The better she did her job, the better I did mine. She was fiercely loyal, and she could fend off even the most absurd requests without provoking anger or offense.

As I introduced myself around, there was plenty to talk about. The leases for the two facilities in Jeddah and Dhahran were up for renewal, and I was concerned that our Saudi landlords were trying to gouge us. The negotiations were arduous, but we finally negotiated the rates down to an acceptable level. We also tried to breathe some new life into the U.S.-GCC dialogue, which had languished owing to lack of attention from Washington.

Early on I found myself in disfavor with the titular head of the American business community. Dick Meade was chairman of the American Business Group of Riyadh (ABGR). His wife Fran was a fixture in the embassy, employed as the social secretary in charge of organizing representational events. She told me shortly after I arrived in April that she was off to the United States for her annual summer vacation and would be back in November. Nothing happens in Riyadh, she argued, between May and November. I pondered this for a day or so and informed her that, if she was going to be away for half the year, I intended to recommend that the Administrative Section hire a replacement. She wasn't prepared to modify her plans and we did hire a new social secretary. Dick Meade was incensed at this decision, and he glowered at me whenever we found ourselves at the same party or reception.

John ("Jack") Farrington was head of USMTM (pronounced youse-mittem) when I arrived. He was an Air Force general, tough, capable, and keenly aware of the chain of command even though a very green DCM was occupying the top rung. When Jack briefed me on difficulties he was experiencing in convincing the Saudi government to accept the reassignment of personnel from Germany to USMTM in Saudi Arabia, I tried to help. If the Saudis were going to drag their feet on allowing U.S. military personnel into the Kingdom, then we could drag our feet on issuing visas to Saudi military personnel planning to visit the United States. The United States, more specifically Disneyland and Disney World, was a favorite vacation destination for senior Saudi military personnel. I asked consular chief Stephanie Smith to slow visa issuance to Saudi military members to a crawl without acknowledging that it was a deliberate decision. After a few weeks, Jack's counterparts in the Saudi Ministry of Defense leaned heavily on him to restart the visa process and, at Jack's request, we did so. As far as I remember, the gambit had little effect on the speed of redeploying personnel from Germany. I was proud of what I thought an ingenious initiative and Saudi-like way of responding, but I learned over time that the Saudis are much better at playing these games than we are.

I also tried to create the close embassy-desk relationship with Office of Arabian Peninsula Affairs director David Ransom that I recalled from my own years as director of Egyptian affairs. Although David and I established a good working relationship, he was never enthusiastic about the idea of a daily official-informal (o-i) telegram. He noted that he was responsible for seven countries rather than just one. We did establish an o-i channel, but it never became quite as useful as the one between Embassy Cairo and Egyptian Affairs.

My first months in Saudi Arabia coincided with the winding down of the Iran-Iraq War and two major disasters, both apparent cases of mistaken identity. The USS *Stark* was attacked by an Iraqi aircraft on May 17, killing thirty-seven and injuring twenty-one. The USS *Vincennes* shot down an Iranian civilian airliner on July 3, killing 290 passengers and crew. Both U.S. ships were in the Persian (Arabian) Gulf as part of Operation Earnest Will, an operation to protect Kuwaiti oil tankers reflagged as American vessels from Iranian attack. Less than three weeks later, Ayatollah Khomeini gave his speech accepting the "poison" of ending the war with Iraq.

Vernon Walters, then U.S. ambassador to the United Nations, came to Saudi Arabia in late May to discuss Iran-Iraq developments. I accompanied him to a meeting In Jeddah with King Fahd on May 29. King Fahd's chief of protocol, a member of the Al al-Sheikh family, descended from the founder of Saudi Arabia's puritanical brand of Islam, Mohammed Abdel Wahhab, met us in Fahd's palace, and we sat down to wait. After about an hour and a half, Walters said to me, "if nothing happens soon, I'm going to do something." Oh no, I thought. My first meeting with King Fahd and Walters is going to walk out on the meeting. What should I do? I didn't do anything except sit nervously. Eventually Walters went over the protocol chief and said something. Shortly, we were ushered in to see the king. I asked Walters after the meeting if he had intended to walk out. "No," he said. "I was just going to say something."

When I was plucked from the senior seminar to go to Saudi Arabia, I extracted a promise from Dick Murphy that the State Department would fly me back to the DC area to attend the high school graduations of my son and daughter. That week happened to coincide with the senior seminar graduation ceremony as well, which I welcomed because I had made many friends in the class. Political counselor Allen Keiswetter took over as chargé during my absence. Sandy and I acted as chaperones as Fairfax (Virginia) High School seniors partied until morning the night after graduation. I headed for the airport to fly back to Riyadh while Sandy accompanied our graduates to Ocean City, Maryland, for more partying.

Sandy arrived in Riyadh to join me in early July after supervising the packing and rental of our home in Fairfax. She brought along our two dogs, Labrador retrievers named Jack and Moose. Most Saudis are not fond of dogs, and canines are only allowed in Saudi Arabia if they are classified as guard dogs. Jack and Moose looked the part at least, but we encountered some dogs during our tour (think Chihuahuas) where calling them guard dogs was a real stretch.

Sandy and I took care of the daunting paperwork for bringing the dogs before I flew back to Riyadh. We had to obtain a health certificate from our veterinarian in Fairfax. Then we drove to Annapolis to the regional U.S. Department of Agriculture office to have the USDA certify that our vet was properly licensed. Then I had to find my way to an office near the back entrance to the State Department, take a number from the machine, and wait. After about an hour I was issued a formal-looking statement granting authority for the USDA to attest to the Fairfax vet's certification. A woman behind the counter took the document, stamped it, and unabashedly signed the document "George C. Shultz." Then we took the document to the Saudi Embassy, where a consular officer stamped the back with an attestation in Arabic that George C. Shultz was indeed competent to determine if the health certificates had been properly prepared. The three documents were then tied together with a ribbon and fastened together with a very formal-looking seal. The dogs were now good to go.

Finally confirmed as U.S. ambassador to Saudi Arabia for the second time in July, Walt Cutler arrived in early August. It was time to find out what it was like to be a deputy chief of mission. I accompanied Walt down to Jeddah on August 17, where he met with King Fahd and presented his credentials. Leaving the meeting, we learned that Arnie Raphel had that day died in a plane crash in Pakistan. The plane was carrying President Zia, Arnie, and a U.S. brigadier general. Arnie was only forty-five years old, the same age as me. We had come into the Foreign Service together twenty-two years earlier and he remained one of my best friends. I was devastated.

According to those in the embassy who worked for Walt during his first tour in Saudi Arabia, he returned a kinder and gentler man. He treated me with respect and included me as often as possible in meetings, and I learned during the eight months he was there how to be an effective DCM. He returned to Saudi Arabia out of a sense of duty because he had already lined up a post-retirement position as president of Meridian House, a nonprofit international education and exchange organization based in Washington DC. Walt's wife Isabel, better known as Didi, was a photographer and a strong personality in her own right. Her stunning photographs of Saudi Arabia hung on walls throughout the embassy. Both the Cutlers loved the social dimension of diplomacy, and they worked very hard to be good hosts and good guests. Walt liked to play tennis, and he had more enthusiasm than ability, which made us a good match.

One of my most vivid memories of Riyadh during this period was my meeting with Mohammed Ali. Ali was, of course, a Muslim and he had made the pilgrimage to Mecca in the past. I don't remember what brought him to Saudi Arabia this time, but he came one evening to a reception hosted by the Cutlers, bringing with him some very religious Muslims. We knew they were particularly pious because they wore *ghutras* (headscarves) without the *agal* (black cord used to secure the ghutra) and their *thobes* (long white dresses) came down only to their shins to avoid contact with any dirt.

I was starstruck by Ali. He was the most famous athlete I had ever met. I did get to meet the Brazilian soccer star Pele later during my time in Saudi Arabia, but Pele did not radiate the larger-than-life magnetism that Ali did. As Ali and I shook hands, I blurted out something like, "you're bigger than I thought." He released my hand suddenly and brought it up as a fist to within an inch of my chin. "What did you say?" he said loudly and indignantly. "What did you say?" My voice quavering, "I said you're bigger than I thought." "Oh," he said, bringing his fist down. "I thought you said, n——." His eyes were twinkling, and I knew that I had been had.

During the eight months that the Cutlers were back in Saudi Arabia, the U.S.-Saudi relationship was uninterrupted by any major crisis. Tensions over Chinese missiles had receded. George H. W.

Bush was elected president, he appointed Jim Baker Secretary of State. The Iran-Iraq War was over, and the new administration now focused on the collapse of the Soviet Union and the reunification of Germany. To the extent Baker's State Department focused at all on the Middle East, it was on the largely unproductive effort to move things forward on the Israeli-Palestinian front.

I had little feel at the time for what was going on in NEA as Baker took over as secretary of state and Larry Eagleburger was appointed deputy secretary of state. Dick Murphy retired, and John Kelly replaced him. Kelly had been U.S. ambassador to Lebanon but, other than that, had no Middle East experience. Under Murphy, NEA had a reputation as the best bureau in the department, one that operated independently, one that stayed in close communications with the embassies it oversaw and took the initiative whenever possible. It attracted the best people and had a real spirit.

Baker thought that regional bureaus showed too much initiative and was particularly concerned about NEA's reputation as having too many Arabists and being insufficiently supportive of Israel. Kelly was selected to clean out the bureau, and he began by replacing all the deputy assistant secretaries. This was the end of the NEA I had known and worked in and, in my opinion, the bureau never really recovered. Although neither Baker nor Kelly took much interest in Saudi Arabia until Iraq invaded Kuwait, I soldiered on with the illusion that the bureau would be there when we needed it. We would find, however, even after Saudi Arabia became the center of the news cycle, that unless Baker and Kelly decided an issue was important, we would get little help from the Department of State.

I made it a point as DCM and as chargé to make sure our junior officers were being challenged. One of the junior officers working in the Political Section was Chuck Forrest. Chuck had made a name for himself as the all-time winningest Jeopardy champion. He identified as a Muslim and traveled to Mecca to participate in the hajj, and he wrote some excellent political reports about it. Working his way up the career ladder in the Foreign Service proved too frustrating for this able and self-confident young man.

He completed his assignment in Riyadh but left the Foreign Service at some point during his subsequent assignment in the UAE. Four other junior officers I worked with, Alice Wells, Kurt Amend, Fletcher Burton, and David Bame went on to successful careers in the Foreign Service. Alice and Kurt married each other. Both Alice and Fletcher went on to be ambassadors.

Alice graduated from Stanford, where I had spent three years as a graduate student. I had long been interested in cultivating Saudis who had graduated from U.S. universities, and I also wanted to play a role in developing junior officers. I asked Alice to seek out Saudis who had graduated from Stanford and to organize a reunion. She tracked down about twenty individuals, and I hosted the group in my residence in Riyadh. One of the Saudis agreed to host a second gathering in Dhahran, which Alice and I attended. Saddam's invasion of Kuwait distracted us from following up. Saudi Arabia, along with most Arab governments, look with suspicion at groups like alumni associations, fearing that they could provide a catalyst for an opposition movement. I was therefore not surprised that the Saudi graduates were unwilling to attract the attention of the Saudi government by turning the gathering into a formal alumni association.

By law, every Foreign Service post should be inspected once every five years by the State Department's Office of the Inspector General. Our number came up in February 1989, and we operated for several weeks under the watchful eye of an inspection team headed by Ambassador Robert Barbour. Inspectors evaluate how well the embassy represents U.S. interests and implements policies, how well it manages resources, and whether management controls are adequate to prevent waste, fraud, and abuse. The inspectors had some useful suggestions for improvement. Overall, they gave the U.S. Mission in Saudi Arabia, and me personally, very positive evaluations.

Walt's last day was April 30, 1989, and I was again left in charge of the embassy until Chas W. Freeman Jr. could be confirmed by the Senate. Chas was a rising star, best known for being Nixon's interpreter when he went to China in 1972. When I read his bio,

I was sobered to learn that he was six days younger than me. His most recent assignment had been principal deputy in the Bureau of African Affairs. Claiborne Pell, then chairman of the Senate Foreign Relations Committee, and Senator Jesse Helms had reservations about Chas's work in the Africa Bureau (particularly, the role he played in negotiating the withdrawal of Cuban troops from Angola), and confirmation was delayed until October.[2]

Running one of the largest U.S. missions in the world is challenging even in the absence of crisis. There were three dimensions to running the mission in Saudi Arabia that were different and perhaps even unique. First, consumption and/or distribution of alcohol in Saudi Arabia is illegal. Nevertheless, it is widely available in the diplomatic community. Many expats outside the diplomatic community became adept at making their own beer, wine, or a vodka-like drink called *siddiqi* ("my friend" in Arabic). Diplomatic establishments import alcohol in great quantities, as do many members of the Saudi royal family, and Saudi Customs turns a blind eye.

During my time as chargé in 1989, the embassy held a contest to name the snack bar located near the pool and the Marine House. Admin counselor Mike McLaughlin and I went through the entries and we agreed that Uncle Sam's was the clear winner. As far as I know, it retains that name. Those outside the American Embassy community required a much-coveted invitation. The Marines had their own bar, but Uncle Sam's became the preferred watering hole for the older members of the American community. I still brag that part of my job was to run the best bar in Saudi Arabia. The huge amount of alcohol that could be found in the Kingdom always amazed me.

A second challenge involved access to television broadcasting. In 1989 the Armed Forces Radio and Television Service (AFRTS) provided the only satellite television available in Saudi Arabia. Everyone in the embassy community received it, as well as a few senior members of the Saudi royal family. In its early days the service was unencrypted, and many enterprising Saudis managed to steal the signal. The Saudi leadership, accustomed to controlling the flow of information that reached its citizens, was displeased about the service's availability, so our military encrypted the signal. I received regular calls from more junior members of the royal family or other prominent Saudis asking how they could get access to AFRTS. I deflected these requests by explaining to the caller that the American Embassy had no objection so long as I received approval from the Royal Diwan (the king's office). The calls eventually stopped.

A third responsibility unique to Saudi Arabia involved opening the embassy to religious services. The country banned the practice of any religion other than Islam. Nevertheless, we would host separate Catholic and Protestant services at the embassy. I don't recall any demand for Jewish services, but we would naturally have agreed to that as well.

Saudi Arabia's puritanical culture presented many challenges. During my career in the Foreign Service, the U.S. Information Service (USIS) was a separate agency charged with what today is called public diplomacy. USIS introduced various aspects of U.S. culture to the world. The agency contracted a superb Cajun band named BeauSoleil to stage a concert in Riyadh. The puritanical religious authorities considered Cajun music unacceptable to a Saudi audience. The government elected not to shut down the concert, held at the American Embassy in the Diplomatic Quarter, but to use the limited access to the area to discourage Saudis from attending. As I looked over the large crowd of Americans and other expatriates at the concert, I spotted a single Saudi with his checkered ghutra. I approached him after the concert and learned that, while he enjoyed the performance, he hadn't realized that he wasn't supposed to be there, and was very anxious about being seen. Sandy and I offered to drive him out of the quarter in our car, which had tinted windows and would pass through the guard station without inspection. He gratefully accepted. BeauSoleil went on to the more relaxed social climate of Dhahran in the Eastern Province, and performed to a crowd that included several Saudis in traditional dress.

One of the toughest issues we faced in Saudi Arabia was "child custody" cases. Many Saudis went to the United States in the late

1970s and early 1980s for a university education. Some met and married American women and brought them back to Saudi Arabia to live. Some of the marriages worked out well. We had many good friends who were in these mixed marriages. Some marriages did not do well, and a number of those produced children. Women, including American women, were not allowed to take their children out of Saudi Arabia without the husband's permission. This was Saudi law and the Saudi authorities were unwilling to bend it. These cases were gut-wrenching, and the embassy and the U.S. government came under withering criticism for selling out these grief-stricken American women to maintain a cordial relationship with Saudi Arabia.

One such case was memorable. Monica Radwan came into the embassy one morning with her children and her luggage. A meeting of an American women's group in the embassy that morning made it easier for her to pass into the lobby. She approached an officer in the consular section and demanded that the U.S. government transport her and her children back to the United States. She pledged not to leave the embassy until that happened. Karla Reed, who had replaced Stephanie Smith as consular counselor, briefed me on the problem, and I confirmed to her that we could not agree to smuggle the Radwan children out of the country and that they could not stay in the embassy indefinitely. The standoff lasted all day until the embassy closed and Marine guards escorted Ms. Radwan and her children out. I did not witness her removal, but learned that she and the children were very upset. Years later, after I retired, I received a call from a congressional staffer, preparing for a hearing on child custody cases, asking me what I remembered of the incident.

Memorable visitors during this period included Arizona senator Dennis DeConcini and his wife Susan. We hadn't yet committed to become Arizona residents, but my father lived in Tucson and my brother had spent many years there. Sandy and I accompanied the DeConcinis to Dhahran, where Saudi Aramco had arranged an air tour of their oil facilities. Sandy had not been invited on the plane tour, but Susan insisted she join, and one of DeConcini's staffers had to be left behind to make room. I first met Adel al-Jubeir, later Saudi foreign minister, on that trip and was impressed by his charm and his fluency in English. He had been a college student at the University of North Texas, a graduate student at Georgetown, and a special assistant to Saudi ambassador to the United States Bandar bin Sultan.

Two foreign policy issues dominated the second interregnum between Cutler's departure in April and Freeman's arrival in November: Afghanistan and Lebanon. The United States, Saudi Arabia, and Pakistan supported the Afghan resistance to the Soviet occupation. The United States provided the training, the Saudis provided the money, and the Pakistanis provided the training ground. Fighting godless communists in an occupied Muslim nation was seen in Saudi Arabia as a good cause, and many Saudis volunteered to go to Afghanistan to support the resistance, including the son of a wealthy Saudi construction contractor named Osama bin Laden.

Peter Tomsen, who was a fellow office director in charge of South Asia when I was director of Egyptian affairs, received a 1989 appointment as special envoy to Afghanistan, with ambassadorial rank. He came to Riyadh at least twice during my time as chargé. I accompanied him to his meetings with Saudi intelligence chief Prince Turki al-Faisal. Like his brother Saud, the foreign minister, Turki was educated in the United States and was a highly respected interlocutor. I gained insight into the world of the Afghan mujahidin, including figures like Gulbuddin Hekmatyar and Abdul Rasul Sayyaf. Sayyaf was then a Saudi favorite, although he later played a role in bringing Osama bin Laden back to Afghanistan.

Peter is a superb diplomat and easy to like, although I must confess that on one occasion, I had to suppress the desire to ring his neck. Never a detail person, Peter called me one night informing me that he planned to come to Saudi Arabia the next day to meet with Prince Turki but had forgotten that he needed a visa. I moved heaven and earth with the Saudi authorities to get him what amounted to an airport visa. In between Peter's visits, the embassy's station chief handled the Afghanistan portfolio but kept me briefed.

While I was still chargé, the Arab League took the initiative to reconcile the various factions involved in the Lebanese Civil War and establish a peace. We had been following the situation in Lebanon closely. Not long after I arrived in Riyadh, Allen Keiswetter took me to meet Rafiq Hariri. Hariri, born in Lebanon, had become a Saudi citizen and had earned billions running a successful construction company. Hariri lived in the same part of Riyadh as I did. In addition to talking with Hariri about the situation in Lebanon, I spoke with one of his sons, who was entering the Massachusetts Institute of Technology (MIT), my alma mater, as a freshman later that year. Tragically, the son died in Boston in an automobile accident only months later.

The Saudis, along with the Algerians and Moroccans, were appointed by the Arab League as a committee charged with making Lebanese reconciliation happen. The Saudis offered Ta'if, a small city in the mountains overlooking Jeddah, as the location of a meeting of all Lebanese parliamentarians elected in 1972 and still living. Lebanese and Saudi culture couldn't be more different, and Ta'if, even by Saudi standards, is not that lively a place. Hariri played a major role behind the scenes in orchestrating the Ta'if meeting. The parliamentarians had a great deal of incentive to come to an agreement quickly. Nevertheless, it took almost a month to reach an agreement to adjust the power sharing agreement between Maronite Christians and Muslims to better reflect 1989 demographics.

The negotiations began in late September and proceeded until late October. Foreign Minister Saud al Faisal spent most of that time in Ta'if. Three times he summoned the British ambassador, the French ambassador, and me on very short notice to Ta'if to brief us. We represented those UN Security Council permanent representatives with which Saudi Arabia had relations. The British ambassador, Alan Munro, and I consulted about where to stay in Ta'if. Alan reported that the French ambassador recommended a hotel called the al-Aziziya. We drove together from Jeddah in a British consulate car to Ta'if and checked into the al-Aziziya. I found my room cavernous and sparsely furnished. In the refrigerator I found pomegranates, a Ta'if specialty, and nothing else. There was a knock on the door. Alan came in and looked around the huge room in amazement, reporting that his room was about the size of a broom closet. We later learned that he had been given his driver's room by mistake, and that the French ambassador, despite his enthusiastic recommendation, had elected to return to Jeddah to stay overnight.

Prince Saud gave us a full briefing on the negotiations with the Lebanese and asked that we send the information as soon as possible to our capitals. I took notes on a small pad designed to fit in a suit pocket. It was well into the evening and dark outside when I returned to the hotel. A table lamp provided my room's only illumination, and the lamp was plugged into the sole electrical outlet. The phone sat on a bedside table on the other side of the room. The only way I could both hold the telephone and read my notes was to lie on the floor between the light and the telephone with both cords stretched to their maximum. I reached Dick Jones, who had replaced Alan Keiswetter as political counselor, and dictated my notes to him, which he would send to Washington via telegram. The phone call had to go through the hotel switchboard. We, of course, knew that the call was likely monitored by the Saudis but, because we were transmitting a message from the Saudi foreign minister, that was not a problem so long as I got it right. The message went out to Washington from Riyadh that night.

Sandy and I came home one day back in Riyadh to find our household staff debating what they should do with a large parrot that had flown into our yard. One of the options discussed may have been to eat it. It was an African gray parrot, which we came to learn was a very valuable bird. We kept it in a dog cage until we could buy a bird cage. Efforts to locate the owner failed, so Bird became a member of the family for about a year. It would say "Ingrid" from time to time, which we thought was a clue as to its owner. *Helwa* was another of Bird's favorite words. It means "sweet" in Arabic, suggesting that Bird in its previous life spent a great deal of time near a TV set broadcasting soccer games. Helwa is a term overused by Arab sports broadcasters to describe a nifty play. Bird quickly learned to imitate the doorbell, the ringing phone, Sandy's sneeze, and my laugh. He also became adept at teasing the two dogs. Once the parrot learned to open his cage and fly around, we decided, preempting a tragedy involving one or both of our dogs, to send him to Dhahran to live with Ken Stammerman, our consul general, and his wife Patty.

During my first two years in Riyadh, the residences of both the ambassador and the DCM were located outside the Diplomatic Quarter, where the embassy stood. New residences were under construction in the Quarter. The ambassadorial residence took the name Quincy House. Abdel Aziz al Sa'ud, the founder of modern Saudi Arabia, had met Franklin Roosevelt on the USS *Quincy* in 1945. The DCM's residence was named Shenandoah, for reasons I never learned. The State Department Office of Foreign Buildings (FBO) chose a woman named Gail Jackson to decorate both homes' interiors. She struck us as a particularly dogmatic and insensitive individual. Jackson did not lack taste, but hers differed greatly from ours. Strange features of the house included a large mirror on the dining room ceiling, and a library filled with exquisitely bound but unreadable books. She wanted her work to be totally undisturbed by the individuals residing in the houses. Shortly after we moved in, Jackson paid us a visit. She expressed dismay at the small things we had done to give the house a personal touch. The final straw came when she went into our bedroom and swept family photographs on a bedside table into a drawer.

The head of FBO, retired admiral Arthur Fort, visited Riyadh a short time later. I had been a youth soccer coach in Fairfax, Virginia, years earlier, and had coached Fort's son Stephen. Art stayed with us in Shenandoah during the visit, and Sandy contrived to put him in a guest bedroom outfitted with curtains that couldn't be shut. Art, Sandy, and I sat down on the upper floor of Shenandoah and worked out a deal. We would leave the first floor pretty much as Gail Jackson had designed it if we could do anything we wanted with the second floor. Shortly after Chas Freeman arrived, he moved into Quincy House and experienced similar problems with Jackson. Chas, according to his oral history, got so fed up that he denied her country clearance (permission to enter the country).[3]

A U.S. ambassador is responsible for all U.S. government personnel working in the country to which he or she is accredited, as well as for all activities undertaken by the U.S. government in that country. Throughout my career, I heard complaints about CIA failures to coordinate with ambassadors, so I expected that agency, because of the secrecy with which it operates, would pose the most difficulties for me. In fact, I never had any difficulties with the CIA station, either in Saudi Arabia or later in Oman. My biggest problem in Saudi Arabia was with the Treasury Department. The problem was not our treasury attaché, Kevin Taecker, who worked next to the economic section in the main embassy building and was a major asset to the embassy. Kevin was smart and knowledgeable, and worked closely with the economic section.

Treasury ran JECOR (U.S.–Saudi Arabian Joint Commission for Economic Cooperation), which was a technical assistance program set up in the wake of the 1970s OPEC oil embargo. JECOR's mission was to set up in Saudi Arabia the bureaucracy of a modern state. The Saudis paid all the expenses and JECOR made sure that any contracts required to pursue that mission went to American companies. The program attracted little scrutiny in Congress because no U.S. appropriations were involved. JECOR over the years was a major contributor to building a very strong U.S.-Saudi relationship.

While JECOR had a U.S. chief resident in Riyadh, the real head of the program was Charles Schotta, resident in Washington. Schotta ran the program as an independent fiefdom, and he reacted indignantly when I suggested that he needed to tell us when he was coming to Riyadh and keep us informed of what JECOR was doing. I asserted that there was a chain of command and that I was, at least temporarily, at the top of it. We had a few heated conversations that failed to reach any resolution. Considering that no one in Washington wished to wade in on this issue, it continued to fester until Chas arrived. He eagerly took on Schotta. Chas denied him country clearance until he acknowledged the chain of command and agreed to keep the embassy informed.

Jack Farrington was replaced by another two-star Air Force general named Don Kaufman in July 1989, who was less sensitive than Jack to how the chain of command works in a U.S. embassy.

I never felt sure I could trust him to tell me what he was up to, and our relationship was a little rocky. My character analysis of Don Kaufman seemed to have been on target, because he was busted down to colonel before retirement after the 1990–91 Gulf War for illegally bringing war booty back to the United States.

At some point during the period between Cutler's departure and Freeman's arrival, I took a visiting deputy assistant secretary (whose name I have forgotten) to the weekly *majlis* (a type of community gathering) of Crown Prince Abdullah. The event began with a group of Saudi citizens who waited in line to petition the Crown Prince. They would advance to the Crown Prince and kiss him on the shoulder and, usually, hand him a petition, which Abdullah would then hand to an aide standing by his side. After the line had dissipated, all sat down to what we irreverently called a "goat grab," a meal of mutton and rice. Honored guests sat at a long head table facing the other guests. The U.S. visitor got into a discussion with Abdullah about George Shultz. Abdullah said something critical of Shultz, which provoked the visitor to protest that Shultz knew the Middle East well and was a friend of the Arabs. Abdullah replied sourly, "a friend who provides you no benefit is the same as an enemy who does you no harm." I will never forget that moment because it captured so well the real meaning of "friend" in the Arab world.

In early 1989, we began a tradition that continued during all four years we were in Saudi Arabia. We hosted a Super Bowl party. We had by then met many Saudis who had done university studies in the United States and become addicted to pro football. Remember that satellite TV was limited to official Americans and the few members of the Saudi royal family who were approved for its use by the king. The party would begin at about 2:00 a.m. Saudi time. I was always amazed at how much our Saudi friends knew about the finer points of the game. We would serve breakfast afterward. Sensitive to Islamic dietary restrictions, we would serve both pork bacon and turkey bacon, with each serving plate clearly marked. The pork bacon would quickly disappear.

The months after Chas arrived were busy, mainly because Chas bristled with energy and ideas about upgrading our reporting. Washington remained relatively indifferent to what was going on in the Arabian Peninsula and elsewhere in the Middle East. I do remember General Norman Schwarzkopf's first visit as the head of CENTCOM in February 1990. I sat in on his discussion with Chas. They agreed that it was no longer appropriate for CENTCOM to plan against a Soviet attack into the Middle East across the Zagros Mountains of Iran, and that more likely scenarios would be either an Iraqi or Iranian invasion of Kuwait or Iran trying to exploit a Shi'a revolt in Bahrain or in the Eastern Province of Saudi Arabia. It made sense to me, but I had no premonition that a few months later we would be dealing with one of those scenarios. Later CENTCOM conducted a command post exercise based on a hypothetical Iraqi invasion of Kuwait. That preparation really bore fruit in the early days of August that year.

One of my biggest headaches as I returned to be a DCM was a proposal to create a day-care center for embassy employees, Americans, and Foreign Service nationals. We had employees from multiple foreign countries but only one Saudi employee. The need for such a center was clear, and logically it should have been run by the U.S. Embassy Recreation Association (USERA). The USERA chair, the embassy budget and fiscal officer, and other members of the board were concerned about liability. There had been lots of recent dramatic stories about abuse at day-care centers in the United States. The embassy asked the State Department for a legal opinion confirming that there could be a liability issue, and recommended directors' insurance for the board members. That wasn't good enough for the USERA chair, and he resigned. Sandy was squarely in the pro day-care faction. Given that a critical mass of people was eager and willing to roll out the day-care center, she was not inclined to wait until USERA got its act together. After the threat of divorce and a sleepless night, I made the decision to go ahead with the day-care center and temporarily accept personal liability. The center began operation and ran successfully for more than twenty-five years. As people moved on and personal animosities faded, USERA got the necessary insurance and took it over. According to former chargé Christopher Henzel (now U.S. ambassador to Yemen), the center is now closed, but only because several private-sector centers have opened in recent years.

Years later when I was reemployed by the State Department and working in Cairo, the IRS out of nowhere began to garnish my salary for unpaid taxes. I suspected that the issue had something to do with the signature I had provided in Riyadh in 1990 to open the day-care center. After I made several appeals to the IRS by phone and by letter and enlisted the assistance of the embassy in Riyadh, the IRS agreed to drop its case and release my salary.

Washington's indifference to events in the Middle East did not discourage Chas from telling Washington what he thought. With help from his colleagues at other NEA posts, Chas persuaded Assistant Secretary Kelly to agree to a meeting of NEA chiefs of mission in Bonn. We suspected that Kelly chose a venue far from Washington to insulate the department from a surfeit of fresh thinking. The Soviet Union was in the process of dissolution, and the German capital would soon move from Bonn to Berlin. Bonn participants were encouraged to submit their ideas ahead of the conference. This led Chas to oversee the preparation of three thoughtful cables that became known as the Woolly Mammoth telegrams. The basic thought was that the end of the cold war would be like the end of the ice age and that we would witness the reemergence of long-dormant ethnic and sectarian conflicts—woolly mammoths long thought extinct emerging from hibernation. Saddam's Iraq was emerging from a long war with Iran with a huge military and crushing debts and with an eye on Kuwait, an arrogant mini-state viewed with little affection by its Arab neighbors.

Shortly before the Kuwait crisis put Saudi Arabia into the center of the news cycle, a disaster during the 1990 hajj left some fourteen hundred pilgrims dead, mostly Muslims from Malaysia and Indonesia. Accounts vary, but the incident took place in one of the tunnels the Saudis had built to facilitate the movement of pilgrims from one location to another. It was early July in Mecca and the heat was intense. The tunnel was air-conditioned, and pilgrims were eager to push into it. For some reason, the crowd stopped moving somewhere in the middle. One version is that they encountered a large group of pilgrims moving in the other direction. It may have been that people stopped to help someone who fainted. In any case, people kept packing into the tunnel, overtaxing the ventilation system and leading to a stampede. It was a grim disaster, not well reported because the Saudis do not encourage critical reports of their management of the hajj.

Chas prepared at the end of July to take home leave, for which he was overdue. April Glaspie, our ambassador in Baghdad, was also scheduled for leave. We were very much aware of the Iraqi military buildup near the Kuwait border, and we knew of the surprise meeting April had with Saddam Hussein on July 25. I had worked closely with April in NEA and greatly respected her ability. I understand perfectly why she didn't say more to discourage Saddam. She had no instructions and no time to receive them. Our policy, which Jim Baker and John Kelly had left on autopilot, was to continue to engage Iraq despite ample evidence that Saddam was a murderous thug. Saddam's threats against Israel and his use of chemical weapons on his own people alarmed many in Congress and the U.S. media but did little to disturb the comfortable assumptions the administration held about Iraq. Kelly, in testimony on Capitol Hill, albeit under relentless pressure from Congressman Lee Hamilton, also confirmed that we had no commitments to defend Kuwait. Nobody in Washington thought to discourage Chas and April from taking well-deserved leave.

In our last country team meeting before Chas left, we discussed the possibility that Iraq might take military action against Kuwait. Most of the country team dismissed the idea, perhaps not wanting to discourage the ambassador from taking leave. I held a contrary view that Iraq would seize the Rumaila oil field that ran under the Iraq-Kuwait border, as well as Warba and Bubiyan, islands that Kuwait controlled but Iraq coveted for use as military bases. I had seen all the reports of substantial Iraqi troop movements to the Kuwait border, and I was dubious that Iraq would put that much effort into running a bluff. Like all my colleagues, I had no premonition that Iraq would seize all of Kuwait. Chas and April departed as planned.

4

·············

RIYADH

·············

Desert Shield and Desert Storm

T he night of August 1, 1990, the Embassy Riyadh communications center called me into the office to read a NIACT Immediate cable (a telegram requiring immediate action outside
normal operating hours). The State Department instructed me to
query King Fahd about a meeting that was scheduled earlier that
evening, hosted by the Saudis in Jeddah between Iraqi Vice President Taha Ramadan and Kuwaiti Crown Prince Saad Al-Abdullah
Al-Salim Al-Sabah. Although it was after eleven in the evening,
we knew from experience that King Fahd would be up for several
more hours. I called Mohammed Suleiman, the king's private secretary. During my four years in Saudi Arabia, I spoke to Suleiman
countless times but only met him once in person, and then only
briefly. He was fluent in English and I could be completely confident that he would relay any message to King Fahd accurately without embellishment and would do the same with Fahd's response. I
relayed the State Department's question, and Mohammed put me
on hold. He returned minutes later to say that the meeting had
gone well and that the two sides had agreed to meet again in two
days in Baghdad. I typed up a brief reporting cable, then gave it
to the duty communicator. He sent it and we both went home.

I was again awakened at 2:00 a.m., this time by a call from the
White House switchboard. President Bush wanted to talk with
the king, and they wanted a number to call. I phoned the king's
office and told Suleiman that the president wanted to speak. He
gave me a number, which I relayed to Washington, and then went

back to bed. At 4:00 a.m. Suleiman called, with a tinge of anxiety in his voice. He said that the king was still awaiting the call from the president but wanted to go to bed. I phoned the White House back and was told that the president was following breaking developments and would call the king when he could. I can't remember if I went back to sleep or not, but someone from the embassy phoned at about 6:00 a.m. to tell me that Iraqi troops were in Kuwait City.

August 2, 1990, was a Thursday, the first day of our weekend in Saudi Arabia, and it was also peak summer vacation time. At the embassy, information flowed in through various channels, including the Defense Attaché Office and the station (CIA). We learned that Americans living in Kuwait were headed south for the Saudi border, so my first action was to call our consul general in Dhahran, Ken Stammerman, and make sure somebody was at the border crossing to shepherd people across. Ken informed me that consular officer Les Hickman was on his way. That was the first day of an incredible seven months for Ken. The embassy staff did what we could to help with his need for more consular staff to help Americans fleeing Kuwait. We told Alice Wells, on a weekend visit to Dhahran, to stay another week and help. Ken was more on the front lines than we were in Riyadh, and he and wife Patty did a magnificent job of rising to the challenges. Much as Sandy did in Riyadh, Patty reached out to the American families in the Eastern Province and demonstrated with her own calm courage that there was no need to panic about the Iraqi threat.

The State Department called to tell me that the United Nations Security Council (UNSC) was in emergency session to condemn the invasion and call for immediate Iraqi withdrawal. Yemen, then the Arab representative on the Security Council, was dragging its feet. Would I ask the Saudis to lean on the Yemenis? I called Suleiman with the message, and I had several back-and-forth exchanges with Washington and with the king's office. The king was clearly unhappy with both the Yemenis and the Jordanians.

Paul Daley from the economic section was in the embassy looking for a way to help. He was a bright, hard-working officer who lacked charisma and probably spent most of his career being over-looked and underestimated. It occurred to me that we were totally focused on the urgent and were giving little attention to the import-ant. I put him to work on a draft cable pulling together our thoughts on what we wanted the Saudis to do and how we would get them to do it. Two hours later he handed me a draft. I thought then that it was inspired, and, in retrospect, I think it was brilliant. We wanted the Saudis to cut the Iraqi pipeline flowing through Saudi Arabia to the Red Sea (and the Turks to cut the pipeline flowing through Turkey to the Mediterranean), and we wanted the Saudis to dou-ble oil production to make up for the loss of Iraqi and Kuwaiti oil on the world market so that oil prices wouldn't go through the roof and lead to a worldwide recession. For the Saudis to stick their necks out with these moves, they needed to know that we would have their back militarily. I read the draft and approved it, and off it went to Washington. I don't know to this day whether it was even read or whether it influenced thinking in Washing-ton, but the Saudis cut off the pipeline and doubled oil produc-tion, and U.S. troops were deployed to Saudi Arabia.

Over the next couple of days, administrative counselor Mike McLaughlin managed to get a twenty-four-hour crisis operation center up and running. He recognized that we had a major challenge in keeping the American community calm. He readily accepted Sandy's suggestion that we set up a separate call center staffed by spouses and volunteers from the American community to field calls from other Americans looking for information or assistance. American community anxiety was a continued problem during the crisis. Anxiety is infectious. The antidote is lots of informa-tion and co-opting as many people as possible to help. When peo-ple are busy and feel a part of the action, they are less anxious.

I was aware that talks were going on in Washington between Prince Bandar and the White House and the Pentagon. The sta-tion chief came to me on August 4 with a terse intelligence report, which he was instructed to bring to my attention to be shared with King Fahd. The gist was that satellite imagery showed that Iraqi forces were undertaking actions that appeared consistent with plans to invade Saudi Arabia. I passed it to the king's office. I don't doubt that the intelligence was accurate, but I was also sure that it was part of a selling job to persuade Fahd of the urgent need to request U.S. forces.

By the next day, we learned that Defense Secretary Dick Cheney was on a plane to Jeddah, accompanied by Schwarzkopf and Chas, to meet with King Fahd. I flew to Jeddah and met the plane, along with Saudi officials. After handshakes and a few minutes with Chas, I found my way to the consulate general in Jeddah. Chuck Angulo, the consulate general's administrative officer, let me use his guest room and promised not to tell anyone where I was. I had been sleep-deprived for four days, so I fell asleep immediately. I slept soundly for twelve hours, the best night's sleep I can ever recall.

I was stunned to wake up and find that at least 150,000 U.S. troops were en route to Saudi Arabia. When the dust cleared, it turned out to be 220,000. I took a moment to drink in what was happening. I had always wanted to be where the action was, and now this had come true. By the next day, the media reported troops were deploying to Saudi Arabia, the 82nd and 101st Airborne, among others. Two squadrons of F-15s were in the air and a carrier task force was repositioning. That triggered one of the biggest challenges we faced in Saudi Arabia. There were at least thirty thousand American citizens in Saudi Arabia, the majority connected in one way or other with the oil industry or the defense industry. Saudi Arabia in general, and especially the oil industry, would not run well without American experts. Many had spouses and children living with them and found themselves overnight in a potential war zone. Boeing, which had a large presence in Saudi Arabia, along with a few other U.S. companies, dispatched planes to take out spouses and children. This sent a chill through the rest of the American community. We asked the department to contact key companies with significant presence in Saudi Arabia and to make appropriate public statements.

The majority of the arriving U.S. military deployed directly to the Eastern Province, which is where the oil is produced and where Saudi Arabia was most vulnerable. Almost thirty years later, it is difficult to remember how unthinkable it was to deploy hundreds of thousands of U.S. troops to Saudi Arabia. What about alcohol? What about women drivers? General Order #1 prohibited the consumption of alcohol in the Kuwait Theater of Operations (which included Saudi Arabia). While compliance was not universal, it largely proved effective. Major General Gus Pagonis, CENTCOM's logistics chief, solved the problem of women drivers. He flew into the Eastern Province ahead of the troops' arrival and met, along with Ken Stammerman, with the province governor and son of King Fahd, Prince Mohammed bin Fahd. He explained that a significant percentage of his soldiers were women and that they had to be permitted to drive. Prince Mohammed said he would give the order that women wearing military uniforms would be allowed to carry out their duties without interference. There were no major incidents, although the presence of American female soldiers behind the wheel no doubt inspired a driving demonstration by Saudi women in November.

The AWACS (Airborne Warning and Control System) unit deployed to Riyadh. Its mission was to provide an around-the-clock radar screen to defend against Iraqi forces. The crews flew hundreds of missions. Sandy and her good friend Sonja Scharles rounded up a few other American women and went to greet them at the local hotel where they were staying in the early days. That led to a very close friendship with the unit. Our home was always open to them, and we saw them frequently throughout the seven months of Desert Shield and Desert Storm. I remember many evenings where multiple members of the AWACS crews were in the house and their gear (gas masks, body armor, radios) was stacked next to the front door in a big heap.

On the evening of August 14, Kent Hinkson and his pregnant wife and four of their six children set off to buy groceries and pick up takeout from a local restaurant. Hinkson had been in Saudi Arabia off and on for eight years, most recently working as a computer programmer for the Riyadh Development Authority. The Mormon family was days away from departing Saudi Arabia for good. They stopped at a traffic light and were accosted by an armed Saudi, who turned out to be a drug dealer on the run. Hinkson was forced to drive at high speed through Riyadh in a futile attempt to evade the Saudi police. In the ensuing shootout, Hinkson's wife and one of his children were killed.

Riyadh by this time was crawling with American media, and the remaining American community in Saudi Arabia was on edge. I received a call from NEA Deputy Assistant Secretary David Mack about the incident. I told him what I knew, that it was a tragedy but that I didn't think it was related to the Iraqi threat. It was the end of another very long day, and I went to bed. That was a clear error in judgment. An incident like this could have set off real panic in the expatriate community. I should have informed Chas immediately and made sure the embassy was in close contact with the Saudi authorities. Fortunately, Mike McLaughlin, our capable administrative counselor, also learned of the incident and called Chas, who in turn coordinated with the Saudis.

We hosted a memorial service for the Hinkson family a few days later in the embassy. Kent Hickson, who had himself been wounded, was one of the most remarkable people I have ever met. He was calm, gracious, and expressed no malice at all toward Saudi Arabia or the Saudi police, even though he had lost his wife and child.

It was roughly during this same period that I first met Air Force General Chuck Horner. Schwarzkopf returned to CENTCOM headquarters in Florida after the August 6 meeting with King Fahd and left Horner behind as commander of U.S. forces in Saudi Arabia. Horner came to the embassy to call on Chas and I sat in. Horner was a tough, no-nonsense military officer who was well-respected and who months later oversaw the remarkable six-week air campaign that kicked off Desert Storm. I remember his concern in August that we did not really have enough forces in Saudi Arabia at that time to do more than slow down an Iraqi advance into Saudi Arabia. He then asked that we set up a system to allow U.S. military members under his command to enter the embassy without any hassle. It was a reasonable request considering there were multiple issues, from intelligence sharing to routine administrative, where the military would be looking for embassy assistance.

I had not served in the military and, although I would in subsequent years come to better understand interservice rivalries, I was still unschooled in August 1990. I sought clarification. "You're asking us to admit anyone who is able to show us an Army ID?" I asked. Chuck Horner, an Air Force general, gave me a withering look and, pointing to the expansive windows in Freeman's office, asked "have you ever been thrown through a plate glass window?"

When Schwarzkopf and his staff moved from Tampa to Riyadh in late August, Marine Major General Bob Johnston, the CENT-COM chief of staff, called on me. Because the DCM is effectively the embassy's chief of staff, we saw ourselves as counterparts. Bob was born in Scotland and immigrated to the United States as a child. He was a Vietnam veteran who had a son in the Marines who was deployed to Saudi Arabia. Bob would walk, arrow straight, into my office carrying his hat and a notebook. We were very much alike, although Bob carried himself with the discipline of a soldier, something I had never learned to do. Our meetings were short, but we got many things done. As I write this, we are both retired in Tucson, and we often see each other in our bike clothes in a restaurant on the east side of the city.

Americans in Saudi Arabia, as well as their friends and relatives in the United States, were watching CNN and learning that Iraq had the fourth-largest army in the world, that Iraq had Scud missiles capable of reaching Riyadh and Dhahran, that Iraq had employed chemical weapons against the Iranians and their own Kurdish citizens, and that Iraq could well have a biological weapons program. The atmosphere in the American and other foreign communities was redolent with anxiety. We knew it was a sensitive subject that we had to get right. We had no way of evaluating the probability of Saddam both having chemical weapons and the means to deliver them on his Scud missiles. If we exaggerated the threat, the likely exodus of Americans could trigger the exodus of other nationalities and seriously degrade the Saudi ability to produce oil and to conduct military operations. If we dismissed a realistic threat, then we could be defaulting on the most serious obligation any American embassy has, protecting American citizens. We needed guidance from our government on what to tell these people. We first asked for such guidance on August 10. The next day, after consulting with the military, we proposed guidance of our own. At no time during the period of Desert Shield (August 2–January 17) did the U.S. government provide coherent and consistent guidance to us about managing the anxiety of civilians living and working in Saudi Arabia. This created a vacuum in which anxious and excitable individuals within the American community were only too happy to fill with dramatic rumors of Iraqi capability and planning. I was in Saudi Arabia begging for guidance and ignorant of the dynamics in Washington that prevented us from meeting our responsibility to protect American citizens. In retrospect, the lack of useful guidance reflected disagreement in Washington about the nature of the threat and indifference to the issue by Baker's inner circle, along with a refusal to delegate the response to a now toothless NEA Bureau. All we got were phone calls from NEA telling us that we would receive no further guidance, and that we should use our best judgment.

The demand for gas masks for protection against chemical weapons surfaced in August soon after the initial deployment of U.S. troops. The military came with gas masks and carried them around in Saudi population centers. The Saudi government announced on August 22 that it would be issuing the devices to its citizens. Some foreign embassies began procuring masks for their citizens.

Without any apparent regard to Saddam's invasion of Kuwait and the fact that Embassy Riyadh was in the eye of the storm, the State Department personnel system kept grinding relentlessly away. Earlier in 1990, I requested an extension of two months because my three-year assignment would end in April 1991 rather than in the summer, when my replacement would be easier to find. On August 1 I received orders to serve on the annual promotion boards beginning in Washington on September 5. It took a message from Chas to Undersecretary for Administration Ivan Selin to get me excused.

Later that month, while I was dealing with the various challenges that Saddam's invasion of Kuwait posed, I received a call

from Deputy Assistant Secretary Teresita (Tezi) Schaffer. Her portfolio was South Asia. She asked me if I wanted to be consul general
in Karachi. I was by now well into my third year of a three-year
assignment as DCM. I don't recall that I gave much thought after
August 2 to the fact that I needed an onward assignment by the
following summer. That moment of silence after she made the offer
was when I found out that I really wanted to be an ambassador
and that I didn't want to be a consul general in a crowded south
Asian city. I had run the embassy in Riyadh, one of the largest in
the world, for well over a year by this time, and I was confident
that I could run an embassy well. Furthermore, I was and am competitive, and winning in the Foreign Service meant becoming an
ambassador. I can't remember how I put it to Tezi, but I declined
the offer on the spot even though the more prudent thing would
have been to ask for time to think about it.

I reported my conversation to Chas and told him I wanted to
extend for a fourth year in Riyadh. I submitted a request for an
extension of one year to June 1992. Two weeks later, the department sent me a message denying my request, because granting
it would schedule me for departure at the same time Chas's tour
would end. Chas went back to work on my behalf and managed to
get the denial reconsidered. I finally was "paneled" (State Department jargon for a personnel decision) into an extra year in Riyadh.

In mid-November, as the war clouds were building, I received a
message from State Department personnel telling me that I would
have to take home-leave as soon as possible or lose it. I drafted a
cable, which Chas approved. It read in part, "I would not care to be
the Department Spokesman explaining why the Embassy Riyadh
DCM could take home leave during the height of the Gulf crisis."

The press of the workload meant that I wasn't getting much
exercise. As the cool weather approached, I began running three
miles on a trail around the Diplomatic Quarter. I chose lunchtime
because it usually coincided with a brief lull in activity. I would do
my run, dive into the embassy pool and float on my back until the
heat flowed out of my body, and then grab a quick lunch at Uncle
Sam's. It became such a relaxing routine that I found I couldn't

give it up when the weather turned hot again in the spring. I would check the outdoor temperature at the Marine House and, if it was less than 110 degrees, I would go on the run. It took longer to cool down, but I never felt endangered by the dry heat.

On November 6, forty-seven Saudi women organized to protest the rule preventing women from driving. Saudi women who wished to venture outside the home had to be driven by a husband or a male family member. Fourteen vehicles with Saudi women behind the wheel drove around a downtown Riyadh shopping center. They were no doubt motivated by the knowledge that U.S. female soldiers were driving military vehicles in Saudi Arabia. U.S. forces were pouring into the kingdom in early November in anticipation of Desert Shield morphing eventually into Desert Storm. Western journalists were also in Riyadh in large numbers, and the demonstrators made sure that their action was well covered. Saudi religious conservatives, already angry about the presence of infidel troops, went ballistic. The Saudi government came down hard on the female demonstrators. They lost their jobs and their passports, and Saudi males were warned of dire consequences if they did not control their family's females in the future. This set back the cause of Saudi women for a generation and reflected the strength of the conservative backlash to the presence of foreign troops.

Early November also brought an announcement that President Bush would visit Saudi Arabia to spend Thanksgiving with the troops. It was my first and only presidential visit. The advance team was led by Sig Rogich, a political operative who worked in the White House and would later be named U.S. ambassador to Iceland. Rogich was competent, but his deputy and many of the young staffers he brought with him were way out of their depth. They were keenly focused on their personal security. The team members wondered where their gas masks were, and we had to explain that American civilians didn't carry gas masks. This reflected a major disconnect between the way we in Riyadh and Dhahran saw the situation and the way Washington saw it. By early November, we were not very concerned about an Iraqi attack into the Eastern Province of Saudi Arabia. The advance team had clearly received a scary briefing in Washington that stressed worst-case scenarios. Because communication between the embassy and Washington was abysmal, no one made a real effort to reconcile our differing assessments.

I accompanied the advance team to the Eastern Province, and we took a helicopter around to the various desert sites that the president would tour. The president's visit went smoothly. The king hosted the president and the first lady in one of his many palaces. Senior embassy officers received invitations, as did prominent members of the American business community. Per Saudi custom, there were separate dinners for men and women. The men's dinner was uneventful. President Bush stood with King Fahd and both shook hands with all the guests. That was my only personal encounter with a sitting president. I had met Nixon, Carter, and Ford at Sadat's funeral.

The women's side was livelier thanks to Barbara Bush. She tolerated the stiff protocol of sitting next to the uncommunicative wife of the king for only so long. Then she corralled Chas's wife Pat and said, "I know you will want to talk with the queen." She then set about working the room, a stunning departure from normal Saudi protocol. Pat Freeman did her best for a short while and then grabbed Sandy and sat her down next to the queen. During their brief conversation, Sandy suggested that she open the palace for tours. The queen had little enthusiasm for that idea. Sandy then managed to pass the honor to the wife of the senior American military officer.

As the event wound down, one of the servants brought incense into the room and proceeded to put it under Barbara Bush's designer dress. Perfumes, fragrances, and incense are integral to Middle Eastern culture, as anyone who had ever walked through a Middle Eastern market (souk) is aware. To expose guests to an expensive fragrance is to honor them. Barbara Bush was totally unprepared for this honor, and Sandy, noting her alarm, quickly convinced the servant to stop.

The president was far from the only official U.S. visitor we received. Virtually every member of Congress found their way to Saudi Arabia to visit the troops. We had difficulty with some, explaining that they couldn't simply arrive in Saudi Arabia for photo opportunities with soldiers. As a matter of courtesy, they were asked to call on the custodian of the Two Holy Mosques, King Fahd. For several of these meetings, I served as the embassy escort. I was struck by the bitterness King Fahd felt toward King Hussein of Jordan. He began virtually every meeting with senators and congressmen by relating his attempts to contact Hussein by telephone on the morning of August 2. King Hussein could not be reached. Fahd was convinced that Hussein had colluded with Saddam. Hussein was a Hashemite, descended from those who ruled the Hijaz until Fahd's father, Abdel Aziz, drove them out in the 1920s. Fahd assumed that Hussein coveted the return of western Saudi Arabia to Hashemite rule.

As far back as August 20, we had begged Washington to restrict all but essential visits. We reiterated the plea in October and again in December. We received no acknowledgment, and the visitor volume never diminished until Iraq started firing Scuds at Riyadh and Dhahran. Owing largely to our capable counselor of administrative affairs, as well as to Ken Stammerman and their staffs and a very cooperative Saudi government, we managed to routinize our support of congressional visits (or CODELS in State Department jargon) so they didn't totally consume our time and resources. We also coped with administration officials at all levels. Chas sent in one of his priceless messages importuning Washington to dial back the visitor volume, suggesting that Saudi Arabia was being treated like a military theme park. Both Secretary of Defense Cheney and Chairman of the Joint Chiefs Colin Powell visited multiple times, but we welcomed their visits, knowing they had a war to run.

By the end of November, we had a pretty good idea that the war would start in mid-January. I was unabashedly rooting for the war to start because I knew that my next day off would not come until the war was over. By now there were five hundred thousand American troops in Saudi Arabia. We knew that keeping them there into the month of Ramadan, which would begin in mid-March, and beyond into the summer heat was unsustainable. Congress had approved, and Jim Baker had orchestrated, passage of a UN resolution (UNSC 678) authorizing the use of force and setting a deadline of January 15 for Iraq to withdraw from Kuwait. It made sense to us to recommend that the department authorize a voluntary departure to coincide with the beginning of the holiday break in mid-December for the American School in Riyadh. Voluntary departure meant that family members and non-essential personnel could (but were not required to) return home at U.S. government expense. Mid-December came and went, and Washington did nothing. Saudi officials, who had long since sent their families to Jeddah or other places outside Scud range, were mystified by our unwillingness to do the same.

Since the end of October, it had been clear that our strategy was moving from defense to offense. The gist of what little guidance we got from Washington was that civilians didn't need gas masks and that, if the situation deteriorated to the point where they would be needed, we would evacuate civilians. We were not encouraged to discuss the dimensions of the threat Americans in Saudi Arabia faced from Iraqi missiles and Iraq's possible chemical and biological warfare capability. This may have reflected the reality that our intelligence community simply had no good answers. More likely, somewhere in the highest levels of the U.S. government, someone determined that leveling with Americans could spark an exodus that would demoralize our Saudi hosts. We, for our part, feared that failure to level with Americans in Saudi Arabia would be more likely to spark such an exodus.

Embassy personnel gave up on help from Washington and worked with the CENTCOM staff in Riyadh to assemble a briefing team to reach out to Americans to discuss the Iraqi threat. Either Chas or I led off the briefing with a general assessment of the Iraqi threat and the state of embassy and consulate general preparedness. Jim Ritchie, our defense attaché, discussed the capabilities of Scud missiles. He explained that the missiles had a circular error probability of three kilometers, which meant that, if they were aimed at a geographic point (set of GPS coordinates), there was a 90 percent probability that the missile would land within three kilometers of that point. Then we turned to the military doctor we called the "Bugs and Gas Man," who took the stage and briefed on what we knew about chemical and biological warfare. He stressed that, even if Iraq had the capability of delivering chemicals on a missile warhead, it would not result in a poisonous cloud forming over the entire city. Those outside in the immediate vicinity of a missile strike would be in severe jeopardy, but those inside homes and buildings would be far less vulnerable. Gas masks alone were inadequate protection, in any event.

We conducted about eight of these briefings in the days leading up to the mid-January launch of Desert Storm. The ambassador led the briefings to a mission-wide staff committee and to the American business community (ABGR). I led several briefings in Dhahran of Americans working for Saudi Aramco and other business leaders, as well as a briefing for JECOR employees and for American employees of the King Faisal Hospital in Riyadh. The briefings were well-attended, and most attendees were respectful, but we did have a few hostile questions. Because we were on our own without Washington guidance, we were vulnerable to surprise decisions. For example, we assured our audiences that we had no evidence that the Iraqis possessed militarized biological agents. Days later, the *New York Times* broke a story that the U.S. military was preparing to inoculate troops against anthrax. That provoked a nasty letter from an American in one of my audiences, accusing me of disseminating misinformation. I wanted to project that we were on top of the situation and prepared to do what was necessary to protect our citizens. Overall, the briefings were successful in reducing anxiety levels.

The majority of embassy employees dealt calmly with the impending war and the heavy workload. The chief of the embassy communications unit was an exception. We knew that he was sharing his fear of various worst-case scenarios with his coworkers. When he applied to take leave over the holidays, I quickly approved it and recommended to the department that it curtail his assignment. This, of course, was not good for his career, and he filed a grievance. I had, as a result, to respond to a battery of questions from Washington, but I believed that maintaining the overall high morale of the post was a higher priority.

My son and daughter, who were in the middle of their junior years at the University of Arizona, came to Riyadh for the holidays. I was tapped to stand in for Vice President Dan Quayle during a rehearsal of his planned visit to the aircraft carrier USS *John F. Kennedy* off the coast of Jeddah, part of his planned visit to Saudi Arabia over the New Year's holiday. Sandy and both children visited the carrier along with the vice president's advance team. Greg and Tina got along well with young men on the team, who were not much older than they. We arrived and departed on a C-2 aircraft. Both landing on and taking off from a carrier involves a couple of seconds of stark terror as you transition from two hundred miles per hour to zero and vice versa.

On January 16, Chas took me aside and told me that the war would start at 3:00 the next morning, and that I should come into the embassy before then to activate the fax net to alert all American citizens. Sandy got some hints from her AWACS friends, so she was not as surprised as she should have been when my alarm went off at 2:15 and I went off to the embassy.

I walked into the embassy crisis center, which had been operating since August 2, at about 2:45. Alfred Leung, our FBO officer, was on duty with his back to a TV set tuned to CNN. He looked totally relaxed but somewhat puzzled by my appearance in the early morning hours. "Alfred," I said. "Anything going on?"

"Not really. It's pretty quiet," he responded.

I rotated his swivel chair 180 degrees so that he was looking directly at the TV screen behind him. CNN was showing the sky over Baghdad lit up with anti-aircraft tracers. "Looks to me like something is happening," I said, and explained why I was there.

Three or four nights later, I was at home late in the evening when a call came in from the embassy telling me that four Scud missiles were in the air headed for Riyadh, and that I should come into the embassy. We had been told that it would take about seven minutes for a Scud to travel from a launch site in southern Iraq to Riyadh. The military had a warning system in place that involved flashing a message to Cheyenne Mountain in Colorado Springs and back to our posts in the region. We typically would receive a warning with roughly three minutes to spare. I had just enough time to tell the duty officer that I wasn't going anywhere "until those suckers hit the ground." Sure enough, we heard several loud explosions. Sandy set off toward the windows to see what was happening. We had briefed everyone in the embassy to stay away from the windows in case of a Scud attack, so I grabbed her and wrestled her away from the windows. The next day, she talked with many of her friends, who told her the show was spectacular. They could see the Patriot missiles launching from the ground and intercepting the Scuds over Riyadh, a real "fireworks show."

Patriots were a huge morale boost for the remaining American community, although I never understood their military value. A Patriot would hit a Scud, and unless it hit the warhead itself, a low probability, it would just alter the Scud's trajectory, and it would still land somewhere in Riyadh and detonate its warhead. The Saudis never reported any casualties and made it difficult for the Western media to verify the information independently. Our guess at the time was that there were perhaps one hundred killed in the Riyadh attacks. There were no American casualties in Riyadh. A Scud did hit the barracks of an army reserve unit out of Pennsylvania near Dhahran on February 25, killing twenty-nine and wounding many more.

There were several more Scud attacks over the next month. The Saudis got an air raid siren system up and running, and we were no longer the only ones who knew the missiles were coming. We and our guests would watch the show from our balcony. Then we would go inside and view a replay on CNN. One night, as I was driving to the embassy after the explosions, I was shocked to see another car driven by someone wearing a gas mask.

Sandy and some of her female friends in the American community decided to prepare fried chicken dinners with all the fixings and take them to the military unit responsible for maintaining the Patriot batteries. General Schwarzkopf's approval was required, but Sandy had established a close relationship with him. Sandy's grandparents and Schwarzkopf's parents were Presbyterian missionaries in China, and both had spent time in Iran in their younger days. Permission was granted. The preparations took days, but finally it was time to deliver the meals. The women made their way across the Riyadh Air Base to the area where the unit was living, in a bunker excavated out the desert. A young female soldier, clearly from somewhere in the American South, halted them at the perimeter and demanded, "State your business."

The ladies explained that they had brought fried chicken. Her eyes lit up. "Fried chicken," she exclaimed happily, and opened the gate. Everyone in the unit greeted them warmly. The soldiers politely answered all the questions thrown at them about the Patriot batteries and what it was like to live in the Saudi desert. They made no effort to eat. As Sandy and her friends drove away, they could see the soldiers tearing into the food.

Although Riyadh was now under missile attack, the White House elected to veto the State Department's belated recommendation for a voluntary departure. Chas followed up with a message, a real zinger, to the department leadership demanding that a decision be taken to authorize a voluntary departure. He had me compose a terse cable to accompany his message. The message consisted solely of three lists: a) a list of all NEA posts under voluntary departure (virtually all other NEA posts); b) a list of posts currently experiencing Scud attacks (Riyadh, Dhahran, and Tel Aviv); and c) a list of all posts experiencing Scud attacks but not under voluntary departure (only Riyadh). The dam finally broke. On January 25, four days after the Scud attacks on Riyadh began, the State Department not only authorized a voluntary departure but also authorized danger pay and an additional R&R for every Embassy Riyadh employee. Washington, in its inimitable way, delayed the authorization of danger pay to consulate general employees in Dhahran for twenty-four additional hours, causing considerable consternation. The danger facing Dhahran employees was significantly more immediate.

By this point the State Department had authorized the distribution of gas masks but shipped to us masks that clearly had been used during World War II. I kept one, admittedly one of the worst in the shipment. It was covered with graffiti; the seal was broken, rendering it useless, and it smelled of mold. As was often the case, we turned to the CENTCOM staff in Riyadh for help. They found a cache of brand-new gas masks that were in a warehouse under U.S. control and designated for the Saudi Ministry of Interior. The Human Rights Bureau at State had held up the transfer to the Saudis, citing the Interior Ministry as a human rights violator.

We set up a center in the embassy (Dhahran had a similar center) where we provided gas masks to American citizens who wanted them, along with assistance in fitting and training in their use. At the same time, we were processing Americans who had elected to depart. All commercial flights out of Saudi Arabia had ceased several days before the war started, so the only transportation out was on military aircraft (backhaul flights). Getting Americans out of Riyadh went smoothly, but Ken Stammerman in Dhahran related accounts of trying to get Americans to the airport and onto a military plane while the airport was under Scud attack.

At one point during the air war, Sandy and I visited Dhahran and stayed overnight with Ken and Patty Stammerman. The Stammermans had become and remained good friends. They came to Riyadh once a month to country team meetings and usually stayed with us. The African gray parrot, which we had given to the Stammermans some months earlier, put on a show for us by imitating with eerie accuracy the sounds of various coalition aircraft that had been flying over the consulate-general nonstop since January 17.

The air war continued, as did Scud attacks. A highlight of each day was a military briefing broadcast on CNN. Whenever I came home from the embassy, I would find our upstairs living area packed with military and civilian friends watching the war on TV. At some point in mid-February, we received a jaw-dropping directive from Washington instructing us to do everything we could to protect American citizens against the effect of a chemical or biological attack and asking for detailed information on what we were doing. That instruction was blatantly ill-conceived and reflective of that the fact that department leaders had paid no attention whatsoever to our pleas over several months for guidance, nor to the fact that we had taken comprehensive action to distribute gas masks and get Americans out who wanted out.

I was inspired to put together a telegram, which I titled "Missiles from Hell," in which I recounted in mind-numbing detail the sorry tale of our multiple requests for guidance before providing the information requested. My favorite line of the telegram was something like, "and then we were instructed to distribute gas masks which we did not have to citizens that, based on previous guidance, we had largely convinced did not need them." I would guess that it annoyed those who read it in Washington, but sending it was therapeutic for us in the embassy.

The ground war began on my forty-eighth birthday, February 24, and was over in one hundred hours. The televised annihilation of Iraqis attempting to flee north at a chokepoint called Mitla Ridge convinced President Bush and senior administrative officials that the war should end. The early termination allowed the bulk of the Iraqi Republican Guard to escape before General Franks and his VII Corps could cut them off.

General Schwarzkopf met with Iraqi military leaders in Safwan on March 3. He had no political instructions and the meeting was strictly military-to-military. Nobody in Washington was prepared to write political instructions because little thought had been given to how we should end the war and ensure that Iraq did not threaten its neighbors in the years to come. Chas had argued repeatedly that we needed to focus on war aims and what we wanted the outcome of the war to be. He had put plenty of thoughts on paper but ideas originating outside Baker's tight circle were not welcome. No political solution emerged from the end of the war the military had fought brilliantly and, consequently, the war continued and arguably continues to this day. It was just one more critical issue that Secretary Baker and his closed circle of advisers could not find the time to address. We fell back on the hope that Saddam could not survive the crushing military defeat that had been imposed on him, and that the future would take care of itself. The Iraqis argued to Schwarzkopf that they needed to be able to keep flying helicopters to meet humanitarian needs. Schwarzkopf agreed.

Skip Gnehm, who had been confirmed as U.S. ambassador to Kuwait long before Kuwait was liberated and had stayed with us in Riyadh on occasion, invited Chas and me to visit Kuwait after he had established himself there. Chas and I could not be out of the country at the same time, so Sandy went with Chas and I visited a week or two later with political counselor Dick Jones and political-military officer Rick Olsen. Saddam, in a last act of defiance, had set as many Kuwaiti oil wells as possible on fire as he retreated. Because of the oil fires, the sky was dark all day. We had experienced darkened skies farther south in Riyadh, and the soot from the oil fires left a dark residue on all the ochre-colored buildings of the embassy complex. We flew over Mitla Ridge, and the wreckage from our attacks on fleeing Iraqis was still visible. We visited a burning oil well and my senses were assailed. The heat from the burning well was intense, as was the odor of burning oil. The smell of decomp from a nearby dead cow was also memorable.

We expected at that time that it could take years to put out all the oil fires. In fact, the last burning well was capped less than seven months after an extraordinary collective effort by a group of companies with expertise in extinguishing oil fires.

Chas was kind enough to nominate me for the Christian Herter Award, which today is awarded to a senior Foreign Service Officer who has "exhibited extraordinary accomplishment involving initiative, integrity, intellectual courage and constructive dissent." In 1991 there was less emphasis on dissent. It was awarded "for extraordinary contributions to the practice of diplomacy exemplifying intellectual courage and a zeal for creative accomplishment," and I was pleasantly surprised to learn that I was the winner. When my dad back in Tucson learned about it, he decided it was the State Department equivalent of baseball's MVP award. That suited me fine. The American Foreign Service Association (AFSA) awards ceremony was scheduled for some time in April, and Chas had planned to take leave in the United States at that time. I stayed in Riyadh to log a few more days as chargé, and Chas attended the ceremony at the State Department and accepted the award for me. We did get a few days off before Chas departed, which Sandy and I used to make a quick vacation trip to Syria. The award came with a check for $1,000, which Sandy spent almost immediately in the Damascus souk on a gold chain.

Dick Cheney came to Riyadh to meet with Saudi Defense Minister Prince Sultan while Chas was in the United States. Cheney's mission was to try to nail down arrangements to pre-position U.S. military equipment in the kingdom. The plan was for the U.S. military to leave as promised but to have all the equipment they might need in place should they have to return. Cheney came with a large DOD delegation, and I accompanied him to Saudi Defense Minister Prince Sultan's office, where a large Saudi delegation including all the Saudi service chiefs were assembled. After a few introductory pleasantries with Sultan, Cheney turned the meeting over to a one-star general who was sitting across the room from Prince Sultan. The general opened a large briefing book and began to read. The first sentence of his briefing contained the word "POMCUS," which I later learned was an acronym for Pre-positioned Overseas Materiel Configured in Unit Sets. The Saudi translator looked puzzled and interrupted to ask what POMCUS meant. While the general tried to explain, the Saudi military chiefs started talking to each other in Arabic. It was clear to me in that moment that the meeting had gone south and that any thought of pre-positioning equipment in Saudi Arabia was dead in the water.

Cheney was in Riyadh for a day and a half, and I had ample opportunity to talk with him as we rode around the city. He was easy to talk to, and his thoughts on the situation seemed sensible. After Cheney became vice president and one of the architects of our disastrous Iraq invasion in 2003, I no longer recognized the secretary of defense I met and liked in Riyadh.

Jim Baker was also a frequent visitor to Riyadh and to Jeddah when the king moved there in the summer months. Baker visited eight times between the end of Desert Storm in March and the Arab-Israeli peace conference that met in Madrid at the end of October. He was intent on turning our Desert Storm success into progress in the Middle East peace process. Baker would arrive in the secretary of state's airplane with several aides, including State Department spokesperson Margaret Tutwiler, and the State Department press corps. They usually stayed in one of the Saudi conference palaces managed by the Intercontinental Hotel Corporation. I retain an image of Tom Friedman striding past me into the Riyadh conference palace with an intent look on his face. Mike McLaughlin and his staff would set up a suite for the embassy contingent and, when Chas was in country, I would spend much of my time either in the suite or the conference palace dining room. The food in the buffet, available 24/7, was superb.

During one of Baker's visits, I was chargé and saw him in action. We were together during a meeting with Saudi Foreign Minister Prince Saud al-Faisal. Baker's objective during his eight visits was to secure commitments from the Saudis to agree to confidence-building measures that Baker could take to Israeli Prime Minister Shamir to encourage Israeli movement toward peace. Examples included Saudi support for the repeal of the Zionism is Racism UN resolution and ending Saudi participation in the Arab Boycott. The Arab Boycott, run out of an office in Damascus, had been instituted in 1949 after Israel won its war of independence. Foreign firms that traded with Israel were not allowed to do business in those Arab countries that observed the boycott. At this meeting, persuading the Saudis to stop enforcing the Arab Boycott was high on Baker's list. After briefing Saud on where his efforts stood, he made his pitch and Saud, in typical Arab fashion, didn't reject the idea but tried to put off any decision. Baker was determined to leave Riyadh with this concession in his pocket and told Saud something along the lines of: "You said that you wanted to help me but if I can't take this back to the other Arabs and the Israelis, you are not helping me." Saud, the consummate diplomat, was a little taken aback but agreed to call the king to seek permission to make the concession. He called the king in our presence. My Arabic wasn't good enough to understand the conversation completely, but Saud reported that the king gave his blessing. I came away impressed with Baker's negotiating skills.

During one of the Baker visits to Jeddah, we learned that a retired U.S. military officer working for USMTM allegedly had killed his Filipina spouse. Consular counselor Karla Reed, who was with me in the conference palace control room, briefed me on what she had learned. I knew we had to think fast about the jurisdiction problem. Because this employee was not an active U.S. service member, he was not subject to the status-of-forces agreement covering USMTM members. I told Karla that I needed a lawyer, and she immediately called the Office of the Legal Adviser in the State Department who, no doubt, coordinated with lawyers in the Pentagon. Eventually, the employee was tried under the Uniform Code of Military Justice (UCMJ) in the United States and acquitted. I wasn't sure, based on what I knew of the incident, that acquittal was the right result, but it would have been a major news story and headache for us if he had been subjected to the Saudi justice system.

I took advantage of our extra R&R to visit the United States twice in 1991, once in May and again in mid-August. Our children had both decided to transfer to the University of Arizona for the 1990–91 academic year. The fact that their grandfather, my father, lived in Tucson may have influenced them. We visited them in May and slept on futons on the floor of their duplex unit. As we prepared to return to Saudi Arabia, my father, who was a real estate agent in Tucson at the time, worked with my daughter to find us a house. The real estate market was in a slump at the time, and we bought the house sight unseen. When we returned in August, we were able to stay in our own house and sleep in a real bed.

Shortly before going back to the United States in August, we received a visit from Senator Joe Lieberman. He visited in his capacity as chair of the Senate Gulf Pollution Task Force. As an example of how Saudi attitudes toward Israel had relaxed, he was the first person allowed entry into Saudi Arabia with an Israeli stamp in his passport. I spent the better part of a day and a half with him and came away with considerable respect for the thoughtful and kind way he dealt with me and with his Saudi interlocutors.

Not long after returning to Saudi Arabia in the fall, I took a call from NEA principal deputy assistant secretary Jock Covey. He told me that NEA was prepared to put my name forward for an ambassadorial post. Would I prefer the United Arab Emirates or Oman? At that point, I hadn't been to either country. I'm sure I told him how much I appreciated their confidence in me and that I would be happy with either post.

The issue that most challenged me during my final year in Riyadh involved collecting Saudi payments for our services in Desert Shield and Desert Storm. The Saudis had already spent many billions of dollars providing host nation support to our troops and had also paid the expenses of the troops from other Arab and African coalition members. Oil prices, after spiking briefly in the weeks after Iraq's invasion, had settled at about $20/barrel. Our objective was to collect roughly $16.5 billion each from Saudi Arabia and Kuwait. The embassy analysis of the Saudi economic situation suggested that this amount would cause real pain. Though many members of the Saudi royal family possessed significant personal wealth, the Saudi economy was about the same size as the U.S. state of Georgia. The State Department's Bureau of Intelligence and Research (INR) had a far different assessment of the wealth of Saudi economy. Their analysis, if applied to the present-day United States, would have assumed that Bill Gates, Jeff Bezos, Warren Buffet, and a host of other billionaires could be counted on to pay off our national debt. I presented the bill to the governor of the Central Bank and the Deputy Minister of Finance, and could see the anguish in their eyes.

Jim Baker was not impressed by our analysis of the Saudi financial situation and decided that we had gone native and were Saudi apologists. He had raised the issue with Fahd more than once, and Fahd had assured him that the Saudis would pay up. In his memoir of this period, *The Politics of Diplomacy*, Baker accused Chas of "clientitis" for his warnings about the impact of this huge invoice on the Saudi economy.[1] We received instructions with deadlines and threats that, if the Saudis didn't pay, deliveries of U.S. military equipment would cease. The Saudis eventually found the money and transferred it to an account in the Federal Reserve Bank of New York.

As I prepared to depart Riyadh in the spring of 1992, the embassy appeared to me in good shape. Our reporting on the internal political dynamics was comprehensive but we sensed that few in Washington were paying attention. It was an election year in both the United States and Israel, and the Middle East peace process had taken on new life since the Madrid meeting at the end of October 1991. The war had not liberalized Saudi society; in fact, the religious conservatives had tightened their grip. The royal family was under pressure as they called for stricter adherence to Islamic values, a reduction of Western influence, and limits on corruption. The Saudi fiscal situation made it difficult to continue the normal Saudi practice of buying off the opposition. Audiotapes of sermons by young religious radicals were widely circulated. Saudi veterans of the conflict against the Soviets in Afghanistan (we called them "Arab Afghans") were back home looking for a new cause. Most U.S. forces departed in the spring of 1991, but a year later a sizable contingent remained to enforce the southern no-fly zone in Iraq. We did our best to make them invisible to the Saudi citizenry, but Osama bin Laden used their presence to mobilize his followers. The Saudi government revoked Osama's passport, and he slipped out of the kingdom to Sudan.

My nomination as U.S. ambassador to the Sultanate of Oman was announced on May 12. After more than four years in Saudi Arabia, Sandy and I headed off to Washington to prepare for the next chapter in our lives.

5

MUSCAT

Leading an Embassy

On the first day of November 1992, I arrived in Muscat as the U.S. ambassador to the Sultanate of Oman. Reflecting my eagerness to get there after enduring a confirmation process that dragged on for more than five months, I arrived only hours after my predecessor, Richard Boehm, departed. This time, Sandy traveled with me. We opened our new home to everyone in the embassy on November 3 for an election-watching party. Because Bill Clinton emerged as the winner, the next day I needed to write the resignation letter required of all George H. W. Bush appointees. I did not expect a response and never received one. In the unlikely event that the new administration had wished to replace me, my resignation would have been accepted. Otherwise, Washington leadership expected me to remain and do my job. We attended the annual Marine Ball at the five-star al-Bustan Palace Hotel two days later.

During those early days, Sandy and I also hosted a dinner party for Cran Montgomery and his wife Carol. Cran had worked for Senator Howard Baker when Baker was Senate majority leader. He visited Oman in that position and liked it enough to wangle a nomination as U.S. ambassador to Oman. Cran, the only non-career ambassador who ever served in Oman, was well-liked and respected by influential Omanis. He and Carol were back in Oman for a few days, and the evening was an ideal way to inherit relationships Cran had established during his time in Oman a few years earlier.

On November 15, a member of Royal Protocol met me at the embassy and escorted me to al-Alam Palace in downtown Muscat. I stood in the courtyard with my hand over my heart and listened with great pride as the Omani Royal Guard played the "Star-Spangled Banner" and the Omani national anthem. I then met for the first time with Sultan Qaboos and presented my credentials. I was very lucky to be in Oman at all, as the Senate confirmed me only in the late evening of its last session before recessing for the balance of 1992.

Oman is an almost magical country of dramatic mountains, beautiful beaches, and friendly people. It was and remains a relatively stable nation, the size of Kansas, of about four million located in the southeast corner of the Arabian Peninsula. Virtually unknown to all but ardent stamp collectors before 1970, when Qaboos came to power because of a coup d'état engineered by the British against his father, oil and sensible leadership transformed it into a relatively prosperous country. Oman's northern province, Musandam, forms the south side of the Strait of Hormuz, choke point for much of the world's oil trade. Iran is a few miles across the strait to the north. This makes Oman of some interest to the United States.

Six months earlier, on May 12, 1992, a White House press release confirmed my nomination to be U.S. ambassador to the Sultanate of Oman. An anonymous letter dated three days later found its way to the desks of several members of the Senate Foreign Relations Committee (SFRC). The seven-page letter alleged that I was guilty of multiple counts of illegal and unethical behavior during my tenure as DCM in Riyadh. I counted nineteen separate allegations. The anonymous letter triggered another letter, dated June 2, to Secretary of State Baker from SFRC chairman Terry Sanford and ranking minority member James Jeffords requesting that the State Department conduct a thorough investigation into these allegations and report back to the committee. I didn't learn of either letter until June 8, when Lorne Craner, deputy assistant secretary in the Congressional Affairs Bureau, contacted me about it. He sent me the texts of both letters on June 11. The immediate fallout was that I would miss the next scheduled confirmation hearing for nominees to Middle East posts later that month.

I knew instantly that the letter was the work of a junior officer in the Riyadh Embassy I had just left. The officer was, as far as I could tell, competent in his job but rather dour and humorless. Of course, my impression may have been colored by the fact that, during my last year in Riyadh, he and his wife were harboring a deep-seated grievance against Sandy and me because they believed we were responsible for an embassy decision not to renew the wife's contract as a community liaison officer.

The wife and Sandy had worked together in the embassy's Community Liaison Office (CLO) and did not get along. Ordinarily the chain of command would have administrative counselor Mike McLaughlin supervising the office, with me next up in the hierarchy. A Foreign Service Officer cannot be in the chain of supervision of his or her spouse, so I had to recuse myself from any responsibility. This was an awkward arrangement that only made sense because we were in a wartime situation. Sandy decided not to apply to continue in the CLO office after the war was over during our final year in Riyadh. When the wife's contract expired, the embassy elected not to renew it and to look for a new candidate on a full-time basis.

The wife, undoubtedly with the help of her husband, filed a lengthy complaint with the Office of the State Department Inspector General (OIG). That led to a request that the embassy supply a copious amount of information about how the CLO office staff were hired and supervised. Chas, with help from Mike McLaughlin, responded with the requested information but expressed concern about the use of the inspector general's office as an instrument of a personal vendetta. The inspector general conducted a thorough investigation and, as I anticipated, found no improper conduct by anyone in the embassy. I gave it little additional thought until the anonymous letter surfaced the following June.

The letter was clearly malicious given that its stated intent was to derail my nomination as ambassador. After a few hours of stunned disbelief, I set about mobilizing as much support as I could to demonstrate that each of the nineteen allegations contained in the letter were false. I briefed Ed Djerejian, the NEA assistant secretary, on my side of the story and met with Nancy Serpa of the Office of the Inspector General (OIG), who was assigned to prepare the response to the SFRC. I did a point-by-point rebuttal of the nineteen allegations based on what I knew and faxed it to Chas back in Riyadh to help him respond to the OIG's request for his comments on the allegations. I also consulted Bill Gardner, a lawyer with Morgan, Lewis, and Bockius whom I had met in Riyadh. My accuser was and still may be a talented writer, and the letter was very cleverly crafted. The veracity of the letter was easy to attack, however, because it overreached by including several allegations that were not credible and easy to disprove. For example, the letter alleged that we had wasted representation funds by entertaining virtually no Saudis. Suzanne Chapman, my secretary during my last year in Riyadh, dug out the vouchers that Sandy laboriously prepared after each event to show that we had entertained nearly 1,400 Saudi guests during our four years in Riyadh. The letter also alleged that I had made racist comments about an African American officer, leading him to file an EEO complaint. No such complaint was ever filed. Sandy stood accused of making a racist comment about the officer's wife, which anyone who knew Sandy would never believe.

The entire episode was distressing to both Sandy and me. Though the letter was anonymous, the burden of proving our innocence fell on me. I was guilty until proven innocent. Had I not received full and enthusiastic support from the OIG office and from Embassy Riyadh (Chas, Mike McLaughlin, and his staff and Suzanne all were magnificent), my nomination would have sunk like a stone. I can't help but wonder how many other capable officers have fallen victim to character assassination masquerading as whistle-blowing. I did draft a letter to the inspector general of the agency that employed my anonymous accuser arguing that an employee who makes false and malicious allegations should not occupy a position of trust in the U.S. government. I discussed it with Bill Gardner, whose judgment I valued highly. He suggested gently that my energy would be better spent getting on with my life rather than on the pursuit of my accuser. I elected not to send the letter. Both husband and wife today occupy positions with significant responsibility in the U.S. government, which should trouble anyone who values integrity in our public servants.

The State Department eventually demonstrated to the SFRC's satisfaction that all allegations were false. The process took more than a month, but I received clearance to participate in a confirmation hearing on August 11. On the day of the hearing, I was sitting in my assigned place in the hearing room, along with John Monjo (going to Pakistan), Bill Rugh (United Arab Emirates), and John Bookout (Saudi Arabia). Monjo and Rugh, like me, were career Foreign Service Officers. Bookout was a retired former chairman of the Shell Oil Company and a political appointee. Sandy sat behind me. Senator Sanford came into the hearing room and announced that, at Senator Pressler's request, the hearing would be postponed. Larry Pressler was a Republican senator from South Dakota. We later learned that Pressler was upset that the Bush administration had not nominated his candidate for a federal judgeship. I remember meeting Pressler in Riyadh during a visit he made before the war. His knowledge of the Middle East seemed to be based on having seen the movie *Lawrence of Arabia*. We had to educate him on the differences between the al-Saud and the Hashemites. "No," we explained, "Abdel Aziz was not the Arab played by Alec Guinness."

With the hearing postponed indefinitely, Sandy and I set off for the third time that summer to our home in Tucson. We had left our Honda prelude in Saudi Arabia and, during our first trip to Tucson, we bought a Jeep Cherokee. We made two round trips from Tucson to DC in the Cherokee. We visited New Orleans for the first time on one of the trips. The highlight was a cooking class where we learned to love Cajun cuisine. Blackened *hamour* (grouper), modeled after blackened New Orleans redfish, became our signature dish when we entertained in Oman.

The confirmation process took five and a half months and that was more time than I needed to learn all I could about Oman from what was available to me in DC. I met with John Countryman and Cran Montgomery, previous U.S. ambassadors in Muscat. Additionally, I met with Arizona Senators Dennis DeConcini and John McCain because I had adopted Arizona as my new and likely retirement home. McCain told me about a meeting he had with Sultan Qaboos when Qaboos was camping outside Muscat on his annual meet-the-people tour. Visitors were required to sit on the tent floor and McCain, because of his war injuries, was left in the awkward position of sitting with the sole of one of his feet pointed in the sultan's direction. McCain was embarrassed because he was aware that showing the sole of your foot has always been an insult in Arab culture. I fretted because knee issues also made it difficult for me to sit cross-legged. Roughly two years later I accompanied then Centcom commander J. H. Binford ("Binnie") Peay to a similar meeting with Qaboos. His Majesty met us in his tent but, to my relief, his staff had set up camp chairs for us.

During our time in Washington waiting for confirmation, we lived in an apartment on Wisconsin Avenue that belonged to a couple we had become friends with in Saudi Arabia. He was Lebanese and she was American. We were given a temporary lodging allowance, which we signed over to them. During our previous assignments in Washington, we lived well outside DC in Fairfax, Virginia. By now our two children were grown and we enjoyed our first opportunity to live in the city.

Sandy and I attended the two-week course given by the Foreign Service Institute for those nominated to be ambassador. We were privileged to get to know Tom and Alice Pickering, who were headed to New Delhi, and Kenton Keith, who would be my counterpart in Qatar. Highlights included a visit to a Secret Service facility where trainers demonstrated how hard it is in a split second to tell a serious threat from an innocent bystander. We watched situational drills where cardboard figures would pop up unexpectedly and armed agents had to decide instantly whether they were hostiles or innocent civilians. My favorite day in the course was a visit to a West Virginia racetrack, where we were instructed on how to use the brake and steering wheel to execute a 180-degree turn at forty-five miles per hour. We also learned how to hit a vehicle deliberately parked to block us and knock it off the roadway. The secret was to hit the blocking car just behind the rear wheel well. We got to practice both moves on the raceway. Happily, I never had to use either skill in a real situation.

The new confirmation hearing was finally rescheduled for September 24. Monjo, Rugh, Bookout, and I were all back in our seats. I went first, starting off with a short statement touting our good relations with Oman and my own qualifications. Committee chair Sanford recognized Phil Gramm, senator from Texas, who made a statement supporting John Bookout's nomination as ambassador to Saudi Arabia. Sanford then asked me several questions touching on our security relationship with Oman and the appropriateness of providing economic assistance to Oman given its human-rights climate and relative prosperity. Senator Jeffords asked about Oman's role in the Middle East peace process. These were questions I had anticipated and was able to answer easily.

Senator Paul Sarbanes took the floor and asked me how I came to be selected for Oman. He wanted to know why I hadn't picked up Arabic during my four years in Saudi Arabia. I explained that we had a war and there were long periods without an ambassador. That led him to ask me what had happened to Hume Horan. I began to understand that this line of questioning from a Democratic senator was setting the table for a grilling of the Republican political appointee sitting next to me. I responded that the events leading to Horan's departure happened before I arrived in Saudi Arabia and I wasn't the right person to ask. Sarbanes pressed on. "It must have been a source of discussion. What happened?"

I recounted the 1988 crisis with Saudi Arabia over the purchase of Chinese missiles, which had triggered the abrupt departure of Horan and the acceleration of my transfer to Riyadh. Sarbanes quoted a Jim Hoagland article in the *Washington Post* suggesting that Horan was forced out because his Arabic was so good that he could speak to Saudis that a non-Arabist would not be able to reach. I acknowledged that such a theory did circulate among my contacts in Riyadh. Pressed further, I said Horan's departure was a joint decision by him and the administration, which the Saudis may have influenced. Sarbanes gave me a backhanded compliment, calling my answer a "stab at a diplomatic statement." He asked if Chas Freeman spoke Arabic and I said that he spoke reasonably good Arabic. Sarbanes relinquished the floor.

Before excusing me, Senator Sanford had me introduce Sandy

and asked if I wanted to say anything else. I interpreted that as an invitation to talk about the anonymous letter, which I declined to do. I didn't get to stay around for the questioning of Bookout, but I surmise that it was tough. The presidential election was less than six weeks away and he did not get confirmed. After Chas left, the post was left vacant for two years, and David Welch, my successor, served as chargé for the entire period. Chas was the last career Foreign Service Officer to serve as U.S. ambassador to Saudi Arabia.

Following the hearing, we then had to wait and see whether the full Senate would get around to voting on those nominations sent forward by the Senate Foreign Relations Committee. We were told that there was a good chance confirmation would be postponed until the following year, so Sandy and I prepared to head back to Tucson for the fourth time since we had left Oman. Because it was an election year, Congress planned to adjourn on October 8. At some point, late in the evening of October 8, we received word that the Senate had confirmed several nominations, including mine.

In most cases, ambassadors are sworn in by the secretary of state or another senior official in a ceremony on the eighth floor of the State Department. I opted to skip that step so I could accelerate my arrival in Oman. We arranged for a brief ceremony in the office of NEA Assistant Secretary Ed Djerejian. One of Ed's staff assistants, Chris Stevens, organized the event. Many years later Chris, then U.S. ambassador to Libya, was killed in Benghazi. A representative of the State Department Protocol Office brought a Bible, which Sandy held while I took the oath of office. The Omani ambassador attended and Chas came over from his new office in the Pentagon. I also invited Lizzie Lee. Lizzie was secretary to the U.S. ambassador, a former governor of Nebraska, when I served in Helsinki as a junior officer from 1969 to 1972. The work in Helsinki was not particularly exciting and I was at the time having doubts about my choice of the Foreign Service for a career. Lizzie befriended Sandy and me, told us stories about other professional ambassadors she had worked for, and assured me that I would have a great future in the State Department. She was an important part of my support group and we stayed in close touch with her over the years.

It is a heady thing to be U.S. ambassador almost anywhere, and Oman was no exception. I was often tempted to marinate luxuriously in my own importance when I was being driven about in a white armored Cadillac fleetwood, equipped with two-way radio and car phone, with Old Glory flying from the right front. As the fleetwood approached the fortified U.S. Embassy compound, located on the beach near the capital city of Muscat and seemingly designed to withstand a nuclear attack, the gate swung open. Omar, the turbaned Omani driver, looking exotic in a white *dishdasha* (the ankle-length Arab dress worn by most Omanis), radioed ahead that the ambassador was one minute from the embassy. As we drove in, Baluchi guards, similarly attired, sprung to attention. An inner gate opened at just the right moment and the fleetwood swept around the fountain to the embassy entrance.

Alighting from the back seat, always to the right, I greeted Khalfan. Khalfan's job, one he had held for twenty years, was to open the door for people entering the embassy. He was dressed like the Baluchi guards but in addition he wore at his waist a *khanjar*, the ceremonial dagger that serves for an Omani male the same function as a tie serves for a Western businessman. If it was summer, the move between car air conditioning and embassy air conditioning invariably fogged my glasses. The Marine guard, behind bulletproof glass, snapped to attention and saluted before pressing the button releasing the door to the innards of the embassy. Two cipher locks later, I entered my own office, greeted my secretary, Suzanne, and settled down to work.

Unlike the situation in Riyadh, the U.S. government had not gotten around to purchasing or building a residence for its ambassador in Oman. We began in the residence that Dick Boehm, my predecessor, had lived in. He was a bachelor and the house didn't lend itself to the kind of representation we expected to do. We asked around and discovered a house belonging to the head of the Royal Omani Police, which had a large yard. With the permission of our new landlord, we took down some interior walls designed to create separate areas for men and women, as conservative Middle East custom requires. As Westerners, we were not expected to strictly segregate men and women in our home, so we opted to create spacious sitting and dining areas.

The most memorable feature of this residence was its stunning view of Qurum Beach and the Indian Ocean from the master bedroom. Better yet, it had a balcony just off the master bedroom that was a wonderful place to watch the sun sink into the ocean. We watched the *shebab*, the Omani youth, playing soccer on the beach. Omani men and women strolled along the brick walkway separating the beach and the houses. The women were dressed modestly but the bright colors of their dresses and headscarves reflected the influence of East Africa and South Asia on Arab Oman. There were often two Royal Omani policemen, looking dapper and efficient, patrolling the beach on horseback. In the cool season, we would look for our friend the Indian roller, a robin-sized bird who often sat on one of the light globes that illuminated the walkway at night. Often, with a flash of electric blue, it would fly off to another perch. From time to time, Omani fishermen converged on the beach. Some came by boat and others in ancient pickup trucks. Soon they were wading in the surf and dragging to shore a full net of squirming sardines.

Woody Allen reportedly once said, "90 percent of life is just showing up." Indeed, a major part of an ambassador's job is to show up or, as diplomats put it more ponderously, "to show the flag." The showing up or protocolary aspects of the job in Oman can be extraordinary experiences. The mother of all protocolary command performances in Oman is National Day. It coincides with the Sultan's birthday on November 18. National Day is meant to commemorate the day in August 1970 when Sultan Qaboos staged a successful coup to unseat his father, a ruler who had kept his people in impoverished isolation and had shown no signs of mellowing as he aged. It is, however, absurdly hot in August in Oman and it would be inhumane to stage a National Day pageant at that time.

The main event occurs on the evening of the eighteenth. It resembles the halftime show during a football bowl game except that it lasts four hours instead of thirty minutes. As with any event the Sultan attends in person, cabinet ministers, other Omani dignitaries, and the diplomatic corps are asked to show up two hours early. I learned the hard way that an hour in advance is sufficiently early to avoid embarrassment. Upon arrival at the stadium, the cheap seats are already jammed with enthusiastic Omanis who alleviate the boredom by chanting. I dreamed idly about teaching them the wave so that we could all get a chance to stretch our legs.

Finally, His Majesty arrives, the Omani national anthem is played, and the festivities begin. Wave after wave of young Omanis march onto the field, often proceeding or following elaborate floats designed to illustrate the theme of the year. My first year the theme was industry, the second it was Omani youth, and the third year we celebrated Omani heritage. Patriotic music blares out of powerful speakers and the songs are simple and repetitive. Even non-Arabic speakers find they can recite the words by the end of the night. Following my second National Day, I was chanting to myself *Ya shebab* (Oh youth) for at least a week. It is a magnificent and impressive spectacle, but it goes on and on and on. I amused myself by watching for the rare spontaneous moments. It is common for a few performers to faint. The explanation is no doubt dehydration resulting from having been at the stadium all day long and nervously standing at attention for long periods in the warm evening air. The bodies are discreetly removed. While most human performers are motivated to stand at attention endlessly, horses can become visibly restive and even disruptive. Finally, and mercifully, it comes time for His Majesty to deliver his National Day address. We cheer long and loud, knowing our ordeal will soon be over. A spectacular display of fireworks caps the evening.

Omani National Day was only one of many events where the entire diplomatic corps was required to attend. There were only about twenty-five countries represented by ambassadors who lived in Muscat. Two of the countries represented by ambassadors were Iran and Iraq. Oman has a policy of maintaining cordial relations with all countries, which struck me then and now as a good idea. The United States had diplomatic relations with neither in the early '90s, and I understood that I was not authorized to conduct substantive conversations with either the Iraqi or the Iranian ambassadors. We shook hands at each event but at no time did either the Iranian or the Iraqi try to engage me in further conversation.

It is difficult to attend one of these ceremonial events and not think about security. I remember well what happened to President Sadat while presiding over a military parade in 1981. The need for security protection has become a harsh fact of diplomatic life. Statistically, more ambassadors than generals are bumped off in the line of duty, and most ambassadors today are provided a significant measure of security. The Department of State's security bureaucracy tries to allocate scarce resources in proportion to the threat, but like any bureaucracy it is a blunt instrument. Not surprisingly, some ambassadors get too much security while others don't get enough.

I found Oman far safer than any place in the United States in which I have lived, and security for me was rarely an issue. I usually traveled to and from the embassy in my Honda prelude and used the armored fleetwood only for official appointments. I surmised that the Cadillac could have stopped a tank round, while someone could have easily shattered the window of the prelude with a rock. If the embassy security officer ever pondered the irony of that, he never let me know.

Those who remember the August 1998 al-Qaeda terrorist bombing of our embassy in Nairobi were no doubt moved by the courage and public anguish of Prudence Bushnell, our ambassador to Kenya, and understand that some ambassadors aren't provided enough security. Being an ambassador can mean taking a bullet or having your embassy literally blown from under you simply because you are a symbol of a government whose policy is abhorrent to some group somewhere in the world. Ambassador Bushnell had to descend twenty-two flights of stairs in fear and shock with blood streaming down her face. Despite her own fear and pain, she had to comfort the other survivors who looked to her for protection as the symbol of the U.S. government. Like Chris Stevens in Benghazi years later, you can become a target simply by being in the wrong place at the wrong time. Being an ambassador means being charged with the safety of a large community of Americans and their families, as well as for host-country and third-country nationals who work for the U.S. government, often without being given adequate resources to do the job.

Like most Americans nominated as U.S. ambassadors, I was impressed when told I should consider myself the personal representative of the U.S. president in Oman. This, shockingly, did not guarantee me an actual meeting with the president. At one time, the president personally telephoned every one of his nominees to offer the job formally. That was judged in recent administrations not a good use of a president's time. By 1992 a nominee would receive a phone call from the director general of the Foreign Service, a fancy title for the head of personnel. Once confirmed by the Senate, an ambassador can try to schedule a photo op with the president. Considering I was nominated by George H. W. Bush and confirmed very shortly before Election Day, the president was, understandably, too busy. He probably could have found the time after he lost the election, but I chose to fly promptly to Oman and start doing my job. Some months later, during a return trip to Washington, I asked the appropriate State Department official if I might have my picture taken with President Clinton. I did not do so out of vanity. Such a picture, prominently displayed in my office, would help to cement the impression that I was indeed the president's personal representative. Rather than tell me to "get a grip," the official directed me, with a twinkle in his eye, to the sidewalk outside the Treasury Department where tourists paid a few bucks to get their picture taken next to a cardboard cutout of the president.

Occasionally, when protocolary demands are few and terrorists have gone to ground, an ambassador can steal a little time to work on what might be called the substance of the U.S. relationship with his host country. As my own experience with the confirmation process demonstrated, a prospective ambassador generally has a great deal of time on his hands as he or she waits around in the United States for the Senate to act. After I learned all I could about Oman and the history of U.S.-Omani relations, I formulated a strategy to take the relationship to a higher level. I learned soon enough that, thanks to the continued erosion of U.S. foreign policy capability, I would have all I could do to maintain the relationship at the level I found it.

The cornerstone of the U.S.-Omani relationship is the agreement granting us access to Omani military facilities. Following the Iranian revolution in 1979, as part of the Carter Doctrine announcing that we would use military force as necessary to protect our interests in the Persian (Arabian) Gulf, we entered into the military agreement and, at the same time, agreed to establish an Omani-American Joint Commission as a mechanism to provide economic and technical assistance to Oman. It was well understood at the time that the economic aid (at a modest level of roughly $15 million per year) was a *quid pro quo* for our military access. Although the agreement was not popular with Oman's neighbors, Qaboos agreed to it because he understood that Oman lives in a dangerous neighborhood and that Oman would benefit from having such a relationship with one of the world's superpowers.

It was my misfortune to be ambassador when the Clinton administration decided to streamline U.S. economic assistance programs. USAID administrator Brian Atwood, operating no doubt under severe budget constraints, announced the closing of twenty-one U.S. foreign aid missions. He combed the list of countries in the Middle East region receiving economic assistance and concluded that Oman and Tunisia were expendable. He may have concluded that Oman had reached a stage of economic development where it should "graduate" from such assistance. He also may have decided that assistance should be concentrated on countries directly involved in the Middle East peace process (for example, Egypt, Israel, Jordan, and Lebanon). Atwood's logic was not flawed, but either he failed to run his thinking by other important players in Washington, including the Departments of State and Defense, or he did coordinate with those agencies and the key players were asleep at the switch. Atwood scheduled a press conference in Washington on the morning of Friday, November 19, 1993. Someone in the State Department thought to alert me first thing on that morning that the United States would announce the end of its assistance program to Oman in a few hours. First thing in the morning in Washington is well into the day in Muscat, and Friday is the Muslim sabbath. I had to track down Foreign Minister Yusuf bin Alawi and give him this surprising and inexplicable news. Yusuf's reaction gave me plenty of raw material for a cable back to Washington reporting Omani outrage over both the decision and the timing. Happily, he was too much of a professional to shoot the messenger, and our good personal relationship enabled us eventually to weather what could have been a crippling blow to our military security relationship.

It only got worse, however, during the days following the initial shock. There is always a lag between the obligation of funds in the USAID budget for an assistance project and the actual disbursement of the funds to an Omani entity. The amount of funds promised but not yet delivered is called the "pipeline." The USAID leadership, with the apparent acquiescence of State and Defense, elected to rescind a portion of the funds from previous year appropriations already promised to Oman. They called this remarkable initiative "rescissions." I remember well the day I had an appointment with Sayyid Haitham bin Tariq, one of the sultan's nephews and then Omani deputy foreign minister, to explain why the U.S. government was going to take back funds already promised to the Omanis. I had that morning taken Jack, my thirteen-year-old yellow Labrador retriever to a British vet, and we made the decision to put Jack down once the vet had diagnosed cancer that was well-advanced. My heart was heavy, and the meeting was difficult, the more so because the talking points Washington had given me were lame.

Driving back to the embassy from that meeting, I pondered the growing dysfunctionality of the State Department. How could NEA, the bureau I had worked in and with for so many years, leave me so out on a limb to deal with decisions that clearly threatened an important security relationship? Warren Christopher was secretary of state, and I doubt that he gave Oman much thought. Deputy Assistant Secretary David Mack was the most senior official I could reach on the subject, and he told me rather bluntly to get used to the idea that Washington didn't think Oman was important.

A month before the Atwood announcement, in late October 1993, the Multilateral Working Group on Water Resources of the

Middle East was meeting in Beijing. The Water Resources Group was one of five groups created at the Madrid meeting in November 1991 under the multilateral track of the peace process. A month before the Beijing meeting, the Oslo Accords had been signed in the Rose Garden by Israeli Prime Minister Yitzhak Rabin and PLO Chairman Yasser Arafat. I received a call from a low-level official in the State Department telling me to approach the Omanis to urge them to support hosting the next meeting of the Water Resources Group in Muscat. This was a big deal because it would be the first time one of the countries on the Arabian Peninsula would be hosting a meeting attended by Israeli government officials. Oman was a logical choice because it was a long way from Israel and did not share the passion of Israel's close neighbors about the Arab-Israeli conflict. Oman had been one of the few Arab countries not to break relations with Egypt after the Egypt-Israel peace treaty in 1979. I told the caller that this would require me to wake up the foreign minister, and I wanted instructions from a higher level. In a few minutes, Dan Kurtzer, my former deputy in Egyptian affairs and now an NEA deputy assistant secretary, was on the phone instructing me to take the action. Action was urgent because the Water Resources Group was concluding a meeting in Beijing and needed to reach agreement on the site of the next meeting. I called Yusuf to make the pitch and he called back within the hour with Omani government agreement.

The actual meeting occurred six months later in mid-April 1994. Deputy Foreign Minister Yossi Beilin led the Israeli delegation, and he was accompanied by several Israeli journalists. I recall that the Omani government, having gone out on a limb to invite the Israelis to Muscat, was very reluctant to issue the journalists visas. The government relented and, after the journalists arrived, they came to the U.S. Embassy for a briefing on Oman. They made no effort to hide their excitement about being in Oman. They were optimistic, as was I, that Israel's relations with the Arab world would continue to improve. Prime Minister Rabin made a surprise trip to Oman to visit Qaboos in late December that year, and there were reports that Oman and Israel would open trade offices in each other's country.

Oman won election as the Arab representative on the UN Security Council for a two-year term beginning in January 1994. That increased the number of instructions from Washington asking for Oman's support of the U.S. position on several issues before the UNSC. This was a good thing considering Oman's enhanced role in the UN, along with their willingness to host a peace process meeting, gave me positive things to say in meetings that might otherwise have been dominated with recriminations about our sudden decision to end the economic assistance program.

Having come from Saudi Arabia where we received, at least during the war, what might have been too much attention from Washington, it was an adjustment for me to be in a place that received very little attention. We nevertheless took initiatives that received positive notice from Washington. Embassy Economic/Commercial officer Dick Eason, with lots of help from Embassy Public Affairs officer Matt Lussenhop, organized an America Week at a local shopping center that showcased a wide variety of products carried by local companies that the U.S. exported to Oman. The center arranged a variety of cultural events to promote the week. Other than Dick Eason's time and my time inaugurating the event, there was no cost to the U.S. government. The Department of Commerce commended us in a message to all U.S. diplomatic posts around the world with the suggestion that they do something similar.

We also took the initiative to organize a modest conference in Muscat of junior officers who were stationed in the Gulf Cooperation Council countries (Kuwait, Bahrain, Qatar, Saudi Arabia, and the UAE). We didn't get any funding from the State Department, but we managed to shame our sister embassies into financing the travel of the junior officers, and it gave them a chance to compare notes. They also participated telephonically in a question-and-answer session with a State Department personnel officer. That initiative also inspired a worldwide message commending the initiative as an example that other regions might emulate at a time when embassy budgets were strapped.

In early 1995, U.S. government attention focused on the upcoming review of the military access agreement that allowed us to utilize the air bases in Seeb, Masirah, and Thumrait for pre-positioning U.S. Air Force equipment. The Omanis were still smarting over the sudden termination of the modest economic assistance program, as well as the confiscation of funds in the pipeline. The review promised to be contentious, and the minds of key people in State and Defense were now more focused on Oman.

Somewhere in Washington, an initiative was hatched to build on Oman's willingness to host Israelis and take the sting out of the disappearance of the aid program. The Water Resources Group meeting in Muscat had agreed to establish a Middle East Desalination Research Center (MEDRC) in Muscat. Vice President Al Gore visited Oman to meet with Qaboos and to deliver a check for $3 million to help establish the MEDRC. He, along with his wife Tipper, visited on a day during the second half of March. Their time on the ground was four hours and forty-five minutes. They had started the day in Jordan and would finish it in Saudi Arabia, and this was only one day of a five-day trip.

When we met Vice President Gore and Tipper at the airport, neither appeared happy. Someone told me later that something had gone wrong with the on-board toilet just after landing. The vice president went about his time on the ground in a very professional manner, not only covered his talking points welcoming Oman's contributions to the peace process and praising the importance of military cooperation, but also pitching a Mobil natural gas project that we had been working hard supporting. Tipper, on the other hand, blew off an event involving Omani women that had been long-planned, and announced that she would prefer to swim in the hotel pool, demanding that someone find her an appropriate bathing suit. Sandy was left with the job of explaining to the invited Omani women, the majority of whom she would frequently see socially in subsequent weeks, that Mrs. Gore wouldn't be attending the event. Though the Gores were not at their charming best, the visit helped repair the damage caused by the abrupt end to the USAID program. The military access review came and went without any major hiccups, and we continue to this day to have access to Omani air bases.

During my time in Oman, I met with Sultan Qaboos on multiple occasions. I accompanied several distinguished visitors who were granted audiences with Qaboos. I also met with him alone roughly twice a year. Qaboos, having lived in England and attended Sandhurst, was fluent in English, unlike other rulers on the Arabian Peninsula at that time. The one-on-one meetings were a great opportunity to pursue items on my agenda. The meetings were long—ninety minutes to two hours—and relaxed. Qaboos talked about whatever was on his mind that day. Sometimes that overlapped with my agenda but, often, it did not. I learned to be alert for when the door began to rattle, for that meant that coffee, *halwa* (a sticky sweet that you scooped with your hand from a dish), and incense would be proffered. This was also a sign that the meeting would soon end and that I had only a few minutes to pursue my remaining agenda items.

We were invited every New Year's Eve to the Sultan's palace northwest of Muscat known as Bait al-Baraka. The American ambassador and the British ambassador and their wives were the only diplomats invited, along with a select group of Qaboos's British and American friends. Don Bosch, retired American missionary doctor, and his wife Eloise were the only other Americans. The British woman who had hosted Qaboos in her home during his time at Sandhurst was also invited and honored. For each expatriate, a senior Omani, including Omar and Qais Zawawi and our landlord, the Royal Oman police chief, was also present. The Zawawis were the Sultan's most trusted advisors, and they were key players in the transformation of Oman from an impoverished backwater to a modern economy. Dr. Omar, as everyone called him, practiced medicine as a young man and became Oman's leading businessman while holding the title of special adviser to the sultan on external liaison. Few questioned the appropriateness of Oman's most successful businessmen also holding key ministerial positions. Dr. Omar's younger brother Qais also started out in business and, after serving as minister of state for foreign affairs, went on to be deputy prime minister for finance. Shortly after I departed Oman, the Sultan and the two Zawawi brothers were involved in an automobile accident in southern Oman. The sultan, who was driving, had stopped at an awkward spot on the road, and a speeding car rammed their vehicle. Qaboos escaped with only minor injuries, but Qais was killed and Dr. Omar badly injured.

The New Year's Eve event would begin at about 8:00 p.m. with a reception at which Qaboos was not present and at which alcohol was served. At about 10:00 p.m., we would be escorted to a spacious garden, where we would be greeted individually by Qaboos. The British ambassador and I were seated at a head table with the sultan while our wives were seated at other tables.

A highlight of the evening was being served buffet-style a piece of cake, inside of which we might find a gold coin. Sandy and I each managed to come away with a gold coin every year, which we still have. During our last New Year's Eve in Oman in 1995, Sandy learned from another guest that it was customary to give one of your coins to your driver, and she confiscated my coin for that purpose. When I sat back down next to Qaboos, he asked me whether I had found a coin. I told him what had happened to my coin, and he summoned a servant who quickly brought me another.

Don and Eloise Bosch were very special people. They came to Oman well before Qaboos became sultan. Don was a surgeon who worked in the American Mission Hospital in Mutrah (just outside Muscat), while his wife Eloise was a teacher in the American Mission School in Muscat. He saved many lives during the nearly thirty years he practiced surgery. When Don retired in the mid-1980s, Sultan Qaboos granted them both Omani citizenship and built them a home along the coast. We have fond memories of attending a party in their home, where we found ourselves square dancing. Oman was a paradise for sea shell collectors. Don began as a collector and evolved into an internationally recognized expert on the seashells of the Arabian Gulf. Don and Eloise and their family discovered more than twenty species of seashells that were new to science. One, the *Punctada eloisae*, was named after Don's wife.

We have an "Eloise," which we received during a trip Sandy and I made to Masirah, a large island off the coast of central Oman. The Royal Omani Air Force Base on Masirah was one of the three

Omani air bases we utilized to store pre-positioned U.S. Air Force equipment. The other two were Seeb (co-located with the civilian airport serving Muscat) and Thumrait, in the desert north of Salalah in Oman's southern portion. Masirah was used as a staging area for the abortive attempt to rescue American hostages held by Iran in 1980. Several of the early U.S. operations into Afghanistan in 2001 also used it as a staging area.

Some of our most enjoyable days in Oman were ones we spent in the company of Dr. Asim al-Jamali. Dr. Asim was a former minister of health who seemed to enjoy the prestige of a ministerial position without the responsibilities. He owned a very modern, very fast boat. Learning of my interest in scuba diving, he invited Sandy and me for a boat trip. According to my dive log book, I went out with Dr. Asim five times. We motored to a place southeast of Muscat along the coast called Bandar Khiran one time and also four times to the Daimaniyat Islands. These were nine uninhabited islands about twelve miles off the Batinah coast, which featured the best diving in Oman.

I had learned to dive along with my son and daughter during my first summer in Saudi Arabia. We received our initial training in the Embassy Riyadh swimming pool and completed our PADI (Professional Association of Dive Instructors) certification off the al-Bilad beach in Jeddah. Diving in the Red Sea was spectacular, but the diving off Daimaniyat Islands was almost as good. Given the distance from the coast, Dr. Asim's fast boat was essential to the adventure. An abundance of coral hosted many colorful fish as well as moray eels, lionfish, and lobsters. Dr. Asim did not dive but Maggie, his English personal assistant, and Bill, the boat captain, did. They were experienced divers, which came in handy during one dive when, because of a BCD (buoyancy control device) issue, I ran out of air and had to return to the surface doing "buddy breathing."

In November 1994, we learned that Oman was on the itinerary of State Department undersecretary for political affairs Peter Tarnoff. He let it be known that he would like to do some diving during his brief visit, so I called Dr. Asim, who agreed to take us out to the Daimaniyat Islands. Peter was no more experienced than I, and he lost one of his fins, and both of us inadvertently grabbed sea urchins and wound up with spines in our hands. Even if removed correctly, the wounds sting. Fortunately, Dr. Asim and his crew had seen this problem before. They made sure we got the spines out and had us soak the wounds in Listerine. Listerine was very effective in reducing the discomfort, but I am not sure Tarnoff was thrilled with his experience.

During my first year and a half, both of my senior military officers struggled. I decided in consultation with regional medical officer Dr. Scott Kennedy and the deputy Centcom commander to send home the army colonel in charge of military assistance for what I considered inappropriate personal conduct. I also decided to curtail the tour of the defense attaché, an Air Force colonel, by a year, largely because he was unable to get along with the strong-willed but very capable Marine major who served under him as the naval attaché. These were decisions that caused me more than one sleepless night but were necessary to maintaining an effective embassy. Both Centcom and the Defense Intelligence Agency came up with replacements who turned out to be excellent, and the military component of the embassy performed strongly during my last year in Oman.

Two of the most memorable adventures Sandy and I experienced in Oman were arranged by the military. The USS *Pasadena*, a nuclear submarine, invited Foreign Minister Yusuf bin Alawi to visit. The sub anchored well off-shore. Sandy and I accompanied the minister on a small skiff. When we arrived, the water was roiling with white snakes. Something about the surfacing of the sub had attracted them. We had to walk carefully up the side to the hatch on top and descend on a ladder. The crew took us for a dive. Foreign Minister Alawi was impressed but our real audience was Sultan Qaboos. The navy had long pushed for Oman to allow nuclear-powered warships into Omani ports. The Omanis had long resisted. During my last months in Oman, a highly placed Omani pointed me toward a training film made by Georgetown University. The film, clearly made during the cold war, developed a scenario where

Oman was taken over by a government allied to the Soviet Union, which led to a "Cuban missile type" confrontation between the United States and the Soviets. Students viewing the film were asked to become policy makers and choose among several options. One option resulted in Muscat being enveloped in a mushroom cloud. My contact suggested that the Sultan had seen this and determined that nothing nuclear would be permitted in Oman.

On another occasion, Sandy and I were invited to observe a Marine Expeditionary Unit (MEU) exercise that took place on an unpopulated beach off Oman's southern coast. The USS *Tripoli*, an amphibious assault ship, took part in the exercise. The captain made his cabin available for Sandy and me for the night before the exercise. Observing the exercise took us ashore on an LCAC (landing craft air cushion), an amazing vehicle that skimmed across the water and up onto a rough beach on an air cushion. Now on shore, we rode first on a Humvee and then on a helicopter to watch the exercise. It happened that my father served on an earlier version of the USS *Tripoli* during World War II. I came away with a USS *Tripoli* hat that I sent to my father, who wore it proudly for much of the rest of his life.

An additional personnel headache emerged when a staffer of my USAID director accused him of sexual harassment. The allegation came directly to USAID in Washington, which kicked off a seemingly endless investigation where guilt seemed to be presumed until innocence had been established. It angered me that I had not been given the opportunity to deal with the allegation at post before its conveyance to Washington. I liked and trusted the aid director, and my gut told me that the allegation came from a poorly performing employee who resented criticism. That I had been the victim of baseless allegations may have colored my judgment.

After the investigation dragged on for nine months, I sent a message directly to USAID administrator Atwood in Washington about the delay in adjudicating the allegation. I complained that, while spending months investigating, USAID didn't find it necessary to send an investigator to Muscat to experience the interpersonal dynamics that I was observing. The most serious issue facing me at the time was the elimination of funding for the USAID program and the rescissions of money in the pipeline. I needed my aid director's full attention. Still, the investigation dragged on. I was eventually deposed over the phone, along with others in the embassy. In the end, the USAID administration took no action. While he completed his tour in Muscat, the aid director sensibly left USAID and went to work for the Pan American Health Organization.

There were no other serious difficulties with my staff. Liz McKune, my DCM, kept things running very competently. The station chief was superb and had an excellent relationship with his counterpart in the Omani government. He kept me in the loop even on the most sensitive issues. He went on to senior positions in the operations side of the CIA. Matt Lussenhop, my public affairs officer, was also excellent. Scott Kennedy, our regional medical officer stationed in Sana'a, helped me in several significant ways. Not only did he assist me in identifying an employee who needed to be sent home, but he helped me get through a personal bout of malaria, which Oman claimed to have eliminated, and a case of shingles. In each case, he promptly identified and located the right drug, and minimized the amount of down time I required.

The State Department's budget crisis came to Oman in 1994, and we had to cut back on expenses by 10 percent. This required us to do more than reduce office supplies and turn down the air conditioning. We had to cut down on the number of Foreign Service nationals who worked at the embassy. I scheduled a mission-wide town hall to explain why we had to take these actions. I promised to involve everyone in the drawing up of a budget-cutting package and to make the process totally transparent. The jobs of American employees were not directly affected by this exercise, but a separate decision in Washington reduced our hardship differential sharply, reducing take-home pay significantly. I was proud of the resilience of the embassy staff in weathering these twin blows. Morale remained surprisingly high.

In 1992 archaeologists discovered the ruins of a city in a remote area in southern Oman known as Shisr. Although many claimed it was the lost city of Ubar, celebrated in the Qur'an and *A Thou-*

sand and One Nights, the claim sparked controversy. The site clearly dated back to the time two thousand years earlier when this region of the Arabian Peninsula was the center of the frank-incense trade. The lead archaeologist, Juris Zarins, a professor at Southwest Missouri State University, invited me down to visit the site outside Salalah. Zarins was a charismatic leader of a group of mostly young American students who were meticulously unearth-ing the site. He told us that the "gold" in the biblical reference to the wise men bearing gifts of gold, frankincense, and myrrh was probably a high grade of frankincense rather than actual gold. As we walked around the site, I spotted what looked like an interest-ing artifact, and I asked Juris what it was. "An AFR," he replied. I fell far too easily into the trap he set for me. "What's an AFR," I asked. "Another f**king rock," he replied.

During my last year in Oman, my seventy-seven-year-old father came to visit, bringing his *Tripoli* hat. He planned the trip with great care so that he could visit the three of his four children who were at the time stationed in exotic places. His twin daughters (my half-sisters) Beth and Polly were both in the Peace Corps, stationed in Morocco and Ivory Coast, respectively. It was a brave decision on his part because he had been diagnosed with emphysema and he would be traveling alone. He left Tucson on February 20, 1995, and didn't arrive in Dubai until February 22, shortly after mid-night. Sandy and I drove the four hours from Muscat to Dubai to meet him at the airport. We stayed the night at the home of the consul general, David Pearce, who we had gotten to know well in Riyadh. David was the political counselor in the U.S. Embassy in Kuwait when Iraq invaded Kuwait. He was outside the country at the time of the invasion, so he was in Saudi Arabia representing the United States to the Kuwaiti government-in-exile.

Shortly after my dad's arrival, Madeleine Albright, then U.S. ambassador to the United Nations, visited Oman with two of her staff on a trip to shore up Arab support for continued sanctions on Iraq. There wasn't time to arrange an official dinner, so we invited her to an informal dinner with my dad and Hank and Sonja, our two friends from Riyadh also visiting. We seated dad next to Madeleine and they got along famously. When my father explained that his cousin George had been named postmaster of Seattle years earlier even though he had no experience with the postal system, Madeleine responded, "Well, he got mail didn't he?"

In a society like Oman, people pay great respect to the older generation, and being the father of the U.S. ambassador ensured that my father received the royal treatment. Dad stayed with us for nearly four weeks and attended virtually all the parties and receptions that Sandy and I hosted or attended. We had officers from the USS *Vandergrift* to dinner at the residence along with Admiral Scott Redd, who was Fifth Fleet commander, living in Bahrain. Dad managed to wangle an invitation to tour the ship the next day. It was a special time for both of us because he had opportunity to witness my work at the pinnacle of my career.

From Oman he flew to Morocco to spend time with Beth and then on to the Ivory Coast, where Polly was serving. Hume Horan, who had abruptly left Saudi Arabia seven years earlier, was ambassador in Abidjan, and he invited Dad and Polly to lunch, a very nice gesture.

Bob Pelletreau, now NEA assistant secretary, visited Oman during my last year. As we rode together to call on Sultan Qaboos, he told me that NEA didn't have any spot for me going forward. This did not come as a surprise. The Foreign Service, like the military, is an "up or out" career service. I knew going into my last year in Oman that I would have to retire. I had risen through the ranks very rapidly in my first fourteen years as a Foreign Service Officer, becoming a senior officer at thirty-seven years of age. Because I had been a senior officer since 1980, absent a promotion to career minister or another presidential appointment, my time was up. Sandy was more than ready for the transition after seven straight years of entertaining and being entertained. "Eating and drinking" for our country had been hard on our health. I was less ready because I liked what I was doing and wasn't sure what I would find to do in retirement.

My three-year tour as ambassador would not be up until November, but I elected to depart for Washington in June to take advantage of the State Department's career transition seminar, which they offered only in the summer. As the time for departure crept closer, we anticipated that there would be a flurry of farewell calls and farewell parties that would challenge our stamina. Our remedy was to schedule a ten-day vacation in Greece. We split the time between two beautiful islands, Corfu and Santorini, and came back to Muscat refreshed and ready to be gracious and charming for our last month.

One of the many farewells was a lunch organized by the protocol chief of the Ministry of Foreign Affairs, where the Diplomatic Corps would say goodbye. That required a short speech from me and I elected to do it in Arabic. My Arabic was still rudimentary, but I thought I could pull it off with some help. The embassy had an excellent language teacher, who I recruited to help me prepare. I wrote out a simple speech in English and he translated it and then worked with me over several days to pronounce the words correctly (more or less). Just to add to the challenge, I read the speech from an Arabic text. The British ambassador grumbled to me when I was done, that I had set a high bar for those non-Arabic speakers who would be leaving after me. It was just the compliment I was looking for.

On my last day, some members of the American business community contacted me about a student who was just graduating from the international school, the American-British academy. I had given the commencement address to the graduates a year earlier. The student was Algerian but had been living in Muscat for several years. He was a bright student and had been accepted as an entering freshman by the Massachusetts Institute of Technology, my alma mater. The problem was that he had been rejected for a visa by the American Embassy in Muscat. I huddled with Manish Mishra, our consular officer, who explained to me that the student did not have strong ties to either Algeria or Oman and thus, in his judgment, did not qualify for a student visa. Over the years, I had never pressured a consular officer to issue a visa, although I often asked them to take another look at a decision. I asked Manish to reconsider his decision as a farewell gift to me, and he agreed. I don't remember the student's name and I never heard how he did at MIT, but I remain confident that U.S. interests were served by granting that visa.

Sultan Qaboos agreed to see me the evening before my scheduled departure. He was at his residence in Sohar, about two hours northwest of Muscat. We arrived at a complex of several buildings, and a staffer asked me to wait in one of the buildings. After several minutes, a member of the Sultan's household came and escorted me out into the June heat and humidity. My glasses immediately fogged, so I took them off. My uncorrected eyesight was terrible and, as I entered the air-conditioned building where Qaboos was waiting with Foreign Minister Yusuf bin Alawi, it was all I could do to find them in the large room. Qaboos was holding an award, which he presented to me before we sat down. He conferred on me the al-Nu'man order of the first class "in appreciation of the effort (I) exerted to strengthen ties of friendship and cooperation between the Sultanate of Oman and the United States of America."

During the meeting we discussed the U.S. contribution to the Middle East Desalination Research Center, an Omani request to relocate pre-positioned equipment away from the civilian airport at Seeb, our proposal to provide M60A3 tanks to Oman, Omani interest in strengthening GCC ties with Yemen, and our concern that Iran might be seeking nuclear weapons. On my own initiative, I presented Qaboos with a copy of *Cadillac Desert*, by Mark Reisner, which I described to him as a cautionary tale about how water resources in the American West had been exploited. It was clear from the atmosphere of the meeting that we had gotten past the abrupt end of our economic assistance program, and that I was leaving U.S.-Omani relations in good shape.

I drafted the reporting cable of the meeting in the car on the way back to the embassy. I turned the award, which clearly contained some valuable jewelry, over to DCM McKune and suggested she ask the State Department for permission for the embassy to retain it and display it in the embassy. The next day, we were on a plane home and getting ready for the next adventure in our lives.

FIG. 1. Meeting Egyptian President Anwar Sadat in Alexandria, Egypt, September 1981, with U.S. Agency for International Development (USAID) administrator Peter McPherson and U.S. Ambassador to Egypt Alfred Atherton (both pictured from behind).

FIG. 2. Presidents Carter, Nixon, and Ford at Anwar Sadat's funeral, with Embassy Cairo staff, October 1981. Only Ford's forehead is visible under the arch. The author is in the back row, with shiny glasses. Ambassador Atherton is on the far right. Deputy Chief of Mission Henry Precht is next to him.

FIG. 3. USAID administrator McPherson, Ambassador Atherton, and the author call on Egyptian President Mubarak in Cairo in 1982.

FIG. 4. Gen. Norman Schwarzkopf with the author's wife, Sandy, and the author in Riyadh, March 1991.

FIG. 5. Departing Saudi Ministry of Defense and Aviation with Secretary of Defense Dick Cheney in Riyadh, April 1991

FIG. 6. Ambassador Chas Freeman presents Christian Herter Award to the author at the U.S. Embassy in Riyadh, April 1991.

FIG. 7. Standing on an Iraqi tank, with a burning oil well in the background (Embassy Riyadh political counselor Dick Jones and political-military officer Rick Olson are on the left) in Kuwait, April 1991. A U.S. Embassy Kuwait escort is in the foreground. Commercial Counselor Dirck Teller is on the right.

FIG. 8. Sandy with Barbara Bush at the White House, September 1992.

FIG. 9. With Suzanne Chapman, the author's secretary from 1991 to 1995, on her birthday, March 17, 1993.

FIG. 10. Sultan Qaboos greets Sandy and the author at his Beit al-Baraka residence near Muscat on New Year's Eve, 1994.

FIG. 11. Madeleine Albright meets with Sultan Qaboos, March 1995.

FIG. 12. Meeting with rural Omanis, 1994.

FIG. 13. Vice President Al Gore with Sultan Qaboos, March 1995.

FIG. 14. With Muscat Diplomatic Corps, June 1995.

FIG. 15. Sultan Qaboos presents al-Nu'man award to the author
at his residence in Sohar, June 1995.

FIG. 16. Members of the MENABANK transition team enjoying a felucca ride on
the Nile in summer 1997. *From left to right*: Dick Goodman, Wafik Grais, Daniel
Yariv, Yomna Adel, Yuki Fukuda, the author, Wim Ritzerfeld, and Rania Sharif.

FIG. 17. Burned and looted Ministry of Foreign Affairs, Baghdad, Iraq, May 2003.

FIG. 18. The Korean couple, pictured with officers from the Second Infantry Division, hosted lunch when they learned that the author had been involved in the construction of their building thirty-nine years earlier. Seoul, Korea, August 2004.

FIG. 19. Scene from the mission readiness exercise (MRX) at the Korea Training Center in August 2004. The Second Infantry Division brigade was preparing to deploy to Ramadi, Iraq.

FIG. 20. Members of the Twenty-Ninth Combat Aviation Brigade participating in a seminar presented by the Leader Development and Education for Sustained Peace Program (LDESP) at the Naval Postgraduate School, Monterey, California, May 2011. (Retired U.S. Army general Dan Petrosky is in the center, while LDESP faculty are in the upper right.)

6

CAIRO

Banking on Peace

I found myself back in Cairo on a warm evening on the last day of May 1997. I was wandering along the east bank of the Nile on the Corniche near the Shepheard Hotel and soaking in the familiar sights (crowds of people), sounds (continuous honking of car horns), and smells (sweat and smoke) of Cairo. I was accosted by a street vendor selling cheap reproductions of pharaonic art. I would normally have walked on, but this was my first day back in Egypt after ten years. I stopped and answered his polite and predictable questions. I had yet to connect with people I knew from a decade earlier and was eager to talk to an Egyptian, any Egyptian. I told him I had once lived in Cairo. I dredged out of my memory some rusty phrases in Egyptian Arabic and soon we were in his shop drinking tea. After a friendly and leisurely conversation, I departed with two papyrus scrolls that I did not want or need and for which I had paid far more than they were worth.

I had been brought out of retirement by the Department of State to head the transition team for the Bank for Reconstruction and Development in the Middle East and North Africa, which sensibly we abbreviated as MENABANK.[1] MENABANK was to be a regional multilateral development bank along the lines of the European Bank for Reconstruction and Development (EBRD) set up six years earlier in London to help meet the financing needs of the countries of eastern Europe and the former Soviet Union. Similar regional multilateral development banks have long serviced other regions of the world (Latin America, Africa, and Asia). They are designed to complement rather than compete with the International Bank for Reconstruction and Development (IBRD) and the other international financial institutions that are a part of the World Bank group. The ongoing Arab-Israeli conflict explained why no such bank yet existed for the Middle East. The transition team's job was to take all the necessary steps to allow the bank to open its doors and begin operation.

The seeming breakthroughs of the Madrid Conference in the fall of 1991, following the first (1990–91) Gulf War, and the Oslo Accords between the Israelis and the Palestinians, signed in September 1993, had led to the MENABANK initiative.[2] The Madrid Conference set up a series of bilateral negotiations between Israel and its Arab neighbors, as well as a multilateral track.[3] As part of the multilateral track, five working groups were set up. As discussed in the previous chapter, Oman's agreement to host a meeting of the Water Resources Working Group led to the initiative to create a Middle East Desalination Research Center (MEDRC). One of the other working groups was the Regional Economic Development Working Group (REDWG), chaired by the European Union (EU). There was considerable discussion in the REDWG about the idea of setting up a regional multilateral development bank. The United States remained opposed to the idea until the core regional parties (Egypt, Israel, Jordan, and the Palestinian Authority) sent a joint delegation to Washington and several European capitals to advocate for the bank. The delegation met with an interagency group in Washington that included Larry Summers, deputy Treasury secretary; Joan Spero, undersecretary of state for economics, business, and agriculture; Al Larson, assistant secretary for economic and business affairs; and Dennis Ross, special Middle East coordinator. All would be key players in fleshing out the details of the initiative, drawing on the EBRD as a model.

The U.S. decision to get behind the bank reflected the atmosphere of optimism (some would say euphoria) that gripped Washington following the Rose Garden handshake between Rabin and Arafat in September 1993. Israeli-Palestinian negotiations were active, and the parties were making progress in the Israeli-Jordanian negotiations (the Israel-Jordan peace treaty was signed in October 1994). International donors had come together to pledge well over $2 billion to the Palestinians and to create a Palestinian aid coordinating agency with strong World Bank technical support. The multilateral working groups were meeting regularly and making progress. Stanley Fischer, the highly respected Israeli-American economist (then at MIT), had also written a long paper in August 1994 advocating for a traditional development bank for the Middle East.

After several negotiating rounds in DC, Moscow, and European capitals, the parties reached agreement at the Amman Economic Summit in late October 1995 to set up the bank. Larry Butcher, the director of the Office of Development Finance (ODF) in the State Department's Bureau of Economic and Business Affairs (EB), and Richard Goodman, a Treasury lawyer with a steel-trap mind who had played a key role in the negotiations to create the EBRD in 1989–90, were significant participants in the negotiations. The actual Articles of Agreement were initialed several months later, on August 28, 1996. Regional members included Egypt, Israel, Jordan, the Palestinian Authority, Morocco, Tunisia, and Algeria. The United States, Canada, Japan, Russia, Turkey, and several European countries also joined. Russia was co-chair with the United States of the multilateral track, and we had high hopes that Turkey, as a donor, would contribute significantly to regional water projects. Notably absent from those initialing the agreement were the UK, France, Germany, and the Nordic countries. The site of the future bank was to be Cairo. The United States, as the largest shareholder with 21 percent, would lead a transition team to set up the bank.

I had settled into an active retirement in Tucson when the Department of State approached me about taking the position as transition team leader. While the Treasury Department would be expected to provide the leader of the team, it seemed that no suitable Treasury officials were available. I understood that Charles Schotta, the Treasury deputy assistant secretary with whom I had butted heads during my days in Riyadh, had turned down the job. Charles had traveled extensively in his Treasury career but, as far as I know, had never lived outside the United States. Treasury seemed happy to allow the State Department to find a candidate to lead the transition team. Given my experience that the Treasury Department jealously guarded its relationships with the World Bank group, the IMF and the regional multilateral development banks, I was surprised by this.

Larry Butcher reached out to me in early March and offered me the job. He was looking for someone with a combination of Middle East and development finance experience. That there were no obvious candidates among active Foreign Service Officers reflected how little depth the Foreign Service had in the late 1990s owing to budget cuts and creeping politicization. Shaun Donnelly, my deputy in Cairo, fit the profile, but he currently held a key deputy assistant secretary position in EB and likely was preparing for his next assignment as U.S. ambassador in Sri Lanka. Years earlier, I had held Butcher's job in ODF, and I had spent three years in Cairo as head of the Economic Section. When the offer came, I was teaching a course for the University of Arizona Political Science Department called the Arab-Israeli Conflict, so I was familiar with the politics that would complicate the work of the transition team.

I was secretly pleased that the Department of State had not forgotten me, but I was also skeptical about leaving the life I was building in Tucson, and I wasn't sure about the level of commitment in the United States and other governments to this project. I agreed to sign on for only six months, although I signaled that I would stay on if the project was thriving but still incomplete and if I was enjoying the experience. I asked a multitude of questions about who I would report to in Washington, how I would relate to the U.S. Embassy in Cairo, what administrative support I could expect, and what resources would be available for carrying out our mission. Larry had good answers to my questions and, over the coming months, I was very happy with the budgetary support the team received and the administrative support from our Cairo Embassy.

My concern about the commitment of governments was well-founded. The Amman Economic Summit took place during the last three days of October 1995. Yitzhak Rabin, the Israeli prime minister, who led Israel into the Oslo Accords, was assassinated on November 4, 1995. Back in Tucson, only weeks after I retired, I attended a memorial ceremony for Rabin at a synagogue within walking distance from my home. Shimon Peres, a stronger supporter of multilateral economic initiatives including MENABANK, became the new Israeli prime minister. Over the next several months, the Palestinian Islamic movement Hamas staged some of its more spectacular suicide bombings. In late February and early March 1996, two separate bus bombings in Jerusalem killed forty-five people. The day after the second bus bombing, on March 4, a bomb set off in a Tel Aviv shopping center killed another thirteen people. In April Israel launched a sixteen-day attack on Hezbollah (Lebanese Shi'a movement) in south Lebanon that did not go well. Israeli rockets hit a United Nations camp in Lebanon, killing four UN soldiers and roughly one hundred Lebanese civilians. Because of the violence in Israel and missteps in Lebanon, Peres's popularity within Israel plummeted. Israel's first-ever direct elections for prime minister took place on May 29, 1996, and Benjamin Netanyahu edged out Peres for the victory. Arab citizens of Israel make up about 20 percent of potential voters, and many reportedly sat out the election because of resentment over the Peres government's harsh crackdown on Palestinians following the Hamas suicide bombings.

Netanyahu had made no secret of his strong opposition to the Oslo Accords. Relations between Israel and the Arab countries, including Egypt, quickly soured. An Israeli decision in late September 1996 to excavate a tunnel along the edge of the Temple Mount in East Jerusalem led to armed clashes between Israelis and Palestinians. Fifty-four Palestinians and fourteen Israelis were killed. The Clinton administration, with special Middle East coordinator Dennis Ross as chief negotiator, soldiered on and in January 1997 produced an agreement between Netanyahu and Arafat that resulted in Israeli redeployment from 80 percent of the city of Hebron in the West Bank. The negotiations were protracted and difficult and left bruised feelings on all sides. On February 26, 1997, the Israeli government announced a decision to proceed with a 6,500-unit housing project on a hill in East Jerusalem known to Israelis as Har

Homa (Jebel Abu Gneim in Arabic). Many around the world considered this an illegal settlement designed to cut off access to Jerusalem from Bethlehem in the West Bank. A few days later (March 7) the United States vetoed a draft UN Security Council resolution calling on Israel to refrain from East Jerusalem settlement activity. On March 30, the Arab League approved a resolution to freeze ties with Israel. This was the political climate during my selection as coordinator of the MENABANK transition team.

My teaching commitment at the University of Arizona kept me in Tucson until mid-May but I did fly out to DC on April 30 for a May 1 meeting of prospective bank members and other interested parties. Conscious of the negative political atmosphere, State Department officials wanted to use the meeting to introduce me as their candidate for transition team leader and revive interest in the bank initiative. The strained relations between Egypt and Israel resulted in both governments electing to send only embassy representatives. The other regional parties (including Jordan and the Palestinian Authority) followed suit. Egyptian and Israeli government support of the transition team remained reserved and low key throughout my tenure on the team.

Once I had posted the final grades for the students in my university course, I packed my bags and flew back to DC for a week of consultations. Two State Department bureaus were involved, the Bureau of Economic and Business Affairs (EB) and the Bureau of Near East Affairs (NEA). I met with NEA Deputy Assistant Secretary Toni Verstandig. As I recall, she was the first political deputy assistant secretary brought into NEA. Others, including Liz Cheney in the George W. Bush administration, would follow. Toni had been a long-time staffer on the House Foreign Affairs Committee before coming to NEA as a Clinton political appointee. She came across in our initial meeting as capable and enthusiastic about the MENABANK project. I understood, however, that her enthusiasm had already started to wane by the time I came on board. There was no NEA assistant secretary, as Bob Pelletreau had retired early in 1997 and Martin Indyk would not take over until later that year. Indyk was a political appointee with experience working for AIPAC and the pro-Israeli think tank the Washington Institute for Near East Policy.

Early on, I met with Dick Jackson, director of Egyptian and North African affairs. I had known Dick from his time as deputy chief of mission (DCM) in Morocco. Sandy and I stayed in his home in Rabat briefly during a vacation trip from Riyadh to Morocco. The Office of Egyptian Affairs I had once directed had been merged with the office handling North Africa (Morocco, Algeria, Tunisia, and Libya), ostensibly for budgetary reasons. I suspect that the merger freed up positions to be added to the Office of Regional Affairs, which fell under Verstandig's supervision. Dick essentially worked for two deputy assistant secretaries. Verstandig dealt with peace process issues and economic issues, including the Gore-Mubarak initiative that addressed the longstanding issue of reforming the Egyptian economy. On peace process issues, and MENABANK fell in that category, Toni reported to special Middle East coordinator Dennis Ross. Art Hughes, a career Foreign Service Officer was the deputy assistant secretary responsible for everything else involving Egypt. I came away from my NEA meetings saddened by the creeping politicization of the bureau, the fragmentation of the chain of command, and the obvious impact on the morale of the professionals working in NEA.

On the economic side, I met with EB Assistant Secretary Al Larson and Philo Dibble, who was on the staff of the then-vacant office of the undersecretary for economic, business and agricultural affairs. Joan Spero, who had played a major role in forging the agreement to set up MENABANK, had departed earlier in the year and Stuart Eizenstat, her replacement, had not yet appeared. I also made the trek over to the Treasury Department to meet Bill Shuerch, the deputy assistant secretary who by this time oversaw U.S. government involvement with multilateral development banks. I met Dick Goodman, who would be Treasury's representative on our team, residing in Washington and visiting Cairo periodically. Larson and Shuerch said all the right things but I didn't sense that they were optimistic about the prospects for the MENA-BANK project.

Given that Dennis Ross had overall charge of the Middle East peace process, I was surprised at how little interest he took in the project. Had he signaled to the leadership of Egypt and Israel as well as to key congressional leaders that it was an administration priority, we might have had more success in 1998 when we made a strong push to breathe life back into the bank.

In addition to Goodman, I also met Lorenzo Savorelli, who was taking a leave of absence from his job at the World Bank to represent Italy on the transition team. Lorenzo was an extrovert, enthusiastic about being a part of the team. After a second meeting with Goodman and Savorelli on my last day in DC, I boarded a flight to Cairo.

Larry Butcher spent several weeks in Cairo in the early part of 1997 working with the Egyptian government and the U.S. Embassy to set up the transition team. The team had already been operating for months when I walked into the office building of the Cairo World Trade Center on June 1. The Japanese representative, Yukimasa Fukuda, the Dutch representative, Wim Ritzerfeld, and the Egyptian representative, Wafik Grais, were working away in a spacious office suite on the fourth floor of one of the two towers. The Egyptian Ministry of Foreign Affairs had provided two capable young women, Yomna Adel and Rania Sherif, who served as our secretaries. Yomna and Rania were both fluent in English and Arabic as well as charming and efficient.

Wim was totally comfortable in the world of computer technology. While I was surprised at the amount of support we were receiving from the Egyptian government, Wim was impatient with how slow-moving the government could be on issues he considered important. Raouf Saad, Egyptian Foreign Ministry official in charge of North American affairs, had been the key Egyptian official involved in the MENABANK negotiations and was also Ministry of Foreign Affairs point man on setting up the transition team. Before my arrival, Yuki, Wafik, and Wim had worked closely with Saad on the level of Egyptian support. At one meeting with Saad before I arrived, Wim committed cultural impropriety. One account held that he was sitting with the soles of his shoes pointed at Saad, and another that he neglected to shake Saad's hand on the way out. Whatever happened, Saad reportedly took umbrage and wanted the team to send Wim home. The team had to apologize profusely to retain him. I was very glad they succeeded because Wim's contributions were critical to our progress.

Yuki was seconded from Japan's aid agency to be his country's team member. He was reliable, hard-working, and totally dedicated to getting the bank up and running. He was the only other team member to have brought his family (wife and young daughter) with him. Yuki had been there for several weeks before I arrived, and he stayed until the team closed its doors in December 1998. Japan was the second-largest shareholder so, when I was away from Cairo, Yuki served as acting team coordinator. Wafik radiated sophistication, charm, and cosmopolitanism. He had family in Cairo, including his mother, but had been working for the World Bank group in Washington for some years when he was selected as the Egyptian representative. Although Wafik and Lorenzo both worked at the World Bank in Washington, they met for the first time when Lorenzo arrived in Cairo shortly after I did.

I set about quickly to touch base with Ned Walker, my predecessor in Riyadh and now U.S. ambassador in Cairo, with Soliman Awad in the Egyptian MFA, and with several Egyptian friends in and out of the government. The embassy, no longer the relatively charming old villa where I worked in the early 1980s, was now an ugly multistory tower surrounded by thick blast walls. Following the truck bomb attack on the U.S. Embassy in Beirut, embassy design gave much higher priority to security. The U.S. Embassy in Cairo was centrally located and an obvious symbol of the imposing American presence. Awad, deputy assistant minister of foreign affairs for regional cooperation, was now our major point of contact in the Egyptian government. I recall that Raouf Saad had been assigned abroad as Egyptian ambassador to the European Union in Brussels. Awad was less supportive than Saad had been, which may have reflected an Egyptian government decision to dial back support for MENABANK as part of the decision to slow the pace of normalization with Israel.

I decided promptly to plan a quick trip to touch base with the other regional MENABANK members. I flew to Amman, where I met Dr. Rima Khalaf, Jordan's minister of planning, and then on to Jerusalem, where I met Gideon Schurr of the Bank of Israel and other Israeli officials. I also drove to Ramallah to meet with Mohammed Shtayyeh, minister in charge of the Palestinian Economic Council for Development and Reconstruction (PECDAR).[4] I received assurance from both the Jordanian and Israeli governments that they would each provide an individual to join the transition team. Israel promptly sent Danny Yariv from the Bank of Israel. The Jordanian government moved more slowly but did finally send Iyad Ahmed. Both proved to be valuable members of the team. Danny was born in Argentina and immigrated to Israel. Iyad, like many Jordanian citizens, had a Palestinian heritage. Though the Palestinian Authority understandably did not contribute a team member, we told ourselves that Iyad represented both Jordanians and Palestinians. Norman Riddell joined us from Canada. Norman came to us from the University of Alberta in Edmonton.

The World Trade Center consisted of an office building and a residence building. The embassy installed me in an apartment on the twenty-eighth floor of the residence building. Ironically, the apartment had previously housed Janet Sanderson, the recently departed and last minister-counselor for economic affairs at the U.S. Embassy in Cairo. My commute to the office involved an elevator ride, a very short walk to the other building, and a walk up three flights of stairs. My experience with elevators during my first tour in Cairo gave me pause about living on the twenty-eighth floor. Happily, I never had an issue with elevators at the World Trade Center. The embassy also rented a car and driver from a local firm to allow me to move around the city.

I was surprised at how little attention we received from embassy economic officers, which probably owed to the puzzling decision to combine the political and economic sections in Cairo. I had worked hard toward upgrading the position of head of the economic section to minister-counselor. Edmund Hull, who had been with me in Cairo in the early 1980s as a political-military officer and was DCM from 1984 to 1986, had been the driving force behind the decision. Embassy Cairo saw itself as a major laboratory for Al Gore's reinventing government initiative, so it received significant support from Washington as well. By 1997 senior economic officers were in short supply in the Foreign Service and the difficulty of finding a strong candidate to run the economic section likely played into the move as well. This struck me as a bad decision given the importance of our economic dialogue with the Egyptians and that the USAID mission was staffed with several senior officers.

I returned to the United States in mid-July for brief consultations in Washington, stopping off in London for a day of meetings with EBRD officials. The EBRD president, Jacques de Larosiere, who had once been IMF managing director, hosted a lunch for me. The EBRD was consistently supportive during the time I was working on MENABANK. We later sent several members of the team to London to seek from EBRD officials on designing an IT system.

In DC I met with the newly installed undersecretary for economic, business, and agricultural affairs Stuart Eizenstat and with Toni Verstandig. I then joined Sandy for a week at Ghost Ranch in northern New Mexico, where I took a course from Robert Gish called "Writing the Land." With Gish's encouragement I finished a short story about the relationship between a young Foreign Service Officer and his experienced boss as they tried to find a missing mountain climber in Ecuador. I had begun writing the story some fifteen years earlier and, with Bob's help, managed to get it published.

On my way back to Cairo, I stopped in Morocco, where I met with officials from the Ministries of Foreign Affairs and Finance and the Royal Palace (Andre Azoulay) to report on the team's work. I took advantage of that itinerary to fly, at my own expense, to Ouarzazate, where both my younger sisters met me and drove me up to Souk al-Khamis, a village in the back of beyond, where they were both working.

Sandy continued to stay behind in the United States largely to carry out our plans to sell our home in Fairfax, Virginia and trade it for a house in Durango, Colorado. We had chosen Durango as the closest place to Tucson with a first-class ski resort. Once the

Virginia house sold, she had only a few weeks to find a house in Durango to avoid tax consequences. She drove up to Durango and spent a day with a real-estate agent and finally settled on a townhome about three miles northeast of downtown. I made several trips back and forth to the embassy to receive, sign, and send back all the documents required for the sale, the purchase, and the financing. Back in Tucson, Sandy filled a rented U-Haul truck with furniture and made the harrowing five-hundred-mile drive to Durango towing a vehicle.

Not long after Sandy's arrival in Cairo, Princess Diana and her companion Dodi Fayed were killed in an automobile accident in Paris on August 31. Sandy watched hours of coverage on CNN International in our apartment. Adel, our driver, provided us a window into what the average Egyptian believed. Given Dodi Fayed's connection to Egypt, Adel was sure that Diana had been killed by the CIA or MI-6 (British intelligence) to prevent Diana from marrying an Egyptian. I spent many hours with Adel stuck in Cairo traffic and we talked about his life and the frustrations he had experienced. His family had sufficient resources to buy his way out of military service, but they lacked the connections to propel him into Cairo's elite.

Sandy had always been fond of Cairo, and she and I settled into apartment life quickly. We could look down from our balcony at the egrets flying up and down the Nile River and across to the seedy elegance of the homes on the island of Zamalek. Two Egyptian-American couples who had become our best friends during our earlier time in Cairo still lived there. Col. Tod Wilson, who had been my military assistance chief during my last year in Muscat, and his wife Sheila were now in Cairo. My job was challenging but we didn't face the crushing burden of entertaining and being entertained that we had experienced in Riyadh and Muscat.

The office hummed with activity during this period. We were nearly at full strength. I presided over a brief staff meeting each morning to go over our progress and next steps. Despite, or perhaps because of, the diversity in our personalities and nationalities, the team members worked well together. The existing staff was already a cohesive unit when I arrived, but I worked to strengthen the bonds. I hosted a small dinner for team members in my apartment before Sandy arrived. The Cairo version of an office lunch or picnic is the hiring of a felucca for several hours to drift along the Nile, eating, drinking, and chatting. Dick Goodman's visit in the fall provided the stimulus. Sandy, Yuki's wife and daughter, and Yomna and Rania joined us, and we ended the day feeling good about each other and the work we were doing.

When I got the call to return to Cairo, my exercise consisted of running and playing tennis. Running in downtown Cairo made little sense, although I remember at least one American colleague from my days there a decade before who ran wearing a face mask. I discovered the residence exercise center several floors below us and worked out on an exercise bike every day. The center director enjoyed American rock, and it seemed like no session went by where I failed to hear Patty Lovelace singing "Try to Think About Elvis." It remains one of those tunes stuck in my head. I was pedaling away one day when a distinguished older Egyptian man mounted the bike next to me. He looked familiar, and I kept covertly stealing glances at him until it dawned on me. I was biking next to the actor Omar Sharif.

Tod Wilson kindly drove me to the house where we had lived in the southern suburb of Ma'adi many years earlier to play tennis. The embassy had renamed it the Ma'adi House and turned it into a recreation center. The house looked much the same, and the gorgeous flame tree in the back yard was in bloom when I first returned. The embassy had added a modern swimming pool and a large children's playground to the tennis court.

In mid-August, I took advantage of an invitation from the Egyptian-American Chamber of Commerce to explain the rationale for MENABANK and to give our project some added visibility in Egypt. The other team members helped me craft the remarks. I tackled the obvious question of how an initiative that emerged from progress in the Middle East peace process could succeed when the process itself had ground to a halt. I also rejected doubts about whether the region, which already had plenty of banks and investment funds, needed yet another bank. I talked about the region's enormous financing needs and the lack of overall foreign direct investment compared to other regions in the world. After describing the bank as outlined in the Articles of Agreement, I listed a few things that the bank would not be:

> It would not be a "Marshall Plan for the region." It would have a modest capital base.
>
> It would not be another concessional aid program. There would be no concessional window like the World Bank group has.
>
> It was not designed to scoop up Arab funds to finance projects proposed by Israel.
>
> It would not compete against existing regional or global financial institutions.
>
> It would target joint ventures and cross-border projects (I provided some examples).
>
> It would not be a retail bank. No ATMs!
>
> It would not be a major employer. We anticipated employing no more than 200 to 250 people.

On September 18, Sandy returned from the embassy commissary with Adel and found the area around the Egyptian Museum cordoned off. Gunman had attacked tourist buses in the museum parking lot with automatic rifles and grenades, killing nine people (seven were Germans) and wounding many others. It served as a reminder that the Egyptian government had been dealing with sporadic terrorist attacks from a radical Islamic group for several years.

In the fall, we received several important visitors to our World Trade Center office. Stuart Eizenstat came to Cairo to meet Egyptian officials. While his primary purpose was to discuss our economic dialogue with Egypt, known as the Gore-Mubarak Partnership, he did visit our office and he made a pitch for MENABANK in his speech to the Egyptian-American Chamber of Commerce. Both the IMF and the World Bank also had active economic dialogues with Egypt. Stanley Fischer, by now deputy director of the IMF and still a strong supporter of MENABANK, visited our offices. I gave little thought to the IMF official who accompanied Fischer. His name was Mohamed el Erian, and he went on to become one of the world's most influential financial experts. Kemal Derviş, then vice president of the World Bank for the Middle East and North Africa region, also visited. The World Bank had mixed feelings about MENABANK, as some saw MENABANK as an unnecessary new entity in a market already crowded with financial institutions. World Bank president Wolfensohn was supportive, as was Derviş, who supported Wafik and Lorenzo's assignments to the transition team. Derviş later became Turkey's minister of economy and then head of the United Nations Development Program (UNDP).

I still had several contacts in the Egyptian business community from my earlier time in Cairo. Business leaders radiated a new energy and optimism, although growing terrorism loomed on the horizon. Mubarak's sons, Alaa and Gamal, were now active participants in the business community. Gamal's star was more noticeably rising. It was also obvious, however, that the relative prosperity was not spreading to average Egyptians.

In mid-October, Egypt staged a production of Verdi's *Aida* in Luxor in the Valley of the Queens. Sandy and I could not resist such a unique event, and we signed up through the embassy travel office for one of the ten performances starring Placido Domingo and Maria Chiara. Tickets cost us several hundred dollars each, but we considered it a "must-see" event. The Egyptian government saw *Aida* as a boon to its tourist industry, which had been struggling because of terror attacks. Egyptian security forces were positioned everywhere during our visit, and the opera was indeed spectacular, although the sound quality suffered somewhat owing to the outdoor venue.

Workers dismantled the set at the end of October and Luxor returned to normal, but not for long. On November 17, six gunmen opened fire on tourists walking toward the Temple of Hatshepsut in Luxor, killing seventy people overall, including at least sixty tourists, mostly Swiss, German, and Japanese. Egyptian hopes

that the *Aida* production would rejuvenate the tourism industry were dashed. Having rediscovered my interest in writing, this
incident inspired me to write a short story about how an average
Egyptian could find himself one day participating in such a terrible massacre. My character was loosely based on Adel and the
many frustrations I imagined that he experienced. For example,
he often helped carry our purchases from the military commissary up to our apartment. I remember him looking down at the
Western women in bikinis lounging around the residence swimming pool. Perhaps he felt frustration seeing a life around him
that he could never aspire to. I never really convinced myself that
Adel could become a terrorist, which may explain why the story
never gained acceptance for publication.

I recall that I was in Doha, the venue for the fourth and last Middle East Economic Summit, when the attack occurred. Several of
us from the transition team attended (Yuki, Lorenzo, Danny, and
Wim), and Stuart Eizenstat joined us. Key Arab countries, including Egypt and Saudi Arabia, elected not to attend, which explains
why Wafik did not join us. Despite the missing Arab countries, nine
hundred business participants from sixty-five countries reportedly attended, and the Qatari government brought cruise ships
into Doha harbor to handle the overflow from fully booked hotels.

Eizenstat and I attended a breakfast in Doha with representatives of those countries who had signed or initialed the MENABANK
articles of agreement. I participated with him in a press conference following the breakfast. Eizenstat stressed that the Clinton
administration would press Congress hard to fund the bank in
the fiscal year 1999 budget. I talked about the pipeline of projects
we were assembling, with emphasis on private-sector and cross-
border infrastructure. Additionally, I spoke about our interest in a
venture capital fund that would involve us in small- and medium-
size industries without turning us into a retail bank. We also discussed the policy forum for the regional members, along the lines
of the Organization for Cooperation and Development (OECD) in
Paris. The bank would serve as the secretariat for the forum, but it
would be up to the regional members to set the agenda.

The team had by this time assembled a detailed pipeline to demonstrate the types of projects we would finance (regional, private-sector, or privatization of public-sector entities), the size ($10 million to $1 billion), and the target sectors (finance, infrastructure, energy, tourism, telecommunications, and agro-industry). Examples of specific projects included a new deep-sea port providing transshipment services and serving the Sinai, a Dead Sea water treatment and production facility, a private wind farm located between Israel and Jordan, an Egypt to Jordan gas pipeline, a Red Sea water desalination plant located in Egypt, a private tourism promotion facility benefiting both Egypt and Jordan, a fiber optic telecommunications link serving Israel and Jordan, a Middle East credit reporting company located in Egypt, greenhouses in Jordan using Israeli know-how to export fruits and vegetables to Europe, and a toll bridge linking Jordan and the northern West Bank. MENABANK's role in these projects could be that of a long-term lender, an equity investor, or a guarantor against political risk. In most cases, the projects in the pipeline were designed to benefit more than one regional member. Though we hadn't yet done as much work on the Maghreb (North African) countries, we envisioned participating in equity or venture-capital funds in places like Tunisia and Morocco.

Not long after my return from Doha, I took a few days off and Sandy and I flew to Barcelona. After a couple of days there, we rented a car and drove to Bilbao. Sandy was excited to visit the Guggenheim Museum, which had just opened. The building, designed by Frank Gehry, was spectacular, but I didn't find the art displayed inside to be memorable.

A few weeks after our return to Cairo, Sandy and I packed up and headed back to Tucson in December. I agreed to continue as coordinator but to reside in Tucson. I don't remember the exact parameters of the applicable regulation, but I could only work the equivalent of roughly six months and continue to get my pension. After that time, I would be working for free.

Before I departed Cairo, I met with Egyptian foreign minister Amr Moussa. I am sure I told him how hard we were working to get the bank ready to open, and I am sure that he told me something along the lines of how Egypt would be pleased to see the bank open once Israel came to its senses.

We agreed to bring the team to DC in December and then again in mid-March to make the best case we could for congressional funding. We created a professional briefing using overhead slides (PowerPoint was still in its infancy). In addition to making the overall case for a development bank in the region, we included specifics for fifteen different proposed projects that would benefit Israel and its Arab neighbors. I recall briefing both the Washington Institute for Near East Policy in DC and the Council of Foreign Relations in New York. Frank Wisner, with whom I worked closely when I was director of Egyptian affairs, was among the attendees in New York. We attempted to visit all the key House and Senate committees. I remember well Danielle Pletka, then a staff member for the Senate Foreign Relations Committee, chaired by Jesse Helms, telling us in so many words that we would not get funding. At least Pletka found time to meet with us. Robin Cleveland, the staff director for the key subcommittee of the Senate Appropriations Committee, was not available. I wrote her a note, recalling that we had met in May of the previous year. We did better on the House side. Lee Hamilton, chairman of the House Foreign Affairs Committee, had long been a strong supporter. Sonny Callahan, the chair of the key House Appropriations Subcommittee on Foreign Operations, was skeptical. He asked us "what was in it (MENABANK) for my people in Mobile, Alabama."

The State Department asked me to return to DC on April 30 to join Stu Eizenstat for a meeting with Callahan and ranking Democratic member David Obey. Callahan eventually agreed to support MENABANK funding within an overall cap to regional funding. During that brief trip, I also met with Martin Indyk and Dennis Ross in Indyk's office.

In addition to the poisonous relations between Egypt and Israel that led Egypt to boycott the Doha meeting, we were facing a Congress intent on reducing overall economic assistance. Prime Minister Netanyahu had already agreed to a reduction in economic aid over a ten-year period (in return for additional military assistance, which meant that Egypt, like it or not, would also be facing significant reductions in economic assistance). Several in Congress argued that our capital contribution to MENABANK was essentially aid to the regional countries and should therefore come out of planned economic assistance to those countries. The Netanyahu government in Israel was not prepared to acquiesce to this logic or arithmetic, and Egypt remained unwilling to agree unless Israel did as well.

I taught for the American Graduate School of International Management (better known as Thunderbird) during the spring semester of 1998 while continuing to work remotely for MENA-BANK. I willingly made the weekly four-hour-plus round-trip commute to the Glendale, Arizona campus because my son, Greg, was now enrolled as a student. I planned to return to Cairo after the semester ended in mid-May. The Canadian Ministry of Foreign Affairs invited me, along with Norman Riddell, to Ottawa for a May 23 meeting and lunch. The Canadians expressed strong support for MENABANK but were concerned that, absent U.S. funding, the project would fail.

I flew from Ottawa back to Cairo and spent a couple of weeks briefing the Egyptian government about what I knew about MENA-BANK's prospects in the U.S. Congress. I also wanted to confirm continuing support with the governments of other transition team members. In July 1997 and January 1998, I sent a status reports to "Prospective Members and Interested Parties" (governments that had signed or initialed the agreement and those that we hoped would eventually join). The January status report enclosed several draft documents covering policies and procedures and asked for comments. We received detailed comments from a few countries, but there was deafening silence from many others, including Russia and Turkey.

Dan Kurtzer, who I first met in Cairo and who was my deputy during my last year in the Office of Egyptian Affairs, had now replaced Ned Walker as U.S. ambassador to Egypt. We met in his office atop the embassy tower. I wanted to thank him for the excellent support his administrative people had provided to the transition team. He assured me of his continuing strong support for the team's work but shared my pessimism about the project's future. On the shelves around us were hats collected from naval ships that had made port calls in Egypt, as well as from other U.S. military units. He complained that the building's architects had designed a skylight in the ambassador's office but had made no provision for cleaning the glass on the outside. The Cairo dust and grime had over time almost completely obscured the once-ample light. I thought about how U.S. and Middle East politics had just about snuffed out the light in our transition team office.

An incident over the summer in the Cairo office captured the spirit of what MENABANK, along with other elements of the multilateral track of the Peace Process, was truly designed to accomplish. Danny Yariv was scheduled to return to Israel and his regular position in the Bank of Israel. Danny was very personable and got along well with all of us. I recall conversations between Danny and Wafik and Iyad comparing words in Hebrew and Arabic. The two are Semitic languages and many words are nearly identical in both. For example, "peace" is *salaam* in Arabic and *shalom* in Hebrew. "Market" is *souk* in Arabic and *shuk* in Hebrew. The team held a farewell event for Danny. I was in Tucson at the time, so I am relying on the account provided by Diane Rudo, our talented consultant who had previously worked at the Export-Import Bank. Iyad got up and explained that, before joining the transition team, he had never met an Israeli and had had no interest in meeting one. He came to the team with considerable anxiety about the prospect of working with an Israeli. Now that he had spent time working with Danny, he realized that it was not only possible to work with an Israeli but also to be friends with one.

By the time I returned to Cairo in August, it was clear that our full-court press on Congress had failed and that the body would not fund MENABANK. We would run out of funding for the transition team at the end of the fiscal year on September 30. I anticipated that my time in Cairo in August would center around decisions about how to wind down the transition team. I met with Soliman

Awad at the Ministry of Foreign Affairs. I told him that, while I didn't yet have any instructions about the future of the transition team, I expected we would be asked to put the project "on blocks." We wanted the work we were completing on policies and procedures to be retained in the files of the Egyptian government so that the project could be restarted without "reinventing the wheel."

I perhaps used too many automobile metaphors and, in my funk about seeing the project founder, I didn't give enough thought to the care and maintenance of my relationship with Awad, which could have led to an abrupt end to Egyptian government logistical support for the team. Yuki let me know that Awad was unhappy that I had skipped town without meeting with him for a second time. I had to do some damage control from Tucson. In retrospect, I had committed a worse offense than Wim, who had reportedly left a meeting without shaking hands. I wrote a very contrite letter to Awad, explaining that we were not "making funeral arrangements" and expanded on the concept of putting the project "on blocks." I requested continued Egyptian government support until there could be a meeting of shareholders and interested parties to determine the future of the team. In the end, our governments concluded that a formal meeting would call unwanted attention to the failure of the MENABANK initiative, and the project died quietly. Knowing that Awad wanted to find a way to keep the team alive, but lacking any guidance from Washington, I floated some personal ideas about maintaining a sort of symbolic or virtual presence in Cairo. I made it clear that the team members were servants of the governments they represented and that it was not appropriate for us to propose our own perpetuation.

Over the next several months the team completed the work we had set out for ourselves, including draft financial and operational policies, a draft organization structure, a draft headquarters agreement, and bylaws and other legal documents. We had also worked further on the extensive menu of proposed projects, which we called our project pipeline. Earlier in the year, we had sent out drafts of many of these documents to the shareholders. The comments that came in from several governments, including the Italian and Egyptian ones, had to be incorporated in the final documents.

We closed the office on December 17, 1998. I submitted my resignation in a letter to Al Larson on December 18. Subsequently, I received a very thoughtful letter from Stu Eizenstat. His office had neglected to put a date on it and I don't recall when it arrived. The letter described the bank as "an idea ahead of its time" and proposed ceasing "active efforts to launch the MENABANK until the environment is more propitious." I imagine that someone in the Office of Development Finance drafted it, but Eizenstat added a handwritten note, which I much appreciated. It read: "You have been great. I wish this project would have gotten off the ground given your team's great work."

All of us on the transition team were proud of the work that we accomplished in the face of very stiff political headwinds. It is hard to believe that success was ever possible given the breakdown in the Oslo process triggered by Rabin's assassination. The Clinton administration, led by Dennis Ross and his team, continued the quixotic attempt to negotiate the implementation of the Oslo Accords with an Israeli leader who was ideologically opposed to withdrawal from the West Bank. Netanyahu's government fell in early 1999, and the Labor Party candidate Ehud Barak was elected prime minister. Clinton administration officials were optimistic that they could work with Barak and get the Oslo process back on the rails.

Shortly after Barak's election, I got a call from an official in NEA asking for thoughts on how to restore the MENABANK initiative. I took a day to reflect. I began my response by recapping the reasons why it had failed. First, there was lackluster support from within the MENA region. Had Shimon Peres become Israeli prime minister instead of Benjamin Netanyahu, the result would likely have been different. Peres embraced regional economic integration, something Netanyahu never bought into. Because of the actions of the Netanyahu government (opening the tunnel, housing construction on Har Homa, foot-dragging on Oslo implementation), the Mubarak government opted to freeze normalization with Israel. In Egyptian eyes, MENABANK was no doubt a component of normalization. The Jordanians saw the bank as a new funding source, but their enthusiasm was less than it might have been because of the decision to choose Cairo instead of Amman for the headquarters. The Palestinians were unenthusiastic because MENABANK would not have a concessional window (no loans available at less than market rates). The Maghrebis (Morocco, Algeria, and Tunisia) were indifferent.

The congressional demand that the modest amount of money requested by the administration for paid-in capital ($52.5 million per year for five years) come out of existing economic assistance to Egypt and Israel was not welcomed in either Cairo or Jerusalem. I understand that Egypt was prepared to acquiesce reluctantly to this approach so long as Israel would do the same. The Israeli government rejected the idea. Although Eizenstat provided MENABANK with enthusiastic support, overall administration support proved lackluster. Clinton's team prioritized aid to the Jordanians and the Palestinians. The Treasury Department was supportive, but they struggled with congressional reductions in support for existing multilateral development banks. With the death of Dick Goodman, Treasury no longer participated on the team and was less engaged.

The absence of key Europeans (the UK, France, Germany, and the Nordic countries) proved a major liability. Because the European Union had strongly supported the bank initiative in the REDWG, the opposition of key Europeans came as an unpleasant surprise. There was a sense in many European countries that the European Investment Bank, along with existing international financial institutions, could satisfy future financing needs. We operated on the assumption that the European holdouts would join later once U.S. funding was assured. Those countries that did provide enthusiastic support (Canada, Japan, the Netherlands, and Italy) received little thanks for it from either the United States or the regional governments.

In the years since the transition team closed its doors, the EBRD has expanded into many of those countries that MENABANK was designed to cover. The EBRD website boasts that it has invested 7.8 billion euros in 179 projects in the Middle East and North Africa (which it calls the southern and eastern Mediterranean region, or

SEMED).[5] I suspect that it has invested in several projects in our proposed pipeline. This provides some validation to those who argued that another financial institution serving the Middle East was not needed.

Our implicit strategy in the transition team was to create enough facts on the ground to build momentum for congressional approval. We gave it our best shot, but it wasn't good enough. I advised against trying that approach in the future. Success in the future, I suggested, would require the following sequence of actions:

Developing full support in the administration (including State, Treasury, and the NSC).

Seeking funding as part of the MDB budget rather than the ESF budget. (While capital contributions were part of the MDB budget, funding for the transition team came from ESF funds.)

Gaining enthusiastic Egyptian and Israeli support (easier if we weren't asking them to fund our capital contribution out of the economic assistance we were providing).

Getting full support of all the EU countries.

Only with all the above, go to Congress.

Only when assured of congressional support, set about reconstituting the transition team. Quality experts will not step forward if the success of the initiative is in serious doubt.

I heard nothing further from NEA or anyone else in the government. I suspect that they were devoting all their energy to working with Barak on his ambitious agenda: a) a negotiated Israeli withdrawal from Lebanon; b) a peace treaty with Syria; and c) a resolution of all the final status issues with the Palestinian Authority. Though Israel did withdraw from Lebanon (unilaterally), negotiations with the Syrians and the Palestinians broke down, and years of violence followed. The 2000 Camp David negotiations were essentially a "hail Mary" pass orchestrated by two lame-duck leaders (Clinton and Barak). Arafat had to be frog-marched to Camp David and he was unprepared to make significant concessions. While much energy has been devoted to the peace process in the years since, there have been no negotiations with a realistic chance of success. MENABANK, I assume, remains "on blocks" somewhere in the Egyptian Ministry of Foreign Affairs.

Following our all-court press on the key congressional committees in March 1998, it was difficult to remain upbeat. My instructions were to keep the team working in the hope that there would be a breakthrough. The Japanese, Italian, Dutch, and Canadian governments were committed to soldiering on. I was able to persuade the Israelis to replace Danny and they selected Mordechai (Morty) Spiegel, another Bank of Israel official. The Jordanian government agreed to extend Iyad's contract. During my return to Cairo for several days at the beginning and the end of the summer, I found morale in the Cairo office still surprisingly good given hope of success had faded away.

The State Department I found when I took the MENABANK assignment differed significantly from the one I left a decade earlier to go to Saudi Arabia. MENABANK was a child of the Middle East peace process. The Clinton administration followed the lead of the George H. W. Bush administration, deciding that the peace process was so intertwined with domestic politics that professional diplomats could not be trusted to handle it. Dennis Ross had worked for Jim Baker and stayed on in the Clinton administration, and was named special Middle East coordinator. Ross had co-founded with Martin Indyk the Washington Institute for Near East Policy, which enjoyed the support of the American Israel Public Affairs Committee (AIPAC). Born in London, Indyk grew up in Australia and immigrated to the United States. He started out working for AIPAC. Indyk served at the NSC for the Clinton administration, was named U.S. ambassador to Israel in 1995, and returned to Washington to be assistant secretary of Near East affairs. Dan Kurtzer joined Ross's negotiating team, along with Aaron Miller. Miller was a long-time civil service employee of the Department of State. Kurtzer, the only FSO on the peace team, left in 1994 because, according to Miller, he "felt shut out by" Ross.[6]

The bottom line for MENABANK was that Middle East peace

negotiations were not being handled by professionals. Ross and Indyk were talented but they were also predisposed by their backgrounds to ensuring that U.S. positions were closely coordinated with the Israeli government. The assassination of Yitzhak Rabin led to the election of Benjamin Netanyahu as Israeli prime minister. Netanyahu had made it clear in his speeches and writing over the years that he wanted no part of making territorial concessions to the Palestinians. The Clinton administration, led by Ross, did manage, after bruising negotiations, to persuade the Israelis to withdraw from 80 percent of Hebron in early 1997. Ross and his team labored on, devoting all their energy to the hopeless cause of trying to convert Netanyahu to support a two-state solution. The multilateral track that emerged from the 1991 Madrid meeting was neglected and allowed to wither and fade away. The last multilateral meeting took place in late 1995. The Doha Economic Summit in November 1997 was the last of four economic summits. The decision to put MENABANK "on blocks" was the last gasp of the multilateral track. The great benefits of the multilateral track were that a) it allowed outsiders like the Europeans, Japanese, and Canadians who were eager to be involved to play a role and b) it brought non-political Arabs and Israelis together in situations that allowed them to get past the stereotypes and realize how much they had in common.

I dutifully plowed through the twenty-six chapters and more than eight hundred pages of Dennis's tome, *The Missing Peace*, when it came out in 2005. I was back to teaching a course for the University of Arizona called the Arab-Israeli Conflict, and the book was required reading for me, if not for my students. I could find no reference at all to MENABANK or a Middle East development bank and almost no mention of the multilaterals. Dennis did join a meeting I had in Indyk's office in the spring of 1998 about MENABANK but provided little comfort about the initiative's future.

Two years ago, in Tucson, I walked over to the nearby synagogue (the same one where I attended a memorial ceremony for Rabin) to listen to Dennis Ross give a book talk for *Doomed to Succeed: The U.S.-Israel Relationship from Truman to Obama*. Ross is a skilled writer and a good speaker. I can't argue with his thesis that the relationship is "doomed to succeed." I have always believed that the United States has a moral obligation to protect Israel, but I would extend that obligation to include protecting Israel from itself. By enabling Israel's colonization of the West Bank (which is what the settlements issue represents), we may have doomed Israel to live permanently as an island in a sea of Middle Eastern hostility.

While the failure of the MENABANK initiative was disappointing, I nevertheless found the time I spent on the project in Cairo, in Washington, and in Tucson to be a very positive experience. I enjoyed the chance to return to the familiar ambience of Cairo and to reconnect with many old friends. As a bonus, I made many new friends. I have nothing but respect for the ability and spirit of the professionals who worked with me in the trenches and didn't become discouraged by the long odds we faced. While it was the nature of my career to work closely with professionals from other countries, this was my first experience working as part of an international team. I drew heavily on this experience when I faced my next professional challenge in Baghdad in 2003.

7

BAGHDAD

Wait, What? We're Invading Iraq?

I was at our gym in Tucson when the first plane hit the World Trade Center in New York. Sandy and I had just finished spinning class and we stood mesmerized by the TV as the second plane hit and as both towers crumbled and fell. I knew immediately that this was the work of Osama bin Laden and that the world had changed.

The day before, September 10, 2001, I was teaching a freshman class on globalization and global government at the University of Arizona, and I had spent fifteen minutes discussing bin Laden. He had spoken at a wedding in Afghanistan, and for the first time in my memory he had invoked the Palestinian cause. His principal grievance had previously been the presence of U.S. troops in Saudi Arabia. I speculated that he must be planning something ambitious because he was evidently trying to expand his support.

As one of Tucson's few resident experts on U.S. Middle East policy, I spent most of September 11 doing interviews with local TV stations. It was the first and only time that I appeared on all four major networks on the same day. Bob Johnston, my colleague from Riyadh days who also retired in Tucson, logged quite a bit of air time as well. When I arrived at my class the following morning, students looked at me with a mixture of awe and suspicion. Had I known this attack was coming?

Over the subsequent months, I watched the invasion of Afghanistan and other unfolding events from Tucson, focused on teaching and giving occasional talks on Middle East issues. Like most

Americans, I was pleased with the administration's initial reaction to September 11. President George W. Bush stressed that we were not at war against Muslims or Arabs. He did not, at least initially, fall into the trap that Osama bin Laden tried to set for us and turn what we dubbed the "War on Terror" into a clash of civilizations. But fear led to what some have called a national nervous breakdown. I was appalled to hear President Bush describe Iraq, Iran, and North Korea as part of an "axis of evil" that threatened world peace. There was a time when White House speechwriters would have run a line like that by the State Department, which would have pointed out its absurdity. The White House was dominated by Vice President Cheney and Secretary of Defense Donald Rumsfeld. Secretary of State Colin Powell was overruled and chose to be a good soldier and support his leadership despite personal reservations. Cheney and Powell turned their attention to Iraq even as al-Qaeda continued to be a threat (Osama bin Laden slipped out of Afghanistan) and violence raged in Israel and the Palestinian territories throughout 2002.

Early in 2003, as war with Iraq now seemed inevitable, the Tucson Committee on Foreign Relations (TCFR) asked me to speak about Iraq. On March 6, I gave a luncheon talk to the TCFR. Gabby Giffords, then an Arizona state senator, sat with me at the head table. The structure of my talk was a list of questions to which the American people deserved better answers before the president led us to war with Iraq. Even though I assumed, like most others, that Iraq had an ongoing nuclear weapons program, I argued that al-Qaeda and North Korea were bigger threats. I was unpersuaded that Iraq had any links with al-Qaeda. I worried about American and Iraqi casualties, about the costs of invasion and our ability to handle the aftermath. I reminded the audience that we had decided not to march to Baghdad in 1991 because we did not want to deliver the mail, pick up the garbage, and organize elections. Now, in 2003, we were making decisions that would lead to that very result.

Nine days later, Jim Larocco, principal deputy assistant secretary in the State Department's Bureau of Near East Affairs (NEA), called to ask me to be a part of the U.S. occupation of Iraq. He talked vaguely about my running one of Iraq's economic ministries (the media term for such a position was "shadow minister") for a couple of months until a U.S. embassy could be established in Baghdad. I knew that the invasion of Iraq would be a train wreck, and my instincts were to turn down the offer. Sandy and my son, Greg (by phone), worked me over, arguing that the war was inevitable and that capable people would be needed to put Iraq back together. I relented and called Larocco back to tell him I would accept the job. The next day, my fax machine started whirring with financial disclosure and security clearance forms.

Sandy and I were at a Tucson restaurant the evening of Wednesday, March 19, and we watched television coverage of the war's opening salvos in all its shock and awe. The next morning, I flew to Washington. I reported to the office of NEA executive director Kathleen Austin-Ferguson on Friday morning. I quickly learned that being recruited by the State Department to go to Baghdad was not a guarantee that I would actually go to Baghdad. I spent the next two weeks as one of eight State-recruited pawns in a protracted struggle between State and Defense over who would control Iraq reconstruction. Early on, I communicated with Robin Raphel, once married to my friend Arnie Raphel, and a friend since my early days in the Foreign Service. Robin, former ambassador to Tunisia and former assistant secretary for South Asian affairs, was one of the eight in the second wave of civilians the government sent to Iraq. The first wave had departed the day after Larocco called.

State had created a Future of Iraq project that produced detailed studies of the various issues that might arise in the reconstruction process. The Pentagon ignored the State studies and created an organization called the Office of Reconstruction and Humanitarian Affairs (ORHA). Rumsfeld chose Jay Garner, a retired three-star general who had distinguished himself by running effectively the Kurdish refugee program in 1991, to lead ORHA. Garner was not an ideologue and he was eager to recruit people with Middle East expertise, whether they be from State, the Pentagon, or elsewhere. He had no problem with the eight people that State had proposed. Rumsfeld and senior Pentagon officials felt otherwise and put our second wave on hold.

At Kathleen's request, I took the necessary steps to be rehired by State in case the hold was lifted. I needed a new State Department pass, a new diplomatic passport, and a Kuwait visa (because I would enter Iraq through Kuwait). The Main State building had become a fortress, surrounded by semi-permanent Jersey barriers and patrolling guards with German shepherds. Until I received my building pass, I underwent a full-body frisk each time I reentered Main State. I was sworn in as a new employee, given a medical exam and vaccinations against anthrax and other maladies, gave up a DNA sample (so my body could be identified), and received a security briefing and bio-chem training. State security personnel noted I would be working for a Pentagon organization (ORHA) and demanded that I get the week-long bio-chem training from the military. Kathleen worked the phones and turned that around. In my spare time, I sought out contacts with officials involved in the substance of Iraq reconstruction. I ran into several friends I knew from my earlier years with State. They were unhappy but resigned to the reality that the Pentagon would run the reconstruction.

When it became clear that the Defense hold would not be lifted soon, I volunteered to run the graveyard shift of the State Department's Iraq Task Force to give some of the regular NEA officers a break. The last State Department task force I had worked on was eighteen years before when the Egyptair plane was hijacked to Malta. In those days, a task force was the center of action in any crisis. By 2003 task forces had become auxiliary staff for the State Department Operations Center (Op Center) down the hall. We were tasked with writing a situation report due to the Op Center by 4:00 a.m. and with composing talking points for an NEA deputy assistant secretary to use briefing congressional leaders the following morning. Each night a competent deputy drafted both documents. National Security Adviser Condoleezza Rice ordered us one night to obtain the fax numbers for the foreign ministers and national security advisers of all current and potential coalition partners. The process of getting those fax numbers signaled to our ambassadors that the White House was planning to bypass them and communicate directly with foreign governments. Tom Miller, our ambassador in Athens, conveyed to me his strong objection to this initiative. I was sympathetic but not in a position to take on Rice about it.

Working on the task force gave me a chance to follow the war's progress. U.S. troops were moving quickly toward Baghdad and there wasn't much for a State task force to do. In addition to CNN, we now could watch Fox, MSNBC, and the BBC on the wall, read incoming telegrams on a computer screen, and surf the Internet. I read about the ongoing dispute between Powell and Rumsfeld. The media quoted Rumsfeld as describing the eight of us still on hold as "too low-profile and too bureaucratic for the job." I filed that away to use as motivation in case I made it to Baghdad.

I spent weekends with our good friends from Riyadh days, Hank and Sonja. I had arranged to fly back to Tucson on Sunday morning, April 6, to wait out the State-Defense impasse. Saturday evening, Ruth Whiteside, deputy director general, called to report that State and Defense had reached a compromise.[1] State gave up four slots, including mine. Ruth offered me a job as deputy to Tim Carney, who would be senior ministerial liaison to the Ministry of Industry. I didn't know Tim Carney, and I was angry and humiliated. I said I would think about it. Robin urged me to go anyway, arguing that I was needed to be part of a critical mass of Foreign Service professionals who could add balance to the Pentagon-centric reconstruction effort. Back in Tucson, after some more soul-searching with Sandy, I decided to accept the deputy position. I did not relish having to explain to all my friends in Tucson why I had not gone to Iraq. I phoned Whiteside and Larocco with my decision. The next day, Ruth called me back to tell me that the retired ambassador designated to be senior ministerial liaison to the Foreign Ministry failed to pass a medical clearance, and that I had been moved into that slot. Ruth said it was my reward for hanging in there. I was elated and did a little jig around the house.

The fax machine soon spat out DOD orders, and TV coverage featured our soldiers pulling down a statue of Saddam in Baghdad. I called my son, Greg, in California and he put my four-year-old granddaughter Samanta (Sami) on the phone. Her father had informed her that I was going to a place that could be dangerous. She had some stern advice for me: "Just don't talk to strangers!"[2]

In Kuwait, I met up with the many military and civilian colleagues who were preparing to deploy to Iraq as soon as the military declared the environment in Baghdad "permissive." We were all staying at the Kuwait Hilton, a large complex of rows and rows of small villas. A central dining area offered a bountiful supply of shrimp and smoked salmon, along with many other menu choices. I shared a room with Ted Morse, a retired Agency for International Development officer. Several other Foreign Service colleagues were either staying in the same villa or nearby. Barbara Bodine would run Baghdad Central, one of the three regions the military had divided Iraq into for administrative purposes. I knew Barbara from my days as director of Egyptian affairs. Then deputy director of the Israel office, she had served previously in Iraq. She went on to be DCM in Kuwait and U.S. ambassador to Yemen. Robin Raphel was assigned to the Ministry of Trade. John Limbert, detailed from his post as U.S. ambassador to Mauritania, was working with the Ministry of Culture. I also met Tim Carney for the first time. He had been U.S. ambassador to both Sudan and Haiti.

All of us, except for Barbara, would be working for Mike Mobbs. Mobbs was chief of the civil administration pillar and oversaw the nontechnical ministries, including foreign affairs, trade, industry, and culture. He was a Pentagon official who had worked closely with Defense undersecretary Doug Feith and was best-known for crafting the legal justification that allowed us to house "enemy combatants" in Guantanamo. Mobbs had no Middle East experience.

I found myself in two daily meetings. One, chaired by Barbara, was nominally a meeting of personnel who would administer the Baghdad Central region. I soon realized that it was also a meeting of State-recruited personnel. We were a State Department cell working inside ORHA attempting to put ORHA on what we considered the right path.

Mike Mobbs chaired the other meeting for those of us working in the civil administration pillar. The other two pillars were humanitarian affairs and reconstruction affairs. I learned how ORHA related to the U.S. military forces now occupying Baghdad, the Coalition Forces Land Component Command (CFLCC). Soon after I arrived in Kuwait, the news of widespread looting in Baghdad and the rest of Iraq had just broken. Getting information from CFLCC was not easy, but eventually we learned that virtually every ministry in Baghdad, including the Foreign Ministry but not including the Ministry of Oil, had been looted. The immediate concern, particularly to John Limbert, was the looting of priceless antiquities from the National Museum in Baghdad.

In between meetings, I assembled a kit of things every civilian should have in a war zone. I got an ORHA badge, a Second Chance vest (stops shrapnel but not bullets), a Kevlar helmet (I had to ask a soldier how to configure it), and an anthrax booster. ORHA issued me a laptop and a satellite phone the next day.

I did not know I would be assigned to the Foreign Ministry (MFA) when I was in DC, so I had no specific guidance. From my time on the task force I knew that State, with limited success, was pressing other governments to close Iraqi embassies in their capitals. I had come across a four-page memo likely prepared by a State Department junior officer that contained some basic information about the ministry. The Kuwait Hilton had both a good Internet connection and good phone service. I could call anywhere in the world and ORHA would pay the bill. I started reaching out to as many people as I could for advice. Tom Warrick, who ran the State Department's Future of Iraq program, gave me some leads. I contacted the Iraqi MFA team located in Crystal City near the Pentagon. This was a group of Iraqi-Americans the Pentagon had assembled and called the Iraq Reconstruction and Development Council (IRDC). I persuaded Gary Sick, a Columbia University professor who ran the Gulf 2000 project, to send notice to Gulf 2000 members that I was anxious to contact people who knew something about the Iraqi MFA. That yielded responses from several, including Dick Murphy, who I worked for when he was NEA assistant secretary. None of what I learned was particularly useful when I arrived in Baghdad, but it kept me busy and helped me think through an action plan.

The visit of Jim Kolbe (R-AZ), a few days after I arrived, gave me an opportunity to get to know the ORHA leadership. Jay Garner and his deputy Jerry Bates (also a retired U.S. Army general) were known in ORHA as the "Space Cowboys," the title of a popular 2000 movie starring Clint Eastwood about aging astronauts who came out of retirement to return to space. I squeezed into a breakfast that Jay hosted for Kolbe because I was a constituent. Jim had contacted me when I was still in Tucson asking if I would be his eyes and ears on the progress of Iraq reconstruction. Jim grumbled to me privately that he had been prevented from entering Iraq by Rumsfeld because he (Kolbe) had been critical of our Iraq policy.

A Pentagon official named Larry DiRita arrived a day or two after I did. DiRita was a close aide to Rumsfeld and he had clearly been sent to monitor ORHA and report back directly to his boss. I got together with my growing MFA team. Drew Erdmann, a very capable civil service member of the State Department's Policy Planning staff, had been in Kuwait when I arrived. Allen Kepchar, a retired Foreign Service consular specialist, had also joined the team, as did Radu Onofrei, a Romanian ambassador, making it a coalition rather than purely American team. Allen, who had strong Arabic skills and long experience in the Arab world, had been charged with working with the Ministry of Interior team on the issue of passports and border crossings. Drew put together a brief PowerPoint that I used to brief DiRita on what we thought we would be doing with the Foreign Ministry. Drew, Allen, and I also put together a memo outlining questions we needed answers to from Jay or CFLCC to do our job. The other shadow ministers would also need answers to those questions. The questions included a) the physical state of the ministry; b) who would run the Iraqi government; c) what the role of the coalition would be; d) how we vet (screen) Iraqi officials; e) where we find interpreters; and f) how we control Iraq's borders. I ran the memo by Robin, who was becoming the driving force among the ministerial advisers, and addressed it to Jay Garner by way of Mike Mobbs. We never received any real answers. These were all questions that should have been thought through much earlier, and we ended up getting answers only through trial and error once we got to Baghdad.

On April 24, eleven days after I arrived in Kuwait, I rode with most of the other shadow ministers on a c-130 to Baghdad piloted by the Tennessee National Guard. A few others, including Drew and John Limbert, had driven up two days earlier in a military convoy. Our trip to Baghdad was a harsh lesson in where ORHA fit in the military's priorities and how dependent we were on the military for logistics. We waited for several hours at the military air base in Kuwait when a general commandeered the plane that had been arranged to take us to Baghdad. He needed it for what he deemed a more important mission. After finally arriving at the recently renamed Baghdad International Airport (it had been Saddam International Airport), we again had to wait a couple of hours for transportation. Our original military greeting party had given up and departed.

We arrived at one of Saddam's palaces (which we were instructed to call a compound) on the Tigris River. Four carved heads of a helmeted Saddam adorned the roof. Opulent but filthy, the palace would be my home for the next seven-plus weeks. Tim Carney, John Limbert, and I shared a room on the second floor. Tim and I had to roam the palace looking for sheets, blankets, water, and MREs. Our room had a broken window, but Drew found some screening somewhere in the palace and helped us install it. During the first couple of days, we had no water or electricity in our part of the palace. Port-a-johns were out the back door of the main atrium, a healthy hike from our room. I spent much of my first evening learning how to operate the satellite phone and how to prepare and consume an MRE.

I concluded quickly that the only practical use for the satellite phone (Thuraya) was to call Sandy in Tucson.[3] As the days passed, however, I learned that I could make a few soldiers very happy by lending them the phone to call home in the United States. Calling another Thuraya in Baghdad was almost useless because the recipient would need to know the call was coming and have his or her phone pointed at a satellite.

Life slowly improved. Kellogg Brown & Root (KBR), employed by the Pentagon to handle ORHA support issues, had coffee ready our second morning in the palace, and coffee and croissants by the following morning. Soon milk and cereal became available and hot dogs and hamburgers began appearing for lunch. KBR converted a big conference room into a dining area. I did my first batch of laundry in a bucket out by the latrines, but laundry service eventually became available. Staffers sent laundry to Kuwait, and it returned in five days. I sent five items and was thankful that four came back.

Tim Carney was my roommate for the entire time I spent in Baghdad. He, like me, is a graduate of the Massachusetts Institute of Technology (MIT) and a retired U.S. ambassador. MIT is not known as a training ground for diplomats, so it seemed improbable that the two of us ended up rooming together in a palace in Baghdad. Tim, as befits a hunter of elephants in Africa, is smart, personable, and fearless. John Limbert, one of the U.S. diplomats held hostage in Tehran, speaks Farsi (Persian) and Arabic and was comfortable wandering around Baghdad and building relationships with key Iraqis. John let me read a draft op-ed he was preparing to submit to the *Washington Post*. He described his living conditions as a hostage in Tehran as better than our living conditions in the palace in Iraq.

My mission was to get the Foreign Ministry back up and running. My shadow minister colleagues and I met with the 352nd Civil Affairs Command the evening of April 26. The 352nd was assigned to facilitate our movement around Baghdad and to provide, within reason, the support we needed. They explained to me that the officer assigned to our Foreign Ministry team would not be available for another week. I pitched a profanity-laden fit. After the meeting, Lt. Col. Alex Sonski approached me and offered to take our team to the MFA. Alex, joined by Tony Ward, also from the 352nd, drove Drew and me the next day to the Foreign Ministry, which was close to the al-Rashid Hotel and the Conference Center. I was grateful that Alex and Tony knew the way. The day before, George Molineux, ORHA's representative to the Central Bank, left a meeting of ministerial advisers with his military escort to head to the Central Bank. He soon returned to ask if anyone had a map because his escort didn't know where the Central Bank was. Tim, who seemed prepared for anything, owned a map, which he shared with them.

When we arrived at the Foreign Ministry, we found it guarded by the Free Iraqi Forces, associated with Iraqi exile and Pentagon favorite Ahmed Chalabi. As we were looking around the obviously looted and burned compound, a young Iraqi named Hamid Radhi walked up and introduced himself. Hamid was in the MFA's protocol section. He readily agreed to round up as many of his fellow employees as possible and meet us back at the ministry in forty-eight hours. I had second thoughts about the security implications of this plan, but Hamid was gone before I could revise my instructions.

Two days later, Drew and I returned with Muyhi al-Khateeb (one of the Crystal City Iraqis who had just arrived) an hour in advance of the appointed time. About 150 employees were milling around the compound. With Muyhi's help, we picked out a group of about two dozen senior Iraqis and walked them over to the Conference Center, where we could find a comfortable meeting room. The main result of this meeting was to schedule a second meeting the next day (April 30) in the Conference Center. The next morning began with chaos. Robin Raphel had prevailed on me to agree to the reassignment of Drew to the Ministry of Higher Education, and Drew had gone off to his new ministry. Drew had arranged our transportation, but the ORHA motor pool professed not to know anything about it. We spotted Jay Garner on his way to the Conference Center and convinced him to take us. By this time, Allen and Radu had arrived in Baghdad and, somehow, we managed to stuff all five of us into Jay's car and his security follow car just as the two vehicles were starting to roll.

Arriving at the Conference Center, we found forty Iraqis waiting at the gate. We waited with them until military police (MPs) arrived to let them in. The chaos continued in the meeting with the Iraqis. There were competing groups professing to represent the MFA: current MFA employees, previous MFA employees who had fallen out of favor, and an individual who claimed to be the head of an employee's association. I made some brief introductory remarks in English. Radu translated when needed. I explained that my authority to reorganize the MFA came from CFLCC Commander David McKiernan through Jay Garner. I stressed that I saw the task as a short-term one but that I wanted the ministry to be representative of the Iraqi people (including all ethnic and religious groups and men and women). I wanted the process to be transparent. I explained that I was not there to redesign Iraqi foreign policy. That would be up to a transitional Iraqi government when it was formed.

Ambassador Ghassan Mushin Hussein emerged as the spokesman for the Iraqi leadership. He was a veteran diplomat, educated in part at St. John's University in New York, and he spoke English fluently. He wanted the dissident Iraqis expelled. When I refused, tensions rose, so I decided to call a short recess. I asked that only currently serving MFA employees who held the title of ambassador stay in the room, along with the ministry's auditing and financial staff. I offered to meet with the others separately. When the smaller meeting resumed, I pressed ahead with my agenda, which included security for the ministry, obtaining a list of personnel who would be eligible for emergency payments of $20 each, and restoring communications with overseas posts. We were able to create several committees, including a steering committee to oversee the entire effort. We agreed to meet again at the ministry on May 4, after the Iraqi weekend. I felt pretty good about our progress as we made the long walk back to the palace in the hot sun.

Mike Mobbs was gone the next day (May 1), ostensibly because his wife had a medical emergency. Garner announced an ORHA reorganization that put Robin in charge of all the shadow ministers. We also learned that day that L. Paul ("Jerry") Bremer would be arriving in a matter of days to oversee Garner and ORHA. Betting was that Garner wouldn't stay long after Bremer's arrival. I was pleased with the news for several reasons. I knew Robin well and believed she would be much more effective than Mobbs had been. Though I liked Jay Garner and thought his instincts were good, ORHA management did not appear to be up to the very difficult mission it had been given. Bremer had a reputation as a strong manager and I was hopeful that he would do better. We and the Iraqis we worked with needed to know who was running the American occupation. Jay was supposed to be in charge but Larry DiRita, Rumsfeld's shadowy man on the scene, clearly had veto power. CFLCC, the land-force component of the Central Command (CENTCOM), controlled most of the resources and Jay had trouble getting their attention. Jay had promised me and others a written delegation of authority to satisfy the basic Arab need for a piece of paper. DiRita held it up, perhaps to allow time for the Pentagon ideologues to arrive. I did not see time as being on our side. Iraqis were initially glad to see us, but I expected that to change quickly if the power vacuum continued and the United States was not delivering on its promises.

The problems we faced were daunting. There were clearly not enough military in Baghdad (or in the rest of Iraq), nor was the military that was there sufficiently resourced to provide the security needed for people to return to work and resume normal lives. Allen requested the military to secure and report on the conditions of the major crossing points to Syria, Jordan, and Iran. The military responded that they did not have the necessary manpower. President Bush had declared the war over, but I was hearing gunfire across the Tigris. Our military lifeline, the 352nd Civil Affairs Unit headed by a brigadier, had many talented and dedicated reserve officers but only one telephone line and no radios. Four members of the unit were shot in the early days of the occupation and they had no way to call for help.

I was also concerned that the Pentagon was pouring more civilians into Baghdad and that the logistical support was not keeping up. DOD wanted to bring the Crystal City Iraqis to Baghdad as fast as possible, four or five per ministry. I knew that their agenda to sweep out the old guard conflicted with my strategy of mobilizing the existing professionals in the ministry. Managing Muyhi proved difficult in itself, and I had no way to employ more exiles. We knew also that the Pentagon was planning to send a large governance group to Baghdad. This group turned out to consist mainly of Republican Party operatives. What we really needed was a Treasury group to accelerate the putting of money into Iraqi hands, but Treasury wasn't prepared to send its people until basic life support, office space, and communications became available. We also needed basic staff support, secretaries, staff assistants, and communicators, not more people coming to provide policy guidance. As of May 1, we did not have a single secretary, staff assistant, or communicator to support the senior people advising twenty-three ministries. Barbara Bodine had a very talented secretary and an experienced communicator but her group, Baghdad Central, was at the far end of the palace from the ministerial advisers (the better part of a mile away).

Mike Mobbs's departure solved a big problem for me. Back in Kuwait, I had drafted a simple instruction, to be signed by whomever I identified as the senior Iraqi in the MFA, to all Iraqi diplomatic posts. It requested that they cease all activities and secure files, seals, passports, and equipment. The directive asked heads of mission (usually ambassadors) to report to the Ministry in Baghdad by a specific date (June 6). Other diplomats were to remain in place. I had sent the draft instruction to Mobbs as well as a copy to the Department of State (which did not respond). Mobbs finally returned the draft to me on April 29 in Baghdad with several suggested changes that I knew no Iraqi could accept. He also proposed a clearance process that would have delayed the issuance of the instruction for weeks, if not months.

May 4 started with a morning meeting chaired by Jay. When my turn came, I had progress to report. I then asked for help with four things: a) security; b) a formal designation of authority; c) more support for lead Treasury official David Nummy so that we could move money; and d) freedom to leave lower-level Ba'athists in place. When we arrived at the MFA, there were two very large tanks parked in the compound. I went over and introduced myself and told the soldiers how glad I was to see them. The Iraqis were walking in from another entrance. Ghassan introduced me to Mohammed Amin Ahmed and explained that he was the senior Iraqi MFA official present and should rightly be the chairman of the steering committee. Mohammed Amin was a Kurd from the city of Dohuk in northern Iraq and had been director general of administration and finance. He did not speak much English but Ghassan stayed close, and communication was not difficult. I had brought with me five Thurayas, which I handed over to be distributed to the various committee chairs. I also presented to the Iraqis on the steering committee my draft instruction to Iraqi diplomatic posts. We had a lengthy discussion about how to distribute emergency payments to MFA employees. By the end of our discussion, the Iraqis came back with an Arabic translation of the draft instruction.

Three other senior Iraqis impressed me that day as competent and energetic. Bassam Kubba had entered the Iraqi diplomatic service with Ghassan and, like Ghassan, spoke English fluently. Zaid Nouri also spoke English fluently and, although he had recently been transferred from another ministry, he was clearly the most knowledgeable about MFA buildings and facilities. Nasir al-Samaraie, also fluent in English, had run MFA technology systems, including the communications and computer systems. That afternoon, I met with an Iraqi named Salem al-Qubaisi at the Conference Center. I understood that al-Qubaisi had recently been appointed as an undersecretary at the MFA and, because the minister, Naji Sabri, had fled along with Saddam, al-Qubaisi was now the highest-ranking MFA official left in Baghdad. I told al-Qubaisi politely but firmly that we considered him part of the Saddam regime and that the only way he could get his old job back would be through whatever political process emerged. I will never forget the look in his eyes when I delivered that news. It was pure hatred.

The next day (May 5), when we arrived at the MFA, I vowed to be more careful about what I wished for. I had asked for the military to provide security. The Third Infantry Division (3rd ID) had the gates of the ministry locked and the soldiers were not letting any of the Iraqis in. They had their orders. The soldiers finally agreed to admit the senior Iraqis, but only after they underwent a dignity-rattling body search. I persuaded the soldiers to put me and those on my team through a similar search. The Iraqis were nevertheless unhappy at being treated in this fashion. This incident no doubt reflected similar ones throughout the city and country that over time turned Iraqis against us.

By the next day, we were ready to go with the instruction to diplomatic posts abroad. A young MFA employee brought in a laptop with an Arabic keyboard and he typed up the message on MFA stationary. Mohammed Amin signed it. The palace did not have a reliable international fax line, so Allen and Alex spent the better part of a day driving around Baghdad in Alex's Humvee looking for a suitable fax machine. Allen lucked out when he ran into a military officer he had worked with previously in Sanaa and Riyadh. His friend made sure the fax reached the Iraqi embassies in Damascus and Amman, with instructions to circulate it to all other Iraqi diplomatic posts. Communications between Iraqi posts abroad had been unaffected. Allen later hatched the idea of setting up a Hotmail account for the Iraqi MFA, and we used that for the rest of our stay for communication with the posts abroad.

Jay Garner came to visit the MFA on May 7. I had prepared one page of talking points for him to use. Allen went out ahead to warn the Iraqis that he was coming. Jay used the talking points but added a promise that we would rebuild the ministry. I reflected that I had to either deliver on the promise or find a way to walk it back. The meeting went well but when Jay and Mohammed Amin met the press afterward, a journalist asked whether the Ba'ath Party still existed. Mohammed Amin, who was a Ba'athist, dodged the question.

I had drafted a message to those U.S. embassies and consulates where Iraqis had diplomatic facilities to let them know about the instruction that had gone out from the MFA. I emailed the text to our embassy in Kuwait and asked that they send it, because we had no way to communicate with our embassies from Baghdad. The next day, I received word that Jim Larocco wanted to talk with me. When I called Jim back on my satellite phone, he complained that I was out of control and had dumped a problem in his lap. He would have to send an instruction to embassies explaining what had happened, as well as explain to official Washington how this occurred without anyone in Washington signing off on it. I assured Jim that

Jay Garner knew about it and had not objected. I later learned that our embassy in Kuwait had been instructed not to send out any more messages from me without State Department approval.

I came away from this conversation sobered and, I suspect, Jim did as well. I realized I was on my own. Although I was being paid by the State Department, I was effectively working for a military organization. I was out of control or, at least, out of the State Department's control. Jim realized that he was not able to instruct me, but he did want to be consulted. My instincts were to coordinate with State and I likely would have tried had effective cooperation been established between ORHA and State. I was sorry that State had become irrelevant to Iraqi reconstruction, but I was working for Garner and I had a job to do and there was no way to get it done in a timely fashion while also keeping two different chains of command happy. As I pondered my situation, I had to smile remembering that Rumsfeld had dismissed me (and others) as too low-profile and bureaucratic. I was now running an Arab foreign ministry, not something low-profile bureaucrats often get to do.

The work I was doing was what I had been trained to do by the Foreign Service, and I continued to be an advocate for a professional Foreign Service. When I read in the May 2 *Washington Post* that Richard Perle, neoconservative critic of the State Department, had equated the aggressiveness of Foreign Service Officers to that of hummingbirds, I was provoked. The *Post* published my letter noting that Perle apparently knew little about either Foreign Service Officers or hummingbirds. "Hummingbirds have more aggression per ounce than any other creature on the planet."[4] The *Post* elected to show me as writing from Tucson, when I would have preferred that they show me as writing from Baghdad. I understood that the letter was posted on a bulletin board at the Foreign Service Institute.

We learned on May 9 that Barbara Bodine had been reassigned back to the Department of State. Word was that she had gone into a fifteen-minute rant that morning in a staff meeting about soldiers speeding through the streets of Baghdad playing loud rock music. Her point was well-taken, but the way she delivered it may have been the last straw for Jay. Barbara was one of the few people assigned to ORHA who understood Iraq, but she wasn't a good fit for the job she was given. Running the central part of the country had become an engineering and reconstruction job. Ted Morse, formerly of USAID, and Army Corps of Engineers General Carl Strock stepped into the role.

Life slowly got better. We were enjoying two hot meals a day, reserving lunch for MREs. Indeed, life was so good that the military all over Baghdad had heard about the "palace with the heads" where you could sightsee, snap photos, and score a hot meal. The first night hot meals were served, nine hundred people showed up, twice the number who lived in the palace. Soon, an ORHA badge was required for entry. Our MFA team got the keys to a dedicated vehicle, a Chevy Suburban. Alex had been driving us. Because Alex's role as our driver was no longer essential, I arranged for him to assume a substantive role on the MFA team.

As we moved deeper into May, heat and the lack of air conditioning became a problem. High temperatures had reached triple digits, and the temperature in our bedroom was above ninety degrees when we tried to sleep. I adopted a technique that I learned from Don Bosch, who had survived in Oman before air conditioning. I would put a wet towel over my body. Allen and I spent two hours one evening trying to put together fans to get the air in our rooms moving. There was now running water most of the time in our bathroom. Copiers and printers were scarce, but I could find them if I really needed to.

Security remained a major concern, although my impression in the early days of May was that it was improving. The rules were that we could only leave what became the Green Zone in the company of MPs, but there were only enough MPs to escort a total of three to four trips per day to service more than twenty different ministries. That was simply not compatible with spending several hours each day at the MFA, which was outside the Green Zone. We decided to ignore the rule because the MFA was much closer to the palace than many other ministries. There were at least a couple of nervous days when we were moving unescorted around Baghdad with thousands of dollars in cash. One day we drove over to the MFA in a single military vehicle with $19,000 in cash for emergency start-up costs. On another day, Allen went unescorted with an Iraqi employee in our Suburban to pick up enough cash to pay each employee $20 (the MFA had roughly one thousand employees) and brought it to the MFA. Once commuting to the MFA in the Suburban became routine, we began to move freely around other parts of the city. Tim and I became regulars at Nabil's restaurant on the east side of the Tigris, where we could get excellent kababs and Efes beer.

One of the most puzzling aspects of those early days in Baghdad was our failure to restore communications in Iraq in a timely fashion. The official explanation offered was that a company known as MCI/WorldCom would be setting up a mobile system but had not done so because the security environment was not yet "permissive." I learned from a journalist that we rejected an offer by a Kuwaiti company to extend its mobile service up to Baghdad on an emergency basis. The bottom line was that Iraqis could not communicate with each other, which complicated the task of putting together a representative government. Those of us in ORHA could not communicate with each other either. That solved for me the problem of getting exercise because I walked miles each day along the marbled corridors of the Palace to find people with whom I needed to coordinate. Finally, and most important, ORHA and later the CPA could not communicate with the Iraqi people. The lack of communications infrastructure was only part of the problem. We did not have the serious and effective public communications strategy needed to manage the unrealistic expectations of Iraqis, who needed to understand that it would take lots of time to make their lives better.

There was a moment I witnessed that encapsulated how damaging lack of communications could be. A U.S. Marine colonel stationed in a provincial city noticed a problem. Iraqis were demonstrating daily about the lack of salaries, and the colonel understood that his troops would face increasing danger if salaries weren't paid. He worked with local authorities for a week to compile lists of employees working for various ministries and other government agencies. He got the lists certified and traveled to Baghdad to the Ministry of Finance to collect the money to pay the salaries. The ministry officials looked blankly at the colonel. The ministry was working with officials of other ministries in Baghdad to have them certify lists of employees throughout the country. They had no instructions about what to do with lists brought by a U.S. Marine from the provinces. The colonel came to our palace, and his face and his voice grew angrier and angrier as he tried in vain to find a way to push the button on salary payments in his province. Imagine how much easier this issue would have been if Americans and Iraqis had the ability to communicate with each other.

On May 10, John Limbert kindly offered to take me along on a trip to Mosul, with Baghdad Museum director Dr. Jaber Khalil, to inspect the damage to the Mosul Museum and to the antiquities at nearby Ninevah and Nimrud. We flew north in two Chinook helicopters flying low over the Tigris valley. The scene below us reminded me a bit of the Nile Delta (very green with mud brick houses and many farm animals) and a bit of the Central Valley of California (there was a four-lane highway below). The Mosul Museum had been looted but the damage was not as bad as what had happened to the Baghdad Museum. When we visited Ninevah and Nimrud, magical sites I had only previously read about, we could see that looters tried, with limited success, to pry carved marble out of the cliffs.

Jerry Bremer arrived on Monday, May 12, and made some opening remarks to the entire ORHA staff that evening. He wore a suit, despite the oppressive heat, and military desert boots. He praised Garner and the ORHA staff and asked us to tell him how he could help us. The next morning, in a more restricted meeting, we met a different Bremer. He led off with his plans for DeBa'athification, leaving us confused about whether he was proposing firing the first three layers of the Ba'ath Party, the first three layers of each ministry, or both. He then demanded that Bob Gifford, then running the Ministry of Interior, do more to get armed Iraqi police on the streets to relieve the military. He recalled that we had shot a few looters in Haiti and that the looting stopped. I thought he was briefing us on new rules of engagement but, when his "shoot the looters" idea appeared the next day in the press, we learned that this idea had not been cleared with the military or the Pentagon. It was a stumble out of the gate for Bremer, who clearly wanted to demonstrate that he was now in charge. It had now become obvious that he wasn't.

Tim, John, Robin, and I knew immediately that Bremer's plans for excommunicating Ba'ath Party members was a formula for disaster. Robin did what she could to convince Bremer to dial it back, but he was determined. He gave a measured preview of the policy's official announcement in a press conference the evening of May 15. That gave me some hope that there would be flexibility in the policy. When I saw the written policy the next morning, however, my faint hopes were dashed.

The first consequence for those of us working with the MFA was that we could not retain Mohammed Amin Ahmed as head of the steering committee. It was the first day of the Friday-Saturday weekend, so we ordinarily would have had two days to plan strategy. It happened, however, that Mohammed Amin was hosting lunch for me the next day (Saturday). I huddled with other members of the MFA team to determine next steps. We were joined by the newest member of the team, Jacqueline Lawson-Smith from the British Foreign Office. She spoke Arabic, and had experience in the Arab world and lots of energy. We decided that I would regret the lunch, pleading illness, and that Muyhi would find Mohammed Amin to deliver the message. Muyhi improvised and elected to tell Mohammed Amin that we needed to meet to consider the new policy. Mohammed Amin got the message, took it gracefully, and agreed to depart. The team had found a classic Arab solution to a difficult problem. We delivered the message through an intermediary, allowing Mohammed Amin to save face and depart without confrontation. I was determined to save the other members of the steering committee.

Although Robin had already tried and failed, I felt it necessary to take one more run at Bremer. I sent him a memo, through Robin, that reported on what we were doing to implement his policy at the MFA. I went on to predict an increase in violence throughout the country, creating security problems for both coalition personnel and for those Iraqis working with us. This, of course, is what happened. I claim no great prescience. The memo reflected what all the professional diplomats in the palace outside Bremer and his immediate staff believed.

The day Bremer arrived, Pentagon-favorite Ahmed Chalabi sent word that he wished to see me at the Hunt Club. He wanted me to meet with four former Foreign Ministry employees who had felt wronged by the Saddam regime and left out of the ongoing reorganization of the MFA. Liked most people in the State Department, I was skeptical of the influence Chalabi seemed to have with the Bush administration. Chalabi greeted me warmly, and I had to admire his obvious personal magnetism. I had a longer chat with his daughter Tamara, who struck me as a bright young woman with excellent political instincts.

I ran into Patrick Tyler from the *New York Times* at the Hunt Club. Tyler had just published a story, reprinted in just about every newspaper in the United States, that I would be leaving as part of a shake-up of ORHA. My roommates, Tim and John, along with Barbara Bodine, were reportedly involved in the shake-up. I told Tyler that he had gotten it wrong. John was departing any day to return to his job in Mauritania. Tim and I had both told ORHA leadership that we were planning to depart on June 16. Tyler invited me to lunch the next day. When we met at a local restaurant, he was more interested in Bremer's suggestion that we start shooting looters.

I was not sure what to expect when I arrived back at the MFA the first working day following the publication of Bremer's DeBa'athification order. The remaining members of the steering committee took it in stride. Our meetings that day were punctuated by the sound of power tools as repairs were underway in the Protocol Building. A generator was up and running. I added a talented female diplomat named Aqila al-Hashemi to the steering committee. Aqila had earned a law degree in Iraq and a doctorate from the Sorbonne in French literature. She joined the MFA as a

French translator for then-Foreign Minister Tariq Aziz. She was in 2003 deputy director of the International Organizations Division of the MFA and had excellent contacts with the UN. It wasn't long before a UN truck pulled up and delivered a conference table and chairs. My second initiative that day was to organize a cadre of young Iraqi diplomats into what I called an executive secretariat and assign them various tasks that the senior Iraqis considered beneath their dignity.

Back in the palace, new faces continued to pour in. Peter McPherson, who I had gotten to know well when he was USAID administrator, had arrived earlier to oversee Iraq's economic recovery. Former NYC police commissioner Bernie Kerik came in to advise the Interior Ministry. Bremer brought in a handful of other professionals, including Hume Horan and Clay McManaway, both well into their retirement years. Pat Kennedy, an experienced administrative officer, arrived to be Bremer's chief of staff. Ryan Crocker was transferred from NEA to add some experience to the ideologues on the governance group.

The MFA team, by mid-May up to five, had to surrender our relatively spacious inner office in the palace to Robin, who was now coordinator of all twenty-three ministry advisory teams. We ended up with a utility table, two chairs, two laptops, and two fans in the hall across from a bathroom. There were window air conditioners in the office next to the hall, so our space was cooler than our bedroom on the floor above. Tim and I concluded that the bedroom would not get air conditioning until we agreed to move to a trailer in the rapidly growing trailer park behind the palace. We were now feeling like short-timers, so we resisted the move. We received a new offer of a room in the al-Rashid Hotel. We again refused. The al-Rashid, the tallest building around, was clearly a target for insurgents. Later that year, after we left, the al-Rashid was attacked on two separate occasions with mortars and rockets.

As Bremer and his staff settled in, getting things done became more and more bureaucratic. I thought of ourselves, the early arrivals, as like the mountain men in the American West. Now the railroad had come and with it the good and bad of civilization. I worked very hard with Jacqueline on a proposal to rescue several hundred Iraqis off the beach in Dubai. They were trapped in Dubai by the war, and we were not allowing commercial shipping to the Iraqi port of Umm Qasr. We proposed to allow a ferry to bring the stranded Iraqis to Umm Qasr as a humanitarian exception. The team researched the draft of the ferry, the depth of the channel, and the details of how the Iraqis would be handled upon arrival. We sent all of this in a memo to Bremer. Later, we learned that Bremer had approved it but that his staff later talked him out of it. They were worried about the optics of dumping Iraqis on the beach at Umm Qasr.

The U.S. military raid on the Palestinian Embassy on Wednesday, May 28, was a fresh disaster. It was the initiative of a "Captain Mike," and I assume he did not realize he was raiding an embassy. We learned about it from Washington when a non-governmental organization in Jordan reported it. I sent one of our young Iraqi diplomats over to the scene to learn the facts. He reported that the soldiers entered the embassy shooting and arrested seven Palestinians, including the chargé. They smashed a portrait of Arafat and seized Palestinian flags.

When I returned to the palace, I briefed Robin and Pat Kennedy and I sent a report to the desk officer at State who was responsible for following developments in the CPA. Our military provided several relatively lame explanations. They claimed it was not an embassy but a private house, and that the soldiers found weapons inside. Virtually all Iraqi households and all foreign diplomatic missions in Baghdad had weapons because of the threat of looting and the overall lack of security. According to the AP, CFLCC Commander McKiernan later acknowledged the break-in but explained that it was a response to the killing of a U.S. soldier in that neighborhood. I was pained that a report from an Iraqi MFA employee turned out to be more reliable than the report from our military.

I was stunned at how the U.S. government reacted over the next couple of days to what seemed to me an egregious violation of international law. We did not apologize. In fact, State Department spokesman Richard Boucher argued that diplomats accredited to the Saddam regime as well as their premises no longer held diplomatic status. I met with Bremer on May 31 to discuss progress at the MFA. We also discussed the raid on the Palestinian Embassy. He fumed that the military had released the Palestinian chargé. In fact, the military was still holding him and continued to hold him and another Palestinian diplomat in the Abu Ghraib prison for about a year. I told Bremer that, although he was the boss, I disagreed with the U.S. response. We had arrested a Palestinian diplomat who represented the Palestinian Authority, an entity with which we had diplomatic relations. Bremer seemed to consider that but took no action.

One day I brought Ghassan, Bassam, Zaid, and Nasir to the palace for lunch, and they wandered around looking wide-eyed at the huge rooms. Zaid had been involved in the palace's construction but the other three had never been in this forbidden zone of the city, much less inside the palace. Zaid, the building engineer, identified marble from Turkey, Greece, Italy, and Iraq in the floor and walls.

May 31 was not a good day. Sandy told me that a package she had sent with some badly needed clothes had been returned to her in Tucson with the notation that I had left ORHA with no forwarding address. I went immediately to C-4 (logistics), where the mail was distributed, ready to tear somebody's throat out but found nobody to talk to. Apparently, the mail clerk confused me with John Limbert, who had departed. I poured my anger into an email to Col. Glen Collins, the administrative head of the palace who we called "the mayor." He never responded, and my wardrobe grew steadily shabbier as my departure neared.

My last two weeks in Baghdad were incredibly busy. The steering committee had stabilized at six members. Qusay Mehdi, a close colleague of Ghassan and Bassam, had been included since the early days along with Ghassan, Bassam, Zaid, and Nasir. Aqila al-Hashemi had been the most recent addition. The talented young Iraqi diplomats in the executive secretariat were working hard. We now had $35,000 to rebuild the Diplomatic Institute on the MFA campus. The Protocol Building now had an air-conditioned conference room on the second floor and a well-furnished air-conditioned reception room on the ground floor.

I was living in sin by keeping Nasir on the steering committee. He had been director of a vocational institute before coming to the MFA and had been given a relatively high rank in the Ba'ath Party. I considered Nasir to be competent, capable, and reliable and I was convinced that he had remained in the party only to protect his job and his family. I stayed in the palace one morning laboring over a detailed justification for an exception for Nasir to the DeBa'athification order. I also wrote one for Salah Abdul Salam al-Azzawi, the former chief of protocol, who had been tortured, sentenced to death, and later pardoned. He stayed a party member because he believed he would be killed if he didn't. I argued that the latter exception was critical to demonstrating the policy's fairness. The two memos got lost on the way to Bremer's office and I had to rewrite them.

Bremer did approve them eventually but only after I left Baghdad in mid-June. Radu, who was interim chief of the MFA team after I left, signed waiver notices for Nasir and Salah. Iraqi Foreign Minister Hoshyar Zebari later named Salah head of consular affairs.

The Hotmail account that we set up to communicate with Iraqis in overseas missions was bringing in dozens of messages daily. Saddam loyalists at one embassy attempted to overwhelm the account with large meaningless attachments, but the channel survived. Iraqi chiefs of mission were required to return to Baghdad by June 6 or lose their jobs. We interviewed each one as they trickled in. We expected only about a third to come back, and the number turned out to be closer to two-thirds. Allen or I would interview each one, often with Bassam sitting in, and produce a memo. We had defined the position of ambassador out of Bremer's DeBa'athification decree, but most also held high-ranking and now disqualifying positions in the Ba'ath Party. One memorable day (June 8), I interviewed returning Iraqi ambassadors from Tripoli, Tehran, and Damascus. The Iraqi ambassador to Libya was from Tikrit, Saddam's hometown, and he struck me as a thug. Leaving the interview, he snarled at Qusay that Qusay would be killed and dragged through the streets for collaborating with the occupation. Those words would turn out to be prophetic.

The interviews revealed the complexity of how Iraqis in government positions related to the Ba'ath Party. I learned that some Iraqis with minimal or no Ba'ath Party affiliation were major collaborators with senior Saddam regime officials and informers to the Iraq intelligence agencies, while other with higher ranks were really victims of the régime rather than collaborators. Formal Ba'ath Party affiliation turned out to be a misleading way to separate white hats from black hats. I concluded that Americans don't do shades of gray very well.

Iraqi missions overseas controlled significant financial and other assets. With the help of Jacqueline, Allen, and the rest of the MFA team, I devised a two-phase proposal to regain full control of these posts. We would close thirty Iraqi diplomatic posts and focus on the remaining posts in significant capitals. The first stage involved sending a small inspection team (with a senior Iraqi diplomat and an administrative expert) to nearby posts with large numbers of resident Iraqis (for example, Amman, Damascus, Abu Dhabi, and Dubai). We would enlist the cooperation of the U.S. and UK Embassies. We could also include Tripoli and Tehran because the UK had embassies in those capitals even though the United States did not. The second phase would consist of assembling Iraqis who remained in embassies or Iraqis sent from Baghdad a skeleton staff to secure assets and to provide limited consular services. I pitched the proposal to Bremer in my May 31 meeting with him, and he agreed that we could go forward so long as we went slowly. When I left in mid-June, the first inspection visit, to Damascus, Amman, and Beirut had already been scheduled. Zaid and the MFA's head auditor, Abdul Baqi Ismael, led the first inspection team. They recovered $10 million from the Iraqi embassy in Beirut and $21 million from the embassy in Damascus. These funds helped pay for subsequent inspection visits, among other things. The team also recovered fifteen thousand unissued Iraqi passports, which were used by the MFA until new passports could be designed and printed and kept out of the hands of Iraqi insurgents.

One of the more annoying issues I had to deal with in Baghdad involved the Iraqi-Americans on the Iraq Reconstruction and

Development Council (IRDC). We called them the Crystal City Iraqis, as they were paid by the Pentagon through a Science Applications International Corporation (SAIC) contract and provided office space in Crystal City in Arlington, near the Pentagon. Jay Garner had resisted bringing more than one per ministry but, no doubt because the political heat from Washington was too searing, Bremer allowed them all to come to Iraq (between one hundred and two hundred individuals). During my last week in Iraq, I had four on my team. The majority of them dreamed of sweeping out the old guard and installing themselves in positions of power. Muhyi, the leader of the MFA team, came in late April and proved a very valuable addition. Unfortunately, I never felt able to trust him. My instincts proved true when I arrived at the MFA one morning to find that he had engineered a nomination by the steering committee to be deputy minister. I vetoed the nomination, arguing that it was a political decision for the next Iraqi government and that the Geneva Conventions require that we leave Iraqi laws in place, including the one that required MFA employees to be Iraqi citizens.

As my time in Iraq wound down, I could see that we were at the end of our honeymoon with the Iraqi people. Attacks on U.S. troops were becoming more common, with serious attacks in Fallujah and on the road to the Baghdad airport. Bremer wanted to slow down uncoordinated initiatives and the momentum toward creating an independent Iraqi authority. His instinct was that coalition forces would need time to get things right, to understand our obligations under the new UN resolution (UNSC 1453), and to organize the Coalition Provisional Authority (CPA) that had replaced ORHA. I continued to believe that time was not on our side. The patience of Iraqis was remarkable because they were now free of the horrors of Saddam's regime, but their restraint was not unlimited. U.S. troops lacked the training or skills to be effective in a peacekeeping mission. In addition, the 3rd ID was being replaced by the 1st Armored Division. This meant that what experience the 3rd ID had accumulated would depart with it.

Shortly after the 1st Armored Division took over security at the MFA, on the morning of June 12, Zaid was agitated because members of the new unit guarding the ministry had broken into the main building, breaking glass and scattering flags and Saddam memorabilia around. I was embarrassed. Allen talked to the captain representing the brigade commander, who acknowledged that members of the unit had been in trouble before. Elsewhere, U.S. convoys routinely barreled through Baghdad streets cutting off and now and then even hitting Iraqi vehicles. They were trained not to stop, not to apologize.

In my conversations with Iraqis, I sensed the beginnings of a slow burn that was playing into the hands of the nascent insurgency, resulting in part from Bremer's May 16 order to remove Ba'athists from the government and the subsequent order abolishing all defense, intelligence, and information organs in Iraq. One of the experienced Middle East hands who I contacted through Gulf 2000 put me in touch with Nizar Hamdoon, then residing in the United States, who had been MFA undersecretary under Saddam. Hamdoon wrote me a long memo about the consequences of Bremer's decrees that seemed to me to be right on point. He argued that we should multiply by seven (the average size of an Iraqi family) the number of Iraqis left by our policies to drift without employment, income, or pensions. The resulting number of angry Iraqis was a sure recipe for trouble. There was also the Shi'a factor. Our governance group was focused on the 80 percent of Iraqi Arabs (not including the Kurds) who were Shi'a. But Shi'a clerics were mobilizing their flocks around anti-Western themes related to alcohol, obscene music, and pornography.

I felt good about what we had accomplished at the MFA. We had come a long way in the few weeks since finding Hamid wandering the grounds of the looted and burned Foreign Ministry. The team had a steering committee and our youthful executive secretariat running daily operations. We had invested $54,000 toward fixing up the Protocol Building and the Diplomatic Institute. A contract had been negotiated with an Iraqi company for reconstruction of the main MFA building. Employees, in Baghdad and overseas, were being paid. We had a draft budget and organizational structure. Senior Ba'athists and Iraq intelligence agents had been removed from overseas posts. Thirty-one chiefs of mission had returned to Baghdad and been interviewed. The majority were fired. With one exception (the Iraqi ambassador in Beijing), those who elected not to return had turned their embassies over to their deputies. We were in the process of closing thirty Iraqi posts and regaining control of the others.

I left Baghdad on June 16. Tim and I elected to take the KBR "pony express," a three-car convoy, to Kuwait. As we passed through the area around Nasiriyah, a group of small boys came running toward us throwing rocks. One bounced harmlessly off the side of the car. This served as a reminder that occupiers are rarely if ever loved. According to the car thermometer, the temperature hit 121 degrees in southern Iraq. We needed the help of Dick Jones, then U.S. ambassador in Kuwait, to shepherd us out of Kuwait without a hefty fine. The Kuwait government had no record of our departure for Iraq and assumed we had overstayed our visas. I stayed with friends Hank and Sonja in the DC area, handling the administrative details of again leaving government employment over the phone. Nobody in the Department of State or the Pentagon ever asked to debrief me.

Shortly after I arrived back in Tucson, Aqila called me from New York, where she was representing Iraq at a UN donors' conference. The following month Bremer named her a member of the Iraq Governing Council. Aqila was gunned down one day in September coming out of her Baghdad residence as she prepared to attend the UN General Assembly as part of the Iraqi delegation. I was in touch with Susan Johnson, the very capable career FSO who eventually succeeded me at the MFA. Susan told me on September 24 that Aqila wasn't expected to live through the night. She died of her wounds on September 25, 2003. This news was like a punch to the gut because, in many ways, Aqila was my greatest achievement. I saw in her a remarkable combination of charm, humility, and competence. Once I brought her into the steering committee, word of her evident ability spread to others in the CPA. I remember with pleasure a morning in early June when I accompanied her and two of her male colleagues to the Baghdad *souk* (open market).

Had she lived, the perfect job for her would have been Iraq's ambassador to the UN. By elevating her, I made her a target for the insurgents as the security situation deteriorated over the summer of 2003.

Bassam was killed outside his home in a drive-by shooting on June 12, 2004. He was the senior career official in the Foreign Ministry at the time. Qusay Mehdi was named Iraqi ambassador to the UAE. During a trip back to Iraq on October 27, 2004, four armed men attempted to force him into their car. When Qusay resisted, the men shot him to death. Following that incident, Allen, Susan Johnson, and I sent a letter to Bill Burns, NEA assistant secretary, expressing our concern that the lives of the three remaining steering committee members were clearly in danger and asking that our embassy work with the interim Iraqi government to protect them. We received a polite response, but events proved that neither our embassy nor the Iraqi government could protect the Iraqis who counted on us to stabilize their country.

Ghassan continued working as the senior official in the MFA until the Governing Council appointed Hoshyar Zebari as foreign minister on September 3, 2003. Later that month, while Zebari was on his first trip abroad as minister, the MFA was hit by two RPGs, followed by gunfire from the street. Nobody was injured but the attack caused considerable damage to the main MFA building. A far more devastating attack occurred on August 19, 2009, when a truck bomb detonated just outside the rebuilt MFA, killing fifty-three and wounding more than five hundred.

The MFA assigned Ghassan in October 2003 as Iraqi ambassador to Bahrain. He retired there in 2010. He no longer felt comfortable returning to Iraq because the Iraqi government at the time considered him a holdover from Saddam's MFA, while insurgents considered him a collaborator. Ghassan and I stayed in contact over the years, and we agreed to coauthor a book about our work together to get the Iraqi Foreign Ministry back into operation.[5]

Nasir received his exception from the De-Ba'athification decree but elected to depart Iraq with his wife Hala for Jordan, mostly owing to the death threats he received. Nasir applied for asylum in the United States and, while it took years, the country finally admitted him as a refugee. He has lived since then in San Diego. He and Hala were sworn in as U.S. citizens on February 22, 2018.

Zaid worked as consul general in Manchester, England for six years and spent a year in Nairobi, Kenya. He is now back in Baghdad, heading the Financial Department at the Ministry of Foreign Affairs.

A suicide bomber attacked Nabil's restaurant on the last day of 2003. The restaurant was crowded with people celebrating the coming of the New Year. Five people died and many more were injured. Several of us had become well-acquainted with Nabil, who was a Chaldean Christian, and his family.

The short time I spent in Iraq was challenging and personally rewarding. My wife and son were right that I needed to seize the opportunity. I believe that I was the right person for the MFA job, and I gave the assignment everything I had. Our invasion of Iraq was, however, a huge strategic blunder, and the decisions made after the invasion destroyed any possibility of success. I watched with sadness and pain as the security situation unraveled and Iraqis I had known, worked with, and become friends with became victims. The experience I gained in Iraq did make me a better teacher and it opened new opportunities working with the men and women being called upon to fix our mistakes in Iraq and Afghanistan, our soldiers and marines.

8

TUCSON

Working with the Troops

I n late July 2004, I found myself standing next to a young U.S. Army lieutenant and a Korean Army officer staring at a wall plaque in the entrance to a nondescript office building in downtown Seoul. I, along with several other American students as well as students from Taiwan, South Vietnam, South Korea, and Japan, had helped dig the foundation for that building thirty-nine years earlier in the summer of 1965.

I was in Korea in 2004 as a "senior mentor" participating in an MRX (Mission Readiness Exercise) to help prepare a brigade of the Second Infantry Division ("Second to None") for deployment to Anbar Province in Iraq. The acronym should have been MRE but, as is widely known, those letters are reserved in the military for "meals ready to eat." A couple of weeks earlier, I had received a phone call from Tim Carney, my roommate in Baghdad a year earlier, giving me a "heads-up" that he had recommended me for the job. That phone call triggered a raft of work with the military that would keep me busy off and on for more than seven years.

Soon after I hung up with Tim, I received a call as promised from Bob Tomasovic, a retired U.S. Army colonel who was running a program called Leader Development and Education for Sustained Peace (LDESP). LDESP, run out of the Naval Postgraduate School in Monterey, California, originally was established to run short education programs for troops (mostly U.S. Army) deploying to the Balkans. By 2004 most of its programs targeted U.S. Army units deploying to Afghanistan and Iraq. Funding came from the

U.S. Army Training and Doctrine Command (TRADOC). Tim had been a participant in several LDESP programs for units deploying to Iraq. The 2nd ID had reached out to Bob to find a senior diplomat with Iraq experience to participate in the Korea MRX. Bob called Tim, who was unable to go, and Tim recommended me. Bob needed someone quickly, which gave me some negotiating leverage, and we settled on a satisfactory rate for eight days of consulting plus travel from Tucson to and from Korea.

After a missed connection and some scrambling to get word about the delay to the 2nd ID folks who were meeting me, I landed in Seoul Incheon International Airport. My escort officer, Cpt. Virginia Hayden, drove me to Camp Casey, northeast of Seoul. For the next eight days, I shuttled between Camp Casey, the Korea Training Center (KTC) where the exercise was taking place, and Camp Red Cloud, the location of the 2nd ID Headquarters and division commander's office and residence. I spent a considerable amount of time with division commander Maj. Gen. John Wood and with Col. Gary Patton, commander of the Strike Force brigade that would deploy to Ramadi. For me, it was an immersion course (like drinking from a firehose) in military culture and acronyms. I had to learn that PIR meant priority intelligence requirements, BUB is a battle update brief, and the meanings of several dozen other acronyms.

The actual exercise took place at the training center (KTC) over a three-day period. I provided a one-hour cultural brief to the brigade and senior non-commissioned officers (NCOs) ahead of the exercise. The KTC consisted of several buildings of different sizes that resembled a hotel, office buildings, apartment buildings, and single-family dwellings. Organizers recruited enough "Arabs" to simulate a crowd. Many were Arab immigrants living in places like San Diego, but the ranks were swelled by Koreans wearing *ghutras* and *dishdashas*.[1] The exercise placed a heavy emphasis on crowd control, with liberal use of concertina wire to cordon off Iraqi civilians. I learned about the 4 Cs (clear, cordon, control, and call EOD—explosive ordinance disposal). Where appropriate, I provided feedback during the exercise, cautioning that many Iraqis speak English and that to assume otherwise was dangerous. I also warned soldiers not to take for granted that an interpreter is conveying what you want him or her to convey.

At some point during the exercise at the KTC, I was introduced to a soldier from Tucson named Robert Unruh. We compared notes on where we lived in Tucson, and I am confident that we talked about the Arizona Wildcats basketball team because that is what people from Tucson who encounter each other in remote parts of the world talk about. I later learned that Unruh had been killed in Anbar Province on September 25.

During the exercise, I sat in on a simulated lunch between Colonel Patton and the "sheikh" of the village and provided feedback to the colonel afterward. I recall warning him that bragging about your humble origins does not play as well in the Arab world. It is interpreted as a reflection on and lack of respect for your family.

The day after the exercise, I participated in the exercise AAR (after-action review). My escorts were amazed to learn that I had never used PowerPoint. They coached me on how to put my comments on slides. Each of my five slides consisted of simple text. There was no background design and no photos. That would be the first of many dozens of PowerPoints I would produce over the next seven years as an LDESP consultant. I became so enamored of the program that I began using it for all my lectures at the University of Arizona, much to the annoyance of some students who complained that I overdid it.

I made several suggestions in the AAR about language and culture. The soldiers were issued an "Iraq Culture Smart Card" with several phrases. I suggested that there be more courtesy phrases like "good morning" and "good evening" to go with phrases like "drop your weapons" and "put your hands where we can see them." I urged that they carefully debrief the departing unit in Ramadi, making sure relationships with key Iraqis were, as much as possible, handed off to the new arrivals. I warned that concertina wire was unlikely to provide the answer to all problems they would encounter in Iraq. Not until more than two years later had the army's new counterinsurgency doctrine stressed the importance of protecting local civilians.

I wrapped up with three final points. First, every soldier who met Iraqis should "always be collecting and always transmitting." I was simply repeating and reinforcing wisdom I had learned from General Wood. "Always collecting" means gathering intelligence about people and places and getting it to the people who can use it. "Always transmitting" means having ready in your head brief talking points about why the brigade is in Iraq and why it is good for the Iraqis (what the military refers to as information operations [10]). Second, I emphasized that, consistent with the mission and force protection, everything a soldier does and says should result in making friends and not enemies. Finally, U.S. soldiers needed to be part of the solution, not contributors to the problem. Some version of these three points found its way into the briefings I gave to many military units preparing to deploy to Iraq and Afghanistan over the next seven years. I did, in later briefings, add a point about keeping the Iraqis out front, drawing on a quote attributed to T. E. Lawrence: "Better to let them do it imperfectly than to do it perfectly yourself, for it is their country, their way, and your time is short."[2] Other than trying to do the best job I could for the 2nd ID, my only agenda item in Korea was to return to the site of the student center I had helped construct in downtown Seoul in 1965. I joined about a dozen other Americans that summer in a work camp organized by the U.S. branch of an international organization called World University Service (WUS). WUS America had participated in a similar project in Japan the year before. We stopped in Japan for three weeks on the way to Korea and were treated to a guided tour of Japan, from Tokyo south to the island of Kyushu. Our guides were the Japanese students who had worked with American students the summer before. We took a ferry to Korea from a port on the west side of Kyushu, landed in Busan, and boarded a train to Seoul. In Seoul we dug the foundation for a student center using shovels to fill baskets of dirt that were loaded onto trucks and carted away. My only clue to finding the site thirty-nine years later in 2004 was an address, 18 Mook Jung Dong. We set out from Camp Casey one morning with a Korean KATUSA (standing for Korean Augmentation to the U.S. Army).

KATUSAS were Korean soldiers integrated into U.S. units, a practice dating back to the Korean War.

We wandered around downtown Seoul for perhaps a half hour, with the Korean soldier asking questions of local shopkeepers. Finally, he pointed to a building and said that we had found it. The area bore no resemblance to the neighborhood I remembered from years ago, but the building did have a plaque dedicating it the year after our work camp. Walking into the building, we encountered the son of the Korean director of the project I had worked on back in 1965. The son was delighted by the encounter and gave me a book that had been produced to celebrate the project. The text was in Korean, but it was illustrated by photos of many of the people I had worked with. He explained that the building had been converted years earlier from a student center to a regular office building. Then he invited me and my Korean and American escorts to lunch at a nearby restaurant.

General Wood invited me to a farewell dinner that evening, which turned out to be a very pleasant way to end an intense experience. After dinner, the general challenged me to throw a tomahawk (an important 2nd ID symbol) at a wooden target and get it to stick. After multiple attempts and noble efforts by my host to teach me the proper technique, I "stuck" the tomahawk. He then presented me with a ceremonial tomahawk, which I keep in my home office in Tucson.

Shortly after I returned to Tucson, I received another call from Bob Tomasovic, who I would soon learn to call Colonel T, asking me to make a presentation on "The Implications of a Failed Iraq State" at Camp Shelby in Mississippi in late August and again at Fort Hood in Texas in early September. In each case, I would be one of several SMEs (subject matter experts) who were part of the "faculty" for a multiday seminar. I hadn't gotten around to figuring out how to jazz up my PowerPoint presentations with designs and photos. Still, I put together a slightly more ambitious PowerPoint focusing on what failure in Iraq could look like and outlining the U.S. interests that could be affected (nuclear non-proliferation, counterterrorism, oil, Israel and humanitarian interests defined to encompass democracy, human rights and economic development). I sent it to Bob and went off to Disneyland with my wife and five-year-old granddaughter.

Colonel (ret.) Bill Spores called me in Disneyland to ask about my travel plans for the Camp Shelby presentation. Bill held responsibility for what LDESP called protocol, making sure the participants were met at the airport upon arrival and returned to the airport for their departing flights. The colonel was affable, totally reliable, and unfailingly kind. A tall man, he was easy to spot as I emerged from airport security.

Bill was part of what I thought of as the "Oregon mafia." Bob, Bill, and Ben Hussey, the LDESP operations officer, who would run the Camp Shelby program, were all from Oregon. They also drew their supporting staff from several former NCOs who had retired in Oregon. It wasn't an absolute requirement that you be from Oregon to be part of the team. Col. (ret.) Ron Halverson, who led many of the seminars I was involved in, hailed from Minnesota. Ron and Bob had become well-acquainted in Bosnia.

Most of the programs included among the participants a retired U.S. Army general. Bill Crouch, a retired four-star general, assumed this role for many of the programs. He was one of the most thoughtful military commanders I have encountered. Crouch had played a key role in our intervention in Bosnia, and he understood then that challenges like Bosnia required training above and beyond training in war-fighting. He put together a training package in Germany to "provide the 1st Armored Division's senior leadership with specific training on historical, ethnic, political and cultural awareness issues in Bosnia."[3] This led to the decision by TRADOC to fund this kind of training and the creation of LDESP. Crouch wasn't available for every program. John Lemoyne and Daniel Petrosky, both retired three-star generals, often covered this role.

I was concerned at first about deconflicting LDESP programs from my teaching schedule at the University of Arizona. The Camp Shelby and Fort Hood programs were each three days long and, if I attended the entire programs, I would miss at least two days of class. In response to my questions, Bob told me that he wanted

me to attend as many of the presentations as possible so that I
could contribute if appropriate and, also, be available for questions from the soldiers during the breaks. He understood, however,
that I couldn't miss too many classes and wanted me available for
other Iraq programs later in the fall that had not yet been scheduled. Over the years, I allowed myself no more than three missed
classes per semester and rationed them to maximize my atten-
dance at LDESP seminars.

During the next seven years, I participated in fifty-three LDESP
programs for military units preparing to deploy to either Iraq or
Afghanistan. Except for a program at Camp Pendleton in California in 2007 for a marine battalion, all the programs were for army
units. A number of the units were regular army, some were army
reserve units, and some were U.S. Army National Guard units. As
the years progressed, many of the units were being deployed for
the second, third and fourth times.

Thirty-one of the fifty-three programs were at one of the fol-
lowing five military bases: Fort Hood (northwest of Austin), Fort
Riley (Manhattan, Kansas), Fort Carson (Colorado Springs), Fort
Bragg (Fayetteville, North Carolina), and Camp Shelby (near Hat-
tiesburg, Mississippi). Eleven of the programs alone were at Fort
Hood. Prior to working with LDESP, I never ate much barbeque.
Multiple visits to Fort Hood, Fort Riley, and Camp Shelby changed
my diet significantly. Although the LDESP headquarters were in
Monterey, California, it wasn't until 2010 that I made it there for
a program. Though I flew to most programs, I elected to drive to
the four programs in which I participated at Fort Bliss in El Paso.
It is an easy five-hour drive from Tucson to El Paso on I-10. It
always pleased me when I received an invitation to a program at
a military facility I had not visited before. The nicest surprise was
a program in Honolulu in July 2008. Being paid to spend a few
days in Hawaii seemed too good to be true.

Four of the programs were at various military bases in Germany.
I became accustomed to compressing each trip to Germany to four
days. On day one, I would fly to Germany (Frankfurt or Munich).
On day two, I would arrive in Germany and perhaps sit in on pre-

sentations by other faculty members. On day three, I would present. On day four, I would fly back to Tucson.

While my brief but intense stint in Iraq in 2003 allowed me to claim expertise on Iraq, the LDESP leadership also asked me to present on Afghanistan. I had read James Michener's *Caravans*, but my overall knowledge of Afghanistan and what we were doing there was thin. Therefore, I embarked on a self-taught crash course. My first Afghanistan presentation coincided with my first presentation in Germany in October 2004 at the Grafenwoehr military base in eastern Bavaria near the Czech border. I used my Iraq presentation as a template to put together a PowerPoint called "Implications of Failure in Afghanistan." For the first time, I inserted something other than lines of text. It was a cartoon that I still use to illustrate the point that the sudden onslaught of American culture in a traditional society can prove unsettling. The cartoon depicts two traditional Afghan men walking down the street in Kabul shortly after the Taliban were driven out in 2001. There are billboards on both sides of the street advertising the Hard Rock Café, an Arthur Murray dance studio, Bud Light, and Victoria's Secret (featuring a bikini-clad model). Two young Afghan girls are also walking down the street, one reading a Harry Potter book. One older Afghan says to the other, "That was fast."[4]

I occasionally felt intimidated by the elaborate PowerPoint slides that some of my fellow faculty members produced. When I noticed that the generals who participated had very basic PowerPoints, I felt reassured. I thought the military's romance with PowerPoint might come to an end in April 2010 when Gen. Stanley McChrystal, then senior commander in Afghanistan, encountered an elaborate and complex PowerPoint side. He reportedly said that "when we understand that slide, we will have won the war."[5] Nevertheless, the romance continues.

It was not difficult to throw together a presentation about what success or failure in Afghanistan would look like, and I grew more confident. In early 2005, LDESP asked me to deliver a presentation on the Bonn process, the international initiative to assemble a government in Afghanistan. LDESP had been using Tom Johnson, a professor at the Naval Postgraduate School in Monterey, to present this module, but he was unavailable for a program at Camp Shelby. Johnson sent me his presentation with sixty-one slides, and I plunged into another crash program to understand it well enough to field questions. I thought I got through the presentation reasonably well. Soldiers were asked, however, to provide feedback at the end of the seminar, and one grumbled that he didn't understand why a former ambassador to Oman was presenting on Afghanistan. I had to admit to myself that the soldier had a point. Over time, LDESP recruited more faculty who had on-the-ground experience in Afghanistan.

When Hurricane Katrina ravaged New Orleans and the Mississippi Coast at the end of August 2005, I had already been to Camp Shelby three times. The LDESP leadership elected to have us stay in Gulfport and make the hour-long drive north to the base each day. I was impressed by the beautiful homes, the casinos, and beaches that lined the coast. In October and November 2005, I returned to Gulfport for programs at Camp Shelby and was stunned by the devastation Katrina had caused. The coastline, and several adjacent blocks inland, was destroyed.

Just three weeks later, Hurricane Rita caused major destruction in Louisiana and Texas. I flew into Lake Charles in February 2006 for a program at Fort Polk, and the airport terminal had not yet been reconstructed. I picked up my luggage and signed for my rental car in temporary structures. The Bush administration suffered heavy criticism for its handling of Katrina, and Americans were reminded of the fiscal impact of the two wars we were waging on the other side of the world.

Following my retirement from the Foreign Service, I took up birding (sometimes called bird-watching) as a hobby. My dad was a birder and in his declining years, he needed me to tag along to carry his telescope and his oxygen tank. Skeptical at first, I began to see it as a treasure hunt and very absorbing. I learned that there are birds almost everywhere, so I would always pack a pair of binoculars for travel to LDESP seminars. Bob and Ron tolerated my hobby and would allow me to slip away from time to time. I would often contact a local birder in advance and ask to go out with them. It made me happy that we stayed in Gulfport, Mississippi, for most Camp Shelby programs, because the Mississippi Gulf Coast was a great birding location. I was lucky to connect with a legendary birder named Judy Toups in Gulfport. Judy had a gravelly voice and a warm heart. She literally wrote the book on Gulf Coast birding.[6] Trips to Fort Riley in Manhattan, Kansas, provided excellent birding because it sat adjacent to the Konza Prairie, another well-known birding location. On one of my Fort Riley trips, I enticed a Kansas State professor to take me to parts of the Konza Prairie that were otherwise inaccessible. During trips to Fort Polk in Louisiana and Fort McCoy in Wisconsin I connected with the employees responsible for managing wildlife on the bases.

I encountered one other brush with a natural disaster in the spring of 2010. A program I participated in at Fort Hood finished on Friday, April 30. I elected to fly directly to Nashville because LDESP asked me to present at their program at Fort Campbell for the Third and Fifth Special Forces Groups that was to begin the following Monday. I checked into a motel south of Nashville that was close to some birding locations I wanted to explore. It began to rain and kept raining hard all Saturday and all Sunday. I had nothing to do except watch the unfolding disaster on television. Nashville received more than thirteen inches of rain that weekend, setting records and flooding the Grand Ole Opry, among many other structures. I kept in touch with Mark Kalber, who was running the Fort Campbell program for LDESP, by text message. Monday morning, I was able to drive to the airport in Nashville and turn in my rental car and get a ride from Mark to Fort Campbell. I sat through the presentations that day and went to lunch with some of the soldiers. My presentation was scheduled for the following day (Tuesday), but the program was cancelled to allow the members of the Fifth Special Forces Group, stationed at Fort Campbell to check on their homes affected by the flooding and spend the day with their families. I flew back to Tucson, having spent a bizarre few days doing little or nothing. For this, I could hardly complain, because I collected my normal consulting rate.

In addition to disasters engineered by Mother Nature, my travel for LDESP intersected with some other horrific events. My one trip to Fort McCoy required flying into Minneapolis–St. Paul on July 31, 2007. During rush hour the following evening, the I-35W bridge over the Mississippi River in Minneapolis collapsed, killing thirteen and injuring 145 people. We were by then staying in La Crosse, Wisconsin, almost three hours away, but we were concerned about getting back to the airport. The bridge collapse was also a stark reminder that the United States was spending hundreds of billions of dollars on wars in Iraq and Afghanistan while allowing our infrastructure to crumble.

On November 5, 2009, an army psychiatrist, Maj. Nidal Hasan, shot and killed thirteen people and injured more than thirty others on the base at Fort Hood. This mass shooting took place within walking distance from the location of many of our seminars. I had been there the previous July working with the 120th Infantry Brigade. The following April, I was back in Fort Hood briefing the 3rd ACR, and emotions were still raw from Hasan's rampage.

One of the more rewarding parts of my experience consulting for the military was the chance to get to know the other members of the faculty. Faculty members came and went, but a core group produced several lasting friendships.

Michael Fahy, an anthropologist who teaches at the University of Michigan, was already a regular on our tour when I came into the program. Michael would present a module on the history of Iraq and, after a break, would do a more generic presentation on culture. Michael had mastered the art of the fake sneeze. In mid-sentence, he would pause and sneeze loudly. Someone in the front row would offer "bless you," and Michael would veer off to explain the Middle Age origin of "bless you" as an example of a cultural trait that we don't give much thought to. I was always delighted by Michael's description of how an American birthday celebration seems to a foreigner. "They sing this horrible song and set a cake on fire."

One of the classes I taught at the University of Arizona was called "Business Environment in the Middle East and North Africa." I would always spend a week of the semester on culture. I adopted a few elements from Michael's culture presentation. He would put up a picture of a sailboat and ask the audience what it was that was invisible in the picture but crucial. He compared the invisible wind in the picture to the invisible power of culture. Understanding culture and adapting to it can mean the difference between success and failure. He also skillfully explained the importance in the Middle East of multiple identities, with slides showing an average American with many identities (for example, Texan, Baptist, Cowboys fan) and an average Iraqi with many identities (for example, Sunni, urban, educated). Our unfamiliarity with the multiple identities of Iraqis with whom we dealt helped explain our many failures there.

Father Mark Sargent, a Canadian military veteran and a Catholic priest, was another popular faculty member. He is a tall extrovert with the build of an NFL linebacker. Mark's subject was Islam. His delivery was salty, humorous, and sprinkled with stories from the time he was deployed to Somalia with the Canadian Airborne Regiment in 1992 in support of a U.S.-led United Nations—sanctioned multinational force. Mark told his audiences about two missteps related to understanding Middle East culture and understanding Islam that got the regiment off to a bad start, from which it never really recovered.

The Canadians found themselves in the middle of a chaotic situation where the Somali infrastructure and national government had collapsed. They assembled the local clan leaders and, speaking through an interpreter, tried to explain they were in Somalia on a humanitarian mission of "peace and support." The discussion became heated at times, leading one of the Canadian junior officers to characterize the senior Somali clan leader as "pig-headed." He could not have chosen a more culturally inappropriate epithet. The mood changed quickly in the village where the Canadians were garrisoned, and Canadian patrols were soon shot at and soldiers wounded. To defuse the situation, the Americans printed leaflets explaining the good intentions of the multilateral force and arranged to have the leaflets drift down through the air from coalition aircraft. One bundle of leaflets, still bound by twine, was released by mistake and crashed through the roof of a local mosque. I recall Mark concluding that the situation quickly became "pear-shaped," which in the Canadian lexicon means that things went horribly wrong.

Mark's basic message was that Christianity and Islam had more commonalities than differences. Recognizing that, in addition to PowerPoint, the U.S. Army also likes organization charts, Mark drew one up to illustrate the close theological relationship between Islam, Judaism, and Christianity. God is on top and Abraham is below. Underneath Abraham comes Isaac, who oversees Judaism and Christianity, and Ismael, who oversees Islam. I thought this an inspired summary of the three Abrahamic religions and quickly adapted it for my own classes back in Arizona. Not everyone loved hearing that Islam and Christianity were closely related. Most of our programs were at military bases in places like Kansas, Texas, and Mississippi where conservative Christianity has a strong hold. Discussions occasionally got so heated that the LDESP administrator running the program or the unit commander had to step in and restore order.

Both Father Mark and I were scheduled to do a program for the Fourth Brigade Combat Team of the Tenth Mountain Division at Fort Polk in February 2006. Mark had a presentation on a Monday at Fort Hood and one the next morning at Fort Polk. Given limited flights between regional airports and seasonal storms, the only way to get to Fort Polk in time was to drive the three-hundred-plus miles. Ron Halverson drove, with Mark in the passenger seat. As luck would have it, Ron missed a moss-covered speed limit sign driving through Leesville, Louisiana, at 2:00 a.m. Tuesday. A local constable pulled Ron over. Ron explained that they were headed to Fort Polk to prepare soldiers for their next deployment. The cop went around to Mark's side and asked Mark similar questions. Mark explained he was a Catholic priest also going to teach soldiers. "What do you teach?" the constable asked. After hesitating a beat, Mark responded that he was coming to teach the fundamentals of Islam. As Ron quietly groaned, the constable shone his flashlight in Mark's eyes and asked, "Where did you learn to speak that?"

Beginning with the program at Fort Benning in January 2005, Dodge Billingsley and I participated together in multiple programs. I was amazed to learn recently from Dodge that he participated in 125 LDESP programs over the years. It may well be that Michael and Father Mark took part in even more than that. Dodge is a journalist and filmmaker who has over the years found his way into the middle of major combat operations in places like Chechnya, Afghanistan, and Iraq. He was an embed with a U.S. Marine Corps unit (3/7 India Company) when we invaded Iraq, and he was embedded with one of the last army units to leave Iraq in 2011. Dodge is founder and director of Combat Films and Research. He lives in Salt Lake City and is a fellow at the David M. Kennedy Center for International Studies at Brigham Young University.

Dodge's role in the LDESP seminars was to explain the role of the media and to suggest how our influence operations can be more proactive and less reactive. He argued that much of the wars we are engaged in are won or lost in the media. His experiences in combat and excellent stage presence gave him considerable credibility as he delivered the message that, while the media will remain independent, the military should seize opportunities to engage the media rather than insulate itself from it. Dodge faced an uphill battle at times because many in the military were conditioned to think of the media as, at best, an annoyance and, at worst, as unwitting collaborators with the insurgents.

Mazen Ayoub, like Michael, was a regular when I first began working with LDESP. Born and raised in Iraq, he now lives in Michigan. His presentation was a comprehensive look at Iraqi culture. Mazen's PowerPoint skills were among the best of all the faculty members. He used photos and fly-ins to excellent effect. His presentation was also strengthened by his understanding of American culture and the most likely mistakes a soldier might make.

Ed McCarthy is a retired army colonel and Vietnam veteran who was associated with the Army War College in Carlisle, Pennsylvania. Ed had served in Bosnia and, I assume, met Bob Tomasovic there and was present at the creation of LDESP. He taught negotiating skills and led a short module on how to use an interpreter.

Ed relied less on PowerPoint and more on audience interaction to make his points. He drew on Roger Fisher and William Ury's book *Getting to Yes*, introducing concepts like BATNA (best alternative to a negotiated solution) and ZOPA (zone of possible agreement) but drew on examples from his career or real-world examples.[7] He would play the role of someone coming into an auto dealership determined to buy a car. He would ask someone from the audience to play the car salesman. Ed would make it clear that he had to have the car and tell the salesman exactly how much he could afford. There wasn't much left for the salesman to do except make the sale on great terms for the dealership. That would lead to a discussion of better ways for the car buyer to proceed.

Ed and I were presenters at a program at Fort Dix in New Jersey in March 2009. He was proud of a portable GPS device he carried with him that he could stick with a suction cup on the windshield of his rental car. Ed's wife had come to join him in her own car. He was planning to return his rental car to the Philadelphia airport, so I asked to go along. I had been picked up by the LDESP protocol officer for that seminar, and I needed to rent a car for personal travel after the program to visit my son, who lived in Delaware, and another friend who lived in New Jersey. Ed set the GPS to take us to the airport, but before long we were off on a backcountry road that didn't look promising. His wife was in the car behind us looking quite puzzled. After a couple of more tries, we still hadn't found a road that looked like it would take us to the airport. Finally, Ed broke the code. The GPS was set to avoid paying tolls. Anyone familiar with that area would realize that you can't get to the Philadelphia airport without paying tolls. We eventually reached the airport in an hour and a half. Using an old-fashioned map, I drove back to Fort Dix in my rental car in forty-five minutes.

Michael Rubin started coming to LDESP seminars perhaps a year or two after I did and quickly became a regular. He is bright, confident, and very conservative, as befits a resident scholar at the American Enterprise Institute. Michael worked in the Pentagon briefly and spent some time in 2004 working for the Coalition Provisional Authority in Iraq. I thought of him foremost as an Iranian expert, but he could hold his own on Iraq, Saudi Arabia, Turkey, or virtually any Middle East topic.

Michael was a proud conservative and had a sense of humor about it. One day we were riding together to or from the seminar location on some military base, and we passed a homeless encampment. Michael looked at us with a twinkle in his eye and wondered aloud why these camp members couldn't just pull it together and go out and find jobs.

Col. Tom Norton, a retired U.S. Army chaplain, lectured on ethics and values. He started out with a joke based on his Tennessee provenance. Tom recounted that his former girlfriend, with the improbable name of Modine Gunch, started a business combining veterinary and taxidermy services.[8] The sign on her business bragged, "Either way, you get your dog back." Tom's analysis of the My Lai massacre as an example of leadership failure was very revealing to me. The core of his presentation was a collection of scenarios involving, for example, questionable orders, the observation of questionable behavior, and dealing with petty corruption on the part of Iraqi counterparts. He would outline the situation and then ask the soldiers in the audience what they would do. There were no easy answers, and I applauded Tom's ability to get the soldiers thinking about such dilemmas before they encountered them on the battlefield. The news of our heinous mistreatment of prisoners at Abu Ghraib had broken before I was involved with LDESP. The Abu Ghraib scandal did great damage to the U.S. image and was a stark example of why ethics training was an essential part of preparation for deployment.

Over my seven years with LDESP, I worked with many other quality people. Tim Carney, who first got me involved with LDESP, was a fellow faculty member in several of the earlier seminars I worked. I lost my luggage flying to Georgia for a program at Fort Benning in January 2005. It was the first of six times an airline lost my luggage over the next two years. I delivered my lecture at Fort Benning wearing my jeans and a shirt and jacket borrowed from Tim. Listening to other presentations at Fort Benning, I found myself sitting next to a charming woman with a pleasant southern accent named Sandra Mackey. I had read two of her books, one about Saudi Arabia and the other (*The Reckoning*) about Iraq, which became required reading for troops deploying being deployed there. We swapped stories about Saudi Arabia and Iraq over the course of the seminar.

Ambassador Peter Tomsen, whom I had known since the mid-1980s, was a fellow faculty member at several of the Afghan programs I attended. Peter had been special envoy to Afghanistan and was working hard on a massive book about the country. I first met Gary Guertner following his retirement in Tucson from the position of dean at the George Marshall Center for European Security Studies in Garmisch-Partenkirchen, Germany. Gary became a fellow adjunct in the University of Arizona's School of Government and Public Policy. He was interested in the work I was doing with LDESP, so I introduced him to Bob Tomasovic and we ended up doing several seminars together. Scott Carpenter was an infrequent participant in LDESP seminars. I first met Scott in Baghdad, where he worked for the CPA in putting together the Governing Council that included Aqila al-Hashemi. Scott subsequently joined the State Department as a political appointee and, after a stint in the Human Rights Bureau, became a deputy assistant secretary in NEA.

Andrew Garfield, a frequent and thoughtful participant, was a former British military (later civilian) intelligence officer. His presentations were called "Winning the War of Ideas" and "Exploitation of the Human Terrain." I learned much from his lectures, but I recall him mainly as breathlessly arriving from some other commitment or breathlessly leaving for a subsequent commitment. Abbas Kadhim was a fellow lecturer at LDESP seminars during the latter years of my participation. Abbas was, at the time, an assistant professor at the Naval Postgraduate School in Monterey. He persuaded me to write a chapter on Saudi Arabia for the *Handbook of Governance in the Middle East and North Africa*, which he edited for Routledge. Routledge paid me the handsome sum of one hundred British pounds for the chapter. I thought it a bargain and I hope Routledge did as well. Kathleen Ridolfo was a fellow participant late in my association with LDESP. She went on to become executive director of the Sultan Qaboos Cultural Center, replacing my former DCM in Oman, Liz McKune. The University of Arizona has been working on and with Oman in recent years, so I have seen Kathleen in Tucson. Bob Kitrinos was working for the State Department's Bureau of Intelligence and Research (INR) when we first met. He went on work at the NSC, then the Joint Staff, and is now with Booz Allen Hamilton. Bob had an encyclopedic knowledge of the various tribes and ethnic groups in Iraq.

I remember well a program at Camp Shelby on Afghanistan but have forgotten the name of one of my fellow presenters, who was a young Afghan-American woman. She likely delivered a presentation on Afghan politics or Afghan culture. Camp Shelby didn't have many dining choices, so we usually ended up having lunch at a barbeque place just outside the gate. The inside walls were covered with drawings of large cartoon pigs. This is "the Muslim hell," she told us.

On another program at Fort Hood, one of my fellow participants was Ahmed Ali, an Iraqi-American associated with the Washington Institute of Near East Policy. Several of us found ourselves at the end of the day with bottles of beer but no bottle opener. After vain attempts to get an opener from the hotel management, Ahmed said he knew of a way to pop the caps. He put a bottle in his teeth and sure enough, the cap came off. Soon we all were enjoying open bottles of beer but sipping them slowly because we weren't sure how long Ahmed's teeth would hold up.

The LDESP staff ran a tight ship. They handled seamlessly airport pick-ups and drop-offs, as well as hotel reservations. We often had a pre-meeting where we learned a little bit about the unit we were briefing and were warned against "faculty fratricide" (airing disagreements we might have with fellow faculty members). Faculty members lined up at the beginning of a program and each of us briefly introduced ourselves and our topics. The LDESP staff brought their own sound system and video projection equipment. They also set up wireless systems (one for the staff and one for the faculty), allowing us to work on our presentations and catch up on the news. I would almost always listen carefully to someone presenting for the first time, but over time I zoned out during the presentations of regular faculty members that I knew by heart.

Complex Solutions, a defense contractor headquartered in Hawaii with an office in Monterey, handled contracts and expense vouchers. Camber acquired this company in late 2007, but that barely impacted us. I cannot recall having any disputes with how they processed my payments. For years I would communicate with Shiba Sumeshwar from Camber. I finally met her in person when we held a program in Monterey.

I gradually developed a stable of presentations for both Iraq and Afghanistan. Sometimes I presented on the stakes in Iraq or in Afghanistan. Other times I presented on Iraq's neighbors or Afghanistan's neighbors. Sometimes I would combine the stakes and neighbors together in one presentation. Occasionally, when LDESP asked me to, I would do a presentation that drilled down into the weeds of Iraqi politics and economics. I began including maps of countries and photos of leaders in my PowerPoints.

In December 2009, Bob invited me, along with several other regular presenters in LDESP seminars, to a one-day workshop in Denver on PowerPoint presentations. I picked up useful tips and received valuable feedback from the instructors, which proved helpful for my teaching. Not only did the training make my presentations to my students better, but I soon encouraged my students to develop their own PowerPoints and gave them appropriate feedback.

In December 2006, the Iraqi government executed Saddam Hussein, in clumsy fashion. That same month, FM 3-24 was published and COIN (counterinsurgency) became the new religion, seen as the antidote to our stumbling performances in both Iraq and Afghanistan. General David Petraeus was the driving force behind the new doctrine. I did not meet him in Iraq in 2003, but I understood his impact because he was willing to take on Bremer's de-Ba'athification policy and because his 101st Airborne Division seemed to be succeeding in Mosul, in contrast to our poor performance in the rest of the country. Petraeus used his time as commander of the Combined Arms Center at Fort Leavenworth to rewrite the U.S. Army's counterinsurgency doctrine.

I felt a degree of vindication because I had long been arguing that our approach to terrorism was counterproductive. My briefings on both Iraq and Afghanistan always contained a segment on terrorism. I would begin by asking the audience to define terrorism, and I would keep pressing until I got across the point that terrorism is a tactic and that the "War on Terror" was a war on a tactic. We would eventually agree that terrorism constituted violence against noncombatants for political reasons. The violence is not senseless, and the victims are not the real targets. Terrorism is political theater. Terrorists are trying to reach a broader audience, and their symbiotic relationship with modern media helps them get the message out. I would ask the audience to consider what would happen if a terrorist event occurred and nobody ever found out about it.

Until FM 3-24, the U.S. government approach was what I dubbed the "Rawhide" approach. I would quote or occasionally sing badly a line from Frankie Lane's song, "Rawhide." "Don't try to understand 'em, just rope 'em, throw and brand 'em." That song hit the pop charts in 1958, long before most members of my audience were born. But thirty years later, the movie *The Blues Brothers* featured a memorable rendition of "Rawhide" by John Belushi and Dan Ackroyd.

I would then ask the audience to distinguish between a terrorist and an insurgent. An insurgency, which is what we were dealing with in both Iraq and Afghanistan, is an organized movement aimed at bringing down a government or driving out a foreign occupation. Terrorism is a tactic that outgunned insurgents often employ. Finally, I would introduce the concept of supply and demand into the discussion of terrorism. Much as in the case of our country's so-called "war on drugs," we focused on supply. We have over the years seized vast quantities of illegal drugs and, yet, the availability of these drugs never seems to decrease. Our focus on the supply side of terrorism leads us to kill or capture as many as possible but, if anything, this leads to an increase in the number of terrorists. Kill one and create ten more. I urged that we focus on the demand side. When you have a bunch of people trying to kill you and they prove to be good at it, it makes sense to ask why. Understanding is not condoning. Understanding is not justification. Our reluctance to probe the demand for terrorism probably stems from fear that it will lead to politically sensitive areas like our support for Israel. It also leads us away from the comfortable assumption that we are always on the side of "good" and the other side is pure "evil."

Whether I was delivering an Iraq or an Afghan program, I always included a slide about Arab or Muslim views of the United States, which would lead into a couple of interactive exercises designed to encourage the soldiers in the audience to examine their own stereotypes of Arabs and Muslims. In one, I would put up a picture of an Afghan woman in a *birka* alongside a cartoon woman in a bikini. I would explain that the birka represented the *abaya* in Iraq or the *chador* in Iran. Then, I would ask them to tell me which was more oppressive to women, the birka or the bikini, and why. This exercise was inspired by an op-ed I had read years before by two women. The typical response was that the birka was more oppressive because women were compelled to wear it, while wearing a bikini was a matter of choice. If I was lucky, someone would offer an alternative view noting the social pressure on young American women to wear a bikini. The topic usually sparked energy in the audience and often provoked the few women soldiers in the room to speak out. I made sure that the soldiers understood that Iraqi (or Afghan) women often could choose to wear the concealing garment because they felt more comfortable doing so, while young American women are bombarded with images of perfect bodies, which most women are not able to emulate. This can lead to psychological issues and, in extreme cases, to conditions like anorexia or bulimia. I would conclude by assuring the audience that there is no right or wrong answer.

I would then turn to a discussion of movies, which can reinforce our negative stereotypes of Arabs and Muslims. My favorite example was *Rules of Engagement*, starring Tommy Lee Jones and Samuel L. Jackson. The film included a scene in which an Arab mob surrounds the U.S. ambassador's house in Yemen. Jackson was the marine general who led a detachment to rescue the ambassador but that, in the process, killed several of the rioters. Most of the movie features the general's military trial, with Jones as the defense attorney. I would ask those who saw the movie if they remembered what the Arabs were angry about. Nobody could answer because the movie script provided no explanation. Presumably, they were angry because they were Arabs and that was what Arabs are like. I then turned to another movie, *Three Kings*, starring George Clooney, Ice Cube, and Mark Wahlberg, which told the story of three U.S. soldiers who went into Iraq after the 1990–91 Gulf War looking for fortune. During the adventure, they met several Iraqis, who were portrayed as individuals with personalities. The Iraqis' good lines rendered them fully developed characters.

I was comfortable with birka versus bikini and contrasting movie discussions because they energized the audience, even though they were a bit edgy. Success consisted of getting the soldiers to rethink the stereotypes I suspected that most came into the room with.

I came to Monterey in March 2010 to present to the 116th Brigade Combat Team. Retired Lt. Gen. Tom Burnette was there in the role of senior mentor for the seminar. Each faculty member was required to send his or her presentation to the LDESP staff in advance, so they could be copied and bound into a volume that was distributed to each soldier. Burnette, who I had not met before and who may have been at his first LDESP seminar, was determined to be proactive. He went through the PowerPoint slides and didn't like what he saw when he reviewed mine. Burnette sent Ron Halverson to see me with a copy of my presentation. Ron showed me the marked-up presentation with angry red lines drawn through about half the slides. Ron was apologetic, but he was a retired colonel and Burnette was a retired three-star general, and his message was that I had to change my presentation. I was at first stunned and then angry. Colonel T had always sought outside experts with experience on the ground to fill out the faculty. The strength of the overall program in my view was that the experts were given free rein to present what they believed to be relevant. Though the LDESP administrators would make suggestions, they rarely leaned on faculty members to change the substance of their presentations. I balked at altering my presentation and told Ron that, if LDESP didn't like what I was doing, then I would be happy to return to Tucson.

I ended up giving my presentation on St. Patrick's Day in Monterey with little change except the addition of a traditional Irish blessing at the end. That was the end of the road, however, for my standard Iraq presentation. No doubt because of Burnette's intervention, I never again received an invitation to deliver either the Iraq stakes or the Afghan stakes presentation.

A week or two after the Monterey seminar, Ron contacted me and asked if I was would tackle a new subject for an upcoming seminar in Fort Hood. At the time (April 2010), another new religion had been sweeping Washington, dubbed the "whole of government" approach (WGA). WGA had its origins in Britain and Australia. The Organization of Economic Cooperation and Development (OECD) picked it up in 2006, and the Obama administration later embraced it. The basic concept was jaw-droppingly obvious. Various government departments ought to work across organizational boundaries to get things done.

Despite my bold assertions with Ron in Monterey, I didn't really want to end my consulting relationship with LDESP. It was lucrative, fun, and rewarding. I thanked Ron for the opportunity and embraced the new challenge. So I embarked on another crash project to put together a "whole-of-government" presentation in time to for a seminar for the Third Armored Cavalry Regiment at Fort Hood in late April. It proved a good investment of time because I used a version of the presentation for seven more seminars over the next year and a half. We changed the name to "unity of effort."

After several years of flying back and forth to LDESP seminars, I was beginning to feel like a real road warrior. I was amassing airline miles on United and American, and was racking up Hilton Honors (we almost always stayed at Hampton or Hilton Garden Inn) and Hertz Gold points. In addition to occasional holidays with my wife and family, I also was involved in two other activities that required I fly somewhere else from Tucson. I held a board position for a nonprofit involved in international exchange called the Association for International Practical Training, and I attended three board meetings a year, usually in Columbia or Baltimore, Maryland. Additionally, I served as a Woodrow Wilson Visiting Fellow, spending a week at small colleges and universities once or twice a year. I also made a couple of presentations for Department of Defense organizations in the Washington area that were not affiliated with LDESP. My frequent flying peaked in 2007, when I counted seventy-seven legs (each involving a takeoff and a landing). I used the miles, among other things, to treat myself to upgrades on all flights back and forth to Germany.

As impressive as my travel was, it paled in comparison to that of Bob Tomasovic. I remember Bob telling us once that he was on the road nearly three hundred days every year. This elevated him to the most elite status on his favorite airline, United. The movie *Up in the Air* came out in 2009 about a business executive who traveled constantly and whose primary goal in life was to achieve million-mile status. We joked that the movie starred George Clooney playing Bob Tomasovic.

Bill Spores was another member of the LDESP staff who had logged an impressive number of air miles. I agreed to present a program in Fort Riley in early December 2009. It was the end of the semester and I had used up my "grace" days, the days I allowed myself to miss class. I flew to Kansas City after my Monday afternoon class, arriving around midnight. Bill picked me up for the two-hour drive to Manhattan, Kansas. For the first hour of the drive, Bill regaled me with what he had learned about the use of airline miles and how to choose the perfect seat in different types of airplanes. I fell sound asleep. The next morning, I gave my presentation, then hitched a ride back to the Kansas City airport with Dodge, arriving back in Tucson in time to teach my Wednesday morning class.

The time I spent working with LDESP was personally rewarding. I worked with quality people and it made me a more knowledgeable and effective teacher and public speaker. The best part of the experience was the extraordinary sense of camaraderie that existed, not just among the regular faculty members but also among the faculty members and the LDESP staff. The staff were invariably friendly, competent, and helpful. Individuals came from all manner of different backgrounds, including the military, academia, think tanks, and government. We represented a diversity of ethnicities, religions, and political views. I looked forward to every LDESP event because I knew I would be working with people I genuinely liked and who liked me. Perhaps the sobering reality of working with soldiers going into harm's way and perhaps not returning contributed to our embrace of our diversity. Many of us remain good friends to this day. Much as I liked to joke about Colonel T's frequent-flyer status and his serial mispronunciation of Oman when he introduced me, I can't help but come away with enormous respect for his success in selecting and molding staff and faculty into a team that performed with consistent excellence. I have trouble reconciling my LDESP experience with the toxicity and hatred that seems to characterize much of American politics today.

Michael helped me recall one magic moment from our mutual association with LDESP. We were in Honolulu in July 2008 working with an MP brigade, and at the end of a long day spent sitting in a strictly utilitarian room in the Schofield Barracks. Father Mark challenged Michael and me to meet him at dawn the next morning on Waikiki Beach for a swim. The temperature of both air and water was perfect, the beach was pristine, and there was little sound other than that of the gently breaking waves. Michael said, in his account to me, "If you had told me only a couple of years ago, that I would be swimming at 5:00 a.m. in the waters off Waikiki with an ambassador and a Catholic priest, I would have said you were crazy." I reportedly responded, "The feeling is mutual, Mr. Anthropologist." We then speculated on what would happen if an anthropologist, an ambassador, and a Catholic priest walked into a bar.

I came away with a great deal of respect for the U.S. military. I told myself that equipping officers and senior NCOs with the basic skills needed for stability and peace operations was saving lives and giving us a better chance of success in Iraq and Afghanistan. Robert Unruh, from Tucson, died in Iraq in September 2004. I am sobered when I wonder how many of the other soldiers we helped train died or were wounded in Iraq and Afghanistan.

While I confess that I spent a great deal of time talking to fellow faculty members, I also befriended a great number of soldiers. We would talk during breaks and sometimes would go to the base DFAC (dining facility) or a fast-food restaurant on or near the base. A substantial percentage of the soldiers were from what we have come to call "flyover" country, particularly those in National Guard or reserve units. I listened to them talking about the jobs they had in their hometowns and how multiple deployments had disrupted their lives. I rarely heard bitterness. Most believed that their country needed them and that they had a job to do. Part of me was angry at our political leaders for sending these men and women to Iraq and Afghanistan to carry out missions that made little sense and had little chance of success.

So much depended on leadership. I do not mean just the president and the secretary of defense but also the leadership of the unit we were training. The unit commander was most often a colonel. Some commanders sat in the front row throughout the seminar and asked penetrating questions of us. That would guarantee an audience that was alert and attentive. If the unit commander was out of the room or looking bored, we would be looking at an audience of glazed eyes, with one or two who were fast asleep.

For the more than seven years I worked with LDESP, my compensation came out of the DoD budget. I was working for the military and had no connection whatsoever with the Department of State. In this role, I was trying to transfer knowledge and skills I had acquired during nearly thirty years as a Foreign Service Officer to our soldiers and marines. They, rather than America's professional diplomats, were the Americans most likely to be on the ground interacting with Iraqis and Afghans.

When the new counterinsurgency doctrine emerged in late 2006, I was a strong supporter. Over time, however, I concluded that asking the U.S. military to do everything that it takes to make COIN operations effective is asking too much. After the 9/11 attack, we asked the U.S. military to handle governance, reconstruction, and development. These are not tasks that the military is comfortable with or can be made comfortable with. Most senior military

214

officers understand this and want the Department of State and the U.S. Agency for International Development to create the civilian capacity to support the military. State and USAID have been slow to respond. A U.S. division commander was heard to complain, "I feel the civilian surge lapping around my ankles." Despite all the brave talk about "whole of government" and unity of effort, Congress simply hasn't provided the funding needed for State and USAID to restore the appropriate balance between diplomacy, economic assistance, and force.

CONCLUSION

Toward an Effective U.S. Diplomacy

There are three main ways a nation can protect or advance its interests with respect to other nations: diplomacy, economic "carrots and sticks," and military force. We have used military force extensively since the 9/11 attack and the results have been, at best, disappointing. One can hardly blame the military, which has been doing the best it could to carry out the flawed policies of our political leaders. We have also made extensive use of economic sanctions. Economic sanctions do not work well unless they are carefully targeted and closely tied to a diplomatic strategy. Too often, the general population suffers, leaving the leadership unmoved. The amount of money appropriated for economic development in poorer countries remains embarrassingly small as a percentage of our gross domestic product. Reflecting on how little we have achieved, and this at great cost in lives and resources since the end of the cold war, with a strategy that relies heavily on economic sanctions and military force, it might make sense to try a little more diplomacy and development assistance. Diplomacy works better if it is carrying out by capable and experienced diplomats.

The United States has over the years created a thoroughly professional military. There are no easy ways to become a general or an admiral. You must begin as a second lieutenant or an ensign and undergo an appropriate combination of training and command experience to win your first star. An ambassador is the diplomatic counterpart to a general officer. A number of our ambassadors have earned their positions following a rigorous combination of training and practical experience. Many others, roughly a third of our ambassadors, are political appointees. Senate confirmation hearings for political appointees can be embarrassing for those who haven't visited the country to which they are appointed and who haven't taken the time for in-depth briefings. Some may not even have read the Wikipedia page for the country they will be going to.

There is a story, which may be apocryphal, but that is well-known to many of us in the Foreign Service that illustrates why entrusting sensitive diplomatic jobs to amateurs makes no sense. Malcolm Toon was a well-respected professional Foreign Service Officer who was our ambassador in Moscow during the height of the cold war. He attended a social event, and was approached by a navy admiral. During the conversation the admiral allowed that he would be retiring from the navy soon. He thought that he would like his next job to be that of an ambassador. Toon looked at the admiral and said, without a trace of a smile, that he was about to retire from the Foreign Service himself and would like to be captain of an aircraft carrier in his next job.

A Dunford family story makes a similar point. My uncle Jim Dunford retired as a captain in the U.S. Navy. He was for several years chief of staff for Admiral Hyman Rickover. Uncle Jim told me the story, also perhaps apocryphal, of an engineer called upon to fix a boiler in a homeowner's cellar. The engineer looked over the boiler for several minutes and then gave it a sharp kick. The boiler started right up. The engineer submitted an invoice for $601. The homeowner protested. "All you did was give it a kick." The engineer replied, "I'm only charging you one dollar for kicking it. The other $600 is for knowing where to kick it and how hard." An experienced diplomat knows where to deliver a message and how to deliver the message so that it has the greatest effect. As George Kennan wrote, the communication should be delivered with "maximum accuracy, imagination, tact and good sense."[1]

The practice of distributing ambassadorships to political allies or large campaign contributors long predates my time in the Foreign Service. Up until the mid-twenties, there were two separate career services: a consular service and a diplomatic service. The

Rogers Act (Foreign Service Act of 1924) combined the two services into the "Foreign Service of the United States." From that day forward career Foreign Service Officers worked side by side with political appointees to design and implement the institutions that have dominated global diplomacy since World War II. The Rogers Act envisioned a merit-based system based on the highest professional standards. In recent years, we have moved further away rather than closer to meeting that goal.

This narrative begins during the last decade of the cold war. The U.S. Foreign Service was far less professional then than the diplomatic services of countries like the UK, France, and Germany, but the 1980s was a time when career diplomats were in a far better place than they are today. Although political appointees ran the majority of the embassies in pleasant places like Europe, Canada, Australia, and New Zealand, career Foreign Service Officers ran most of the embassies in the Middle East and North Africa. Morocco, one of the more attractive places to live in the region, was an exception. Cairo was far more important, and professionals like Roy Atherton and Henry Precht were entrusted with managing that key relationship. Quality young officers, many of whom went on to run their own embassies in later years, staffed it. The embassy managed the relationship in partnership with the Bureau of Near East and South Asian Affairs in Washington, which was also run by real pros like Dick Murphy and Arnie Raphel.

By the time I came to Cairo, I had logged fifteen years as a Foreign Service Officer. My apprenticeship consisted of working as a rotational junior officer in four different embassy sections in Quito and as an economic-commercial officer in Helsinki for three years. Based on my performance in those assignments, I earned tenure. Tenure is a certification by the Foreign Service that I had the potential to serve as a Foreign Service Officer over a normal career span.

I ran two separate divisions in the State Department's Office of International Trade, the Economic Bureau's Planning and Analysis Staff, and the Office of Development Finance. I was seconded for a year and a half to the Executive Office of the President to work as a deputy assistant U.S. trade representative. The State Department provided me with two months of basic training when I first entered the Foreign Service, four months of Spanish-language training, nine months of Finnish-language training, and six months of in-house economic training. The State Department also financed an academic year of graduate economic training at Stanford University. Many of my colleagues had assembled a similar package of training and experience. Our résumés were very different, but the depth of training and experience was comparable. Those entering the Foreign Service today do not have the benefit of a training assignment as a rotational junior officer like I had in Quito. They must choose a specialization before getting any on-the-ground experience in the Foreign Service.

Just prior to my assignment to Cairo, I was promoted across the "senior threshold." The four senior ranks in the Foreign Service are roughly equivalent to generals and admirals in the military. Once I settled into my new job in Cairo in 1981, I realized that Embassy Cairo was the career Foreign Service at its best. Running the Embassy Cairo economic section drew upon every bit of my training and experience (except the language training), but I was far from the ideal candidate. I did not speak Arabic and I had no Middle East experience. Neither Spanish nor Finnish was particularly useful in Cairo. I learned by doing and by working for and with career Foreign Service Officers like Atherton, Veliotes, and Precht. They thoroughly understood the culture of the Middle East and they had mastered the practice of diplomacy. After three years, my Arabic remained rudimentary, but I was comfortable working in the Middle East and I had learned a great deal more about how to be an effective diplomat.

Moving back to Washington as the director of Egyptian affairs was an easy transition. I knew, from working with Henry Precht and seeing how he related to the Office of Egyptian Affairs, what the embassy expected of me. The NEA Bureau was responsible for the Middle East, North Africa, and South Asia in 1984.[2] NEA was known to those who served there or who had served there as the "mother" bureau and was considered one of the most well-run bureaus in the State Department. April Glaspie, Phil Wilcox, and Peter Tomsen, all talented career officers, were fellow office directors. George Shultz, the secretary of state, relied heavily on the bureau and, as a result, bureau morale was high. I was working with some of the best the Foreign Service had to offer, like Dick Murphy, Arnie Raphel, and Frank Wisner. On a daily basis I was in touch with Embassy Cairo and Egypt's ambassador in Washington. I never felt "out-of-the-loop" on any issue involving Egypt.

The Shultz era was far from perfect for Middle East policy. Al Haig's decision to give a green or yellow light to Israel's invasion of Lebanon led to the rise of Hezbollah and to one crisis after another. That was followed by a series of amateurish decisions emanating from the National Security Council (NSC) known as Iran-Contra. The lack of progress in the Middle East peace process led to a Palestinian uprising in Gaza and the West Bank known as the Intifada. Shultz, however, relied heavily on the NEA bureau and his embassies in the Middle East and North Africa to manage the many crises that afflicted the region. Officers serving in NEA in Washington or in our embassies in the Middle East and North Africa had a great deal of job satisfaction because we knew Shultz relied on us and we knew that he had our backs. I did, during that era, witness three of our finest diplomats get pulled from the field because they were scapegoats for policy decisions that went wrong. Henry Precht never got to be an ambassador because of his association with our Iran policy. Nick Veliotes was scapegoated for Mubarak's embarrassment in the *Achille Lauro* affair, and Hume Horan took the heat when the Saudis were caught secretly buying missiles from the Chinese. Shultz might have done more to defend all three men.

Training should not end once Foreign Service Officers reach senior status. Following three years in the Office of Egyptian Affairs, I lobbied successfully to be admitted to the senior seminar, the nine-month State Department equivalent to the National War College or one of the other war colleges. Half of the participants were from other U.S. government agencies, and the seminar was an intense education about what makes the United States tick. Although I was pulled from the seminar two months early to fill the unexpected gap in Riyadh owing to Hume Horan's departure, the months I spent contributed significantly to my understanding of my own country. It also allowed me to focus on the qualities that make a good leader before I was thrown into an actual embassy leadership position. I made many new friends in the seminar who contributed to my professional growth.

After I retired from the State Department, the senior seminar was abolished. I searched in vain for some reference in the media to the sudden disappearance of this important building block of a professional foreign service. There was always tension in the Department of State between training and filling open positions at home and abroad. Unless the secretary of state is a strong believer in the value of training, the need of the personnel office to fill vacant positions will always win out. George Shultz strongly believed training was important, and that is why the National Foreign Affairs Training Center in Arlington carries his name.

After some digging, I learned that the senior seminar was abolished in 2003 during the George W. Bush administration.[3] Then-Secretary of State Colin Powell was reportedly a strong supporter of training, including senior training, but he did not like the senior seminar. It required four full-time employees, it was expensive, and it trained only a select group of senior officers. From what I can gather, more than once the associate dean who ran the program was plucked for what the State Department considered a more important assignment. The department had established during that period a "capstone" training course for all new senior officers, which to the State Department leadership made the senior seminar seem redundant.

After I arrived in Riyadh and even before the change in administrations in January 1989, I noticed that Department of State support for the embassy in Riyadh was much less "hands on" than support for the embassy in Cairo had been. The Office of Arabian Peninsula Affairs had to support seven different embassies. High-level U.S. government attention to Saudi Arabia had also faded rapidly after the Chinese missile crisis receded and the Iran-Iraq War ended. When Jim Baker took over as secretary of state, his management style was markedly different from that of George Shultz. Baker thought that the regional bureaus held too much power. He was particularly intent on remodeling the NEA bureau, which he reportedly thought was filled with FSOs who were too sympathetic to Arab positions and not sufficiently supportive of Israel. John Kelly, whose Middle East experience was modest, was his choice as assistant secretary with a mandate to clean out the bureau. David Ransom, who directed the Office of Arabian Peninsula Affairs during my first two years in Riyadh, did not get along well with Kelly.

Sitting in Riyadh, I did not really understand the dynamics in Washington, but I sensed that the close cooperation I was accustomed to between Cairo and Washington no longer existed for me in Riyadh. During the nine months of Walt Cutler's second tour in Riyadh, there were few significant events in U.S.-Saudi relations, and Walt was less concerned about the weak support he received from the Department of State. When Chas Freeman arrived, he brought an ambitious agenda, and he soon grew unhappy with the level of Washington inattention and incompetence.

Iraq invaded Kuwait in August 1990, and Riyadh became the center of attention for the next seven months for the Washington foreign-policy establishment. Baker, Cheney, and Powell did a superb job of managing the major elements of the U.S. response. But the unfolding crisis soon exposed the weakness of the centralization of decision making among a few individuals on the seventh floor of the State Department. The marginalization of NEA under Kelly meant that we had little support from Washington on issues that did not interest Baker, like managing the security and anxiety of American citizens in Saudi Arabia. Working-level NEA hands had no ability to answer our pleas for guidance. Our inability to get the answers we believed we needed made us increasingly angry. Chas became notorious for his messages chastising Washington officials for their stupidity and incompetence. While he was usually right, my experience over the years was that people who are criticized for being stupid and incompetent do not believe that they are stupid and incompetent and react badly. Chas paid a price.[4]

Baker did not often look to either NEA or his embassy in Riyadh for recommendations on the way forward. The result was often a huge disconnect between the way Baker and his close associates saw the situation and the way we in Riyadh saw it. For example, Baker was convinced that the Saudis could easily absorb the costs of the war, including the $16.3 billion invoice we presented them. We not only did the financial analysis, but we also saw the anguish in the eyes of Saudi officials when we presented the bill. We argued that taking such a financial hit would cause real pain. Baker prevailed, and we transferred most, if not all, of the costs of the Gulf War to the Saudis and other countries. The seeds for the rise of bin Laden and al-Qaeda were planted and we eventually found ourselves in wars that cost us trillions of dollars.

We managed the seven months of Desert Shield and Desert Storm despite Washington dysfunctionality largely because of the superb working relationship between Chas and Norm Schwarzkopf and their respective staffs. We hosted the hordes of unnecessary visitors, we set up multiple briefings for American citizens, and we eventually secured gas masks and military flights home for Americans who wanted them. We fought off the mindless bureaucratic requirements coming from the State Department personnel system. When I was director of Egyptian affairs, I would run interference with the personnel system on behalf of the Embassy Cairo leadership. When I was in Riyadh, there was nobody in NEA willing or able to play that role.

I arrived in Oman just before the election of Bill Clinton as president. New administrations take time to get organized, and the Clinton administration was no exception. They seized on the concept of reinventing government to make it more effective and less costly. This led to USAID Administrator Brian Atwood's decision to close twenty-one aid missions, including the one in Oman. I understood Atwood's thinking. He was under pressure to cut costs and had to fend off Senate Foreign Relations Chairman Jesse Helms, who sought to abolish USAID. Oman's need for development assistance was real but not compelling. What I do not understand was the supine posture of the Department of State. Somebody, somewhere in State should have known that the aid program was a *quid pro quo* for our ability to pre-position Air

Force equipment on three Omani air bases. It was inconceivable then and now that State did not give me the chance to explain to the Omani government well in advance of the announcement the reasoning behind the decision. Vice President Al Gore himself paid the price for this oversight, having to travel to Oman in the middle of an already packed Middle East trip to save our military arrangements with the country.

By the time I returned to government in 1997, reinventing government had been transformed into further diluting the clout of career diplomats and reducing their number. The Office of Egyptian Affairs had disappeared as an independent entity, as had the economic section in Cairo. Political appointees were routinely placed in State's regional and functional bureaus at the deputy assistant secretary level and even below. The Middle East peace process was being handled almost entirely by non-career people. Since the Reagan administration, presidents and their administrations have bought into the notion that career Foreign Service Officers cannot be trusted to manage the U.S. relationship with Israel. The quality of our diplomacy suffered, as did the morale of professionals in the Foreign Service. The results, or lack thereof, in our Middle East peace process diplomacy in the 1990s and since speak for themselves. The MENA-BANK initiative died because of negligence. Keeping it alive was important but never urgent, and it expired because our political leaders didn't take the time or put in the effort to make it work.

Throughout my career I understood that protecting Israel was an important U.S. interest and a moral imperative. Our interest in Israel, however, must be balanced against other interests, such as oil, counterterrorism, and nonproliferation of weapons of mass destruction. Protection of Israel should also be consistent with our values, which include the promotion of democracy and human rights and with the provision of development assistance to less-fortunate nations. Our interest in protecting Israel should not require blind support of every Israeli government policy (for example, continued expansion of settlements in the West Bank). In fact, such unquestioning support undermines Israel's long-term survival as a democratic Jewish state.

The shock and trauma of the September 11, 2001, attack further accelerated the decline of our diplomacy. While we had a capable and highly respected secretary of state in Colin Powell, he could not compete with Vice President Dick Cheney and Secretary of Defense Donald Rumsfeld for President George W. Bush's ear. Cheney and Rumsfeld were strongly influenced by neoconservative views that the response to the terrorist threat required strong military action to remake the Middle East, and that Iraq was the place to begin. State dutifully began to put together the building blocks for a strategy to remake Iraq. Rumsfeld ignored the Future of Iraq project and tried mightily to keep Foreign Service professionals out of the action. He did not want to hear career diplomats whine about the many reasons remaking Iraq into a Jeffersonian democracy would be difficult. Some of us made it to Iraq, but our ability to influence decisions about Iraq's future was minimal. The Bush administration did find a retired career FSO (Jerry Bremer) to run Iraq, but he was Rumsfeld's man calling plays straight out of Rumsfeld's playbook. Many superb career FSOs, like Dick Jones and Ryan Crocker, were brought in eventually to try to get Iraq back on track, but the damage of Bremer's initial decisions could not be undone. The seeds for ISIS had been planted.

I quietly slipped out of Iraq in mid-June 2003 and returned to retirement in Tucson. Neither the State Department that hired me to go to Iraq nor the Department of Defense for which I had worked in Iraq showed any interest in debriefing me. After-action reviews have never really been a part of the culture of the Foreign Service. Overlaps are rare and lessons, once learned, usually must be learned all over again.

Consistent with Rosa Brooks's narrative in her book "*How Everything Became War and the Military Became Everything*," the only real future for someone with my professional skills lay in working for the military.[5] The military was also where the money was. That the military reached out to retired ambassadors like Tim Carney and me directly rather than asking the Department of State for help reflected the increasing irrelevance of State. Working for Colonel T and his capable staff and getting to know the extraordinary individuals that Colonel T recruited for the LDESP program was a highlight of my career. The U.S. Army does perform after-action reviews (AARS), as I learned in South Korea in 2004.

Six years later in April 2010, I received an invitation to participate in a Culture Summit, held in a hotel northwest of Tucson. The event was sponsored by the TRADOC Culture Center at Fort Huachuca. The organizers offered me an embarrassingly large amount of money to speak at a break-out session about "developing diplomatic skills inside the military/overseas/intercultural environment."[6] By this time, I had participated in nearly fifty LDESP programs. I elected to turn the Culture Summit talk into my AAR.

I began my program by asserting that you can turn a soldier into a diplomat within a very short time; just not a very good one. I stressed the difficulty of taking a raw recruit who has never been out of his own country, who thinks all Arabs are terrorists, who has poor communication skills, and who has difficulty relating to others and make him or her into a diplomat. Soldiers are often asked to memorize a list of cultural dos and don'ts, but the real key is a mindset that is open to cultural differences. Changing mindsets is not something that is easy to do in a three-day LDESP seminar. The *birka* versus bikini discussion became a part of almost all my presentations because I knew the subject would grab their attention and because I hoped the majority of them would walk out realizing that there were could be two sides to the issue. Maybe that insight would translate to other cultural issues.

I kept my advice simple. I stressed that soldiers should always be collecting and always transmitting. They should learn a few courtesy words of the language and they should be aware of basic cultural differences. They should invest in relationships and keep promises. Soldiers will rarely turn into seasoned diplomats but, with proper leadership, their actions can result in our military making more friends than enemies, and our soldiers can become part of the solution instead of part of the problem.

I continued that you can turn a diplomat into a soldier in a very short time; just not a very good one. The military leadership understood the limitations of their soldiers and were clamoring for more civilians to be sent to the battlefield. FSOS from State and USAID, often with little experience and little language, were sent to work on provincial reconstruction teams (PRTs) in the deadliest provinces. They were housed in forward operating bases (FOBS) and would venture out in heavily armed military convoys to meet with local leaders to plan and implement local projects. The numbers were modest, and the dream of a civilian surge was never realized.

We had tried putting civilians on the battlefield earlier in our history. The civil operations and revolutionary development support (CORDS) program in Vietnam was an earlier attempt at counterinsurgency and nation-building. CORDS integrated the efforts of the Departments of State and Defense under a "single manager concept" designed to achieve civil-military unity of effort vital to success. It was rare to find anyone responsible for making decisions in Iraq and Afghanistan who had a grasp of the lessons learned in the Vietnam War. The basic lesson we should have learned in Vietnam, Iraq, and Afghanistan is that the highest priority for members of the population is security for themselves and their families. Every citizen in a conflict zone weighs each day who can better protect them and their families. If they decide they are better off supporting the insurgents, then we cannot win.

Once we recognized that we were bogged down in nation-building in both Afghanistan and Iraq, efforts addressed creating a cadre of civilians to take part in stabilization operations with the military. In July 2004, Congress created the Office of the Coordinator for Reconstruction and Stabilization (S/CRS), initially funded out of the Department of Defense budget. Based on a proposal by Senators Richard Lugar and Joe Biden, Secretary of State Condoleezza Rice announced in 2008 the creation of a civilian response corps (CRC) managed by S/CRS. It was to have a self-contained logistics capability, its own doctrine, and it would hold exercises. Many other committees, frameworks and teams came into existence, all with new acronyms, but the whole process foundered on lack of congressional funding, lack of strong administration leadership, and lack of interagency acceptance. Someone made the decision to not employ the CRC in either Iraq or Afghanistan. Given that both the Bush and Obama administrations were preoccupied with Iraq and Afghanistan, the reconstruction and stabilization initiative quickly became marginalized within the State Department. s/cRs morphed into the Bureau of Conflict and Stabilization Operations (cso) in November 2011 but continues today to operate in relative obscurity, and its impact is modest.

The military will continue to bear most of the burden in a conflict situation. Expeditionary civilians exist neither in the numbers nor with the skill sets required for stability operations. Civilians aren't good at providing for their own security. Even if the numbers existed, it doesn't make sense in many instances to send them into situations where the danger is too high. This means that, in conflict situations, many in our military will continue to be called on to do a mediocre job of diplomacy, when warfighting is what they do best. The answer, it seems to me, is to create a robust professional diplomatic capability that can prevent many conflicts in the first place.

I have not discussed the role of the Central Intelligence Agency in this chronology largely because the details of my relationships with CIA officials do not belong in the public domain. I can say that working with CIA officials in Washington, in Cairo, in Riyadh, in Muscat, and in Baghdad left me with great respect for the men and women of the Company. The CIA officials, true professionals, that I worked with respected the role of an ambassador or chargé and I was always confident that they were telling me everything I needed to know.

The threat of terrorism and its place in the American political consciousness has also contributed to the weakening of the Foreign Service. Palestinian terrorism dates to the 1967 war but rarely targeted Americans directly. When I first walked into the State Department in 1966, I did not have to show any identification. We could board an airplane without going through a metal detector. After Israel invaded Lebanon in 1982, the world changed. Lebanese terrorists deliberately targeted Americans. The bombing of the U.S. Embassy in Beirut in April 1983, killing at least seventeen Americans and many others, led to the Inman Report, which in turn led to the creation of a Diplomatic Security Service in the Department of State and the construction of fortified embassies around the world.

Diplomacy has never been risk-free. There are 250 names of fallen diplomats on the memorial plaques as you enter the State Department from C Street. Steven Haukness, who entered the Foreign Service the same day Arnie Raphel and I did, died during the Tet offensive in Vietnam in 1968. Arnie died in a plane crash twenty years later in Pakistan. The September 11 attack, which killed nearly three thousand Americans, led to the further militarization of foreign policy and further weakened the career service. The American diplomatic presence in Iraq and Afghanistan was dwarfed by the number of Americans there to provide security. The tooth-to-tail ratio, as the military would say, was quite low. Terrorism and our response to it has become highly politicized. Chris Stevens, who was U.S. ambassador in Libya when he was murdered in September 2012, was the prototypical NEA professional. He was, twenty years earlier, an NEA staff assistant, and it was he who arranged my modest confirmation ceremony when I went to Oman. Chris spoke Arabic and was totally comfortable moving around the Arab world and building relationships. He would be appalled at the political circus his death in Benghazi created. It has now become more difficult than ever for diplomats to move around the Middle East and other third-world countries without surrounding themselves with a bubble of security.

There are two other impediments to effective U.S. diplomacy that did not affect me during my career but do impact professionals today. One is the proliferation of special envoys, special representatives, coordinators, and senior and/or special advisors. In its 2015 study entitled "American Diplomacy at Risk," the American Academy of Diplomacy counted forty-five such positions. These positions are usually staffed by political appointees who often bring in their own staffs and usually operate without doing much coordination with the rest of the government. Looking at the already imposing State Department organization chart, you can find most of them subsumed in a little box on the lower right labeled "Special Envoys and Special Representatives."[7] The other new factor is the increasing likelihood, thanks to Wikileaks and Edward Snowden, that sensitive communications between our diplomats and senior officials of the governments they work with will become public. This, of course, means that foreign officials are much less willing to discuss sensitive issues with U.S. ambassadors. The result is that our country is less safe and less influential.

As a college student, I spent two and one-half years studying aeronautical engineering before deciding that my future lay elsewhere. One of the building block courses for that major is thermodynamics. I have always been fascinated by the Second Law of Thermodynamics and the concept of "entropy."[8] The First Law states that the total quantity of energy in the universe stays the same. The Second Law concerns the quality of energy. The natural tendency of energy is to become less concentrated, more diluted, and no longer useful. Entropy is a measure of the amount of energy that no longer has any utility. It is therefore often interpreted as a measure of disorder in any closed system. True scientists and engineers get off at this stop, but I am happy to continue on by drawing an analogy to the amount of disorder in the international system. The natural order of things in the international system is to move in the direction of disorder. Governments and international institutions are created to stop, slow, or reverse the otherwise inevitable movement toward greater disorder.

What we have experienced since the end of the cold war is the failure of governments and international institutions to deal with the inevitable tendency of the international system to slide into disarray. As the world's most powerful country, the United States bears a significant share of the responsibility for this failure. The slide of the world into disarray has coincided with the decline of professionalism in our diplomatic service and the increasing use of our military, which has maintained its professionalism, to address problems that do not lend themselves to military solutions. A strong military is an important asset to our diplomacy, but is must be used sparingly. War is about remaking the system or, at least, significant parts of it, and it is very costly in terms of lives and resources. Diplomacy should always be the first tool out of the toolbox because it is much better at strengthening the existing system and managing disorder.

What was a gradual decline has become a complete hollowing out of our diplomatic capability in the Trump administration. My hope is that the inevitable negative consequences will serve as a wake-up call and create public demand for a professional diplomatic service. My fear is that it will take a cataclysmic event like the 9/11 attack or another costly war to convince the American public of the need to invest in our diplomats. It will take a generation to repair the damage already done, but we should resolve now to build a new and better career service to protect our country and our role as a world leader. U.S. diplomats should be hard at work in every capital in the world and in every international institution. We should be building relationships, gathering information, promoting U.S. trade and investment, protecting American citizens, and pursuing U.S. interests in all these places. Most of the time, diplomacy is invisible, and its most important successes often involve preventing bad things from happening. Diplomacy is relatively inexpensive. Our defense budget now exceeds $700 billion, while money spent on international affairs is roughly $52 billion. The latter figure includes our development assistance budget.

Diplomacy should be a profession like law, medicine, and the military. Professionalization of the Foreign Service should lead to expanding the size of the Foreign Service to allow us to fully staff our embassies and consulates worldwide as well as all essential positions in the Department of State, except the secretary of state. Trainee positions should be reestablished in major embassies and consulates to provide for a period of apprenticeship for incoming officers. The National Foreign Affairs Training Center should be fully resourced, with special attention to conducting after-action reviews of major diplomatic events. The senior seminar or something new comparable to the military's National War College should be established or reestablished.[9] This will not happen without a strong commitment from the president and congressional leaders. It will require the appointment of an enlightened secretary of state who is fully committed to restoring diplomacy to its rightful place.

NOTES

Introduction

1. Adam Entous and Devlin Barrett, "The Last Diplomat," *Wall Street Journal*, updated December 2, 2016, https://www.wsj.com/articles/the-last-diplomat-1480695454.

2. Afghanistan is not generally considered part of the Middle East, but U.S. troops are there because of terrorism that has its roots in the Middle East.

3. For a revealing work about the Trump Administration and the State Department and the Foreign Service, see Ronan Farrow, *War on Peace: The End of Diplomacy and the Decline of American Influence* (New York: W. W. Norton, 2018).

4. For a comprehensive discussion of the skills professional diplomats need to have, see remarks by Chas W. Freeman Jr. at the Foreign Service Club on January 11, 1995, https://chasfreeman.net/diplomacy-as-a-profession/ or his remarks to the Watson Institute of International and Public Affairs on April 17, 2018, https://chasfreeman.net/diplomacy-as-risk-management.

1. Drinking from the Nile

1. Throughout the book, I will use NEA as the acronym for the Bureau of Near East and South Asian Affairs, which in 1992 became the Bureau of Near East Affairs. A separate Bureau of South Asian Affairs was created in 1992.

2. Egypt and Crisis Management

1. For a concise description of the Iran-Contra affair, see https://www.history.com/topics/iran-contra-affair.

2. Thomas L. Friedman, *From Beirut to Jerusalem* (New York: Picador, 1995).

3. Chinese Missiles

1. *Foreign Affairs Oral History Collection, Association for Diplomatic Studies and Training,* Arlington VA, www.adst.org, Ambassador Hume Horan, 134.

2. For a summary of this issue, see Paul Lewis, "Angola and Namibia Accords Signed," *New York Times*, December 23, 1988, https://www.nytimes.com/1988/12/23/world/angola-and-namibia-accords-signed.html.

3. *Foreign Affairs Oral History Collection, Association for Diplomatic Studies and Training*, Arlington VA, www.adst.org, Ambassador Chas W. Freeman Jr., 227.

4. Desert Shield, Desert Storm

1. James A. Baker III, *The Politics of Diplomacy* (New York: G. P. Putnam's Sons, 1995), 373.

6. Banking on Peace

1. Those of us working on or with the Transition Team used the acronym MENA-BANK with all capital letters. Other variations of this acronym were common in the media and elsewhere.

2. While the Oslo Accords technically were totally separate from the bilateral and multilateral tracks that emerged from the Madrid Conference, they contributed to the atmosphere that gave birth to the MENABANK initiative.

3. For a concise summary of the 1991 Madrid Conference, see https://history.state.gov/milestones/1989-1992/madrid-conference.

4. We met in a building later destroyed by Ariel Sharon during the Israeli crackdown on the al-Aqsa Intifada.

5. See https://www.ebrd.com/the-ebrd-and-the-semed.html.

6. Aaron Miller, *The Much Too Promised Land: America's Elusive Search for Arab-Israeli Peace* (New York: Bantam Paperback, 2009), 244.

7. We're Invading Iraq?

1. The director general of the Foreign Service is the director of human resources for the Foreign Service. He or she, the equivalent of an assistant secretary requiring confirmation by the Senate, oversees the Bureau of Human Resources. The position is traditionally filled by a senior career Foreign Service Officer.

2. Sami's warning inspired the title of the book that I later coauthored about my experience in Iraq.

3. Thuraya is a mobile satellite communications company located in Dubai that manufactured the satellite telephones, known as Thurayas, widely used by the United States in Iraq.

4. It appeared on the editorial page of the *Washington Post* on May 14, 2003.

5. Ghassan Muhsin Hussein and David Dunford, *Talking to Strangers: The Struggle to Rebuild the Iraq's Foreign Ministry* (Winfield KS: Southwestern College Academic Press, 2013).

8. Working with the Troops

1. A *ghutra* is the headscarf widely worn in the Arab world. A *dishdasha* or *thobe* is the long robe or dress worn by men in the Arab world.

2. This quote was found on the wall of the U.S. Embassy in Saigon after we withdrew. The actual quote from T. E. Lawrence is "Do not try to do too much with your own hands. Better the Arabs do it tolerably than that you do it perfectly. It is their war, and you are to help them, not to win it for them."

3. See https://www.usip.org/publications/1999/10/training-us-army-officers-peace-operations-lessons-bosnia.

4. Cartoon was drawn by Steve Breen, *San Diego Union-Tribune*.

5. "The McChrystal PowerPoint Slide: Can You Do Any Better," *Guardian*, April 29, 2010, accessed online at https://www.theguardian.com/news/datablog/2010/apr/29/mcchrystal-afghanistan-powerpoint-slide.

6. Jerry L. Bird, Judith Toups, and Stacy John Peterson, *Guide to Birding Coastal Mississippi: and Adjacent Counties* (Mechanicsburg PA: Stackpole, 2004).

7. Roger Fisher and William L. Ury, *Getting to Yes: Negotiating Agreement Without Giving In* (London: Penguin, 1981).

8. An author named Modine Gunch has written or co-written at least three books of humorous essays, one entitled *Never Sleep with a Fat Man in July*.

Toward Effective Diplomacy

1. "George Kennan on Diplomacy as a Profession," *Foreign Service Journal*, July/August 2015, retrieved from http://www.afsa.org/george-kennan-diplomacy-profession.

2. The Bureau of South Asian Affairs was created in 1992 through legislation sponsored by Congressman Steven Solarz and Senator Daniel Patrick Moynihan. Robin Raphel was named the new bureau's first assistant secretary in 1993.

3. *Foreign Affairs Oral History Collection, Association for Diplomatic Studies and Training*, Arlington VA, www.adst.org, Ambassador Prudence Bushnell, 136–37.

4. Chas retired from government service in 1995. He was Director of National Intelligence Dennis Blair's choice to head the National Intelligence Council in 2009 but was forced to withdraw his name after his nomination was opposed by supporters of Israel.

5. Rosa Brooks, *How Everything Became War and the Military Became Everything: Tales from the Pentagon* (New York: Simon & Schuster, 2016).

6. I donated 60 percent of my fee to the University of Arizona Center for Middle Eastern Studies.

7. State Department organization chart retrieved from https://www.state.gov/documents/organization/263637.pdf.

8. The First Law of Thermodynamics states that energy cannot be created or destroyed; the total *quantity* of energy in the universe stays the same.

9. For a comprehensive list of recommendations on improving our diplomacy, see "American Diplomacy at Risk," published in 2015 by the American Academy of Diplomacy, retrieved from https://www.academyofdiplomacy.org/publication/american-diplomacy-at-risk/.

INDEX